JESUS

CARL
THEODOR
DREYER'S

JESUS

THE DIAL PRESS

NEW YORK

1972

Library of Congress Cataloging in Publication Data

Dreyer, Carl Theodor, 1889–1968.
  Jesus.

  1. Jesus Christ—Drama.
PN1997.J43   1972   791.43'7   73–37443

Contents

JESUS

INTRODUCTION

Carl Theodor Dreyer, by Ib Monty

Carl Theodor Dreyer was the master of the tragic film. Not merely because his films often lay greater emphasis on man's suffering and martyrdom in this world, but chiefly because his heroes, and more particularly his heroines, have to wage their struggle against the world's evil singlehanded. The struggle often takes place on the inner stage: Joan of Arc's doubt rages within her: Gertrud has to make her choice independently of everyone else. In all Dreyer's films man is central, to use a hackneyed phrase, and the heart of the matter as Dreyer saw it was not how the world's evil can be combatted, for evil is indestructible, but how man maintains his integrity in the face of evil. This human struggle is always a spiritual one, and always in Dreyer's films it ends with the spiritual victory of the individual.

Dreyer was fascinated by man's spiritual greatness, and in order to project it he adopted psychological realism. Although he was always a naturalist, his ability to recreate the most diversified environments was remarkable. It is well known that he had a large set built for *Joan of Arc* and yet never used it for entire scenes. The main intention was to surround the characters with a milieu which would help to bring out psychological realism in the acting. When directing *The Word,* which takes place in and around a large moorland farm in West Jutland, he made the film crew equip the kitchen with everything he considered right for a country kitchen. Then with his cameraman, Henning Bendtzen, he set about removing the objects. Finally only ten to fifteen objects remained, but they were just what were wanted to create the right psychological illusion. External naturalism to Dreyer was unimportant. He knew that only internal realism matters. That is why he could stylize reality with such sureness.

Carl Theodor Dreyer was born in Copenhagen on February 3, 1889. He began to write theatre reviews for provincial Radical papers about 1909. Later he became a working journalist, first on *Berlingske Tidende,* the largest Copenhagen daily, and then from 1912 to 1915 on the afternoon paper *Ekstrabladet.* In 1913 he was appointed script reader by Nordisk Films Kompagni, and by 1918 had written a long succession of scripts and adaptations of novels for leading directors.

Then in 1918 he was given an opportunity to direct a film, his first effort being a melodrama, in Nordisk style, *The President,* based on a novel by Karl-Emil Franzos. It is a sentimental story of a presiding judge's struggle between love and duty. Dreyer tried to improve on the traditional melodrama by emphasizing the authenticity of the sets and by typecasting the extras. His second film, *Pages from Satan's Book* (1919–21), was inspired by D. W. Griffith's *Intolerance.* It shows, in four sections, the temptation of man by Satan in all ages. It lacks its model's mastery of composition, but Dreyer's attempt to intensify the authenticity of sets and types is persisted in.

Dreyer's third film, *The Parson's Widow* (1920), was made in Sweden. It is an entertaining film about a young curate who has to marry an old parson's widow in order to obtain a living. Shot entirely on location, it has a fine lyrical-documentary character. This time Dreyer was inspired by the Swedish lyrical nature films of Sjöström and Stiller. The film was highly realistic in performance and had a rough rural humour, though also real sympathy for the old widow, who in the end lies down to die and so enables the young clergyman to marry the girl he loves.

Dreyer then went to Germany, where, in Berlin in 1921–1922, he filmed Aage Madelung's novel *Love One Another,* under the title *Die Gezeichneten.* It gives a picture of a Russian pogrom of Jews in 1905 and is impressive in its representation of Russian environments. Back in Denmark, Dreyer in 1922 filmed Holger Drachmann's *Once Upon a Time,* a romantic fairy-tale opera of pronounced national character. Dreyer was rather dissatisfied with this film and only two-thirds of it has survived, though sufficient to show that at least it has much elegant irony in the court scenes, and the finest Danish landscape scenes one can recall in a Danish film. It was shot by George Schnéevoigt, the cameraman of four Dreyer films in the twenties.

In Germany again, Dreyer in 1924 filmed Herman Bang's novel *Mikaël,* about artists, with Benjamin Christensen as the master. In it Dreyer wanted to create an intimate film, based on acting and close-ups, about unhappy people in a sham environment, and the milieu was convincingly depicted.

Dreyer made his seventh film in Denmark. *Thou Shalt Honour Thy Wife* is based on Svend Rindom's melodrama *The Fall of the Tyrant,* but from it Dreyer created an intimate everyday drama about the petit bourgeois, in all his monumental limitation and egoism. In this film Dreyer's understanding of the authenticity of milieu and the psychological realism which he had refined coalesced perfectly. There was an intimate connection between the recreated three-room flat and the consistently natural acting. Inspired to a certain extent by Dreyer's own childhood experience, the film was imbued with an almost savage aversion to the petty, pedantic, closefisted and bad-tempered petit bourgeois, and in the picture of his wife Dreyer again drew a portrait of a suffering woman.

Thou Shalt Honour Thy Wife aroused interest in France by its painstaking everyday realism. Dreyer was invited to make a film there, and following the light, and slight, *Bride of Glomdal,* improvised during the summer of 1925 in Norway after a novel by Jakob B. Bull, there came *Joan of Arc* made in France, which brought Dreyer world renown. In *Joan of Arc* Dreyer peeled off every superfluity in order to concentrate on an intense spiritual portrayal of the suffering Joan. His control of cinematic form was now masterly, and in *Joan of Arc* every single picture, every single movement, every single camera angle, has profound spiritual significance. The film was dominated by close-ups, the camera resting almost endlessly on the faces, from which Dreyer draws the spiritual mysticism that was the object of his art. In *Joan of Arc* he achieved a climax of inner realism, of "realizing mysticism," to use his own expression. *Joan of Arc* shows suffering and martyrdom in close-up.

In 1932 he made his first sound film, *Vampyr*, also in France, but in both a French and a German version. This is a horror film, inspired by a tale by Sheridan le Fanu. It is a suggestive and demonically poetic pictorial poem and perhaps Dreyer's most superbly visual film, one which can be seen over and over again.

Then followed the far too long interval in Dreyer's production. In the early thirties he was in touch with the British documentary movement associated with John Grierson, but no film came out of it. In the mid-thirties Dreyer returned to Denmark as a journalist and did not return to filming until 1942, with the documentary *Maternity Aid*. The next year he reverted to the feature in *Day of Wrath*, a triangular drama dealing with the time of witch trials, again with a suffering woman at the center. The film recreated the period in lingering, pictorially beautiful pictures, but once more the milieu description was closely connected with the portrayal of people. The loving woman becomes a sacrifice and a martyr to the narrowmindedness of her time and environment.

In Sweden in 1944–1945 he made *Two People*, with only two characters. It was an experiment that failed, because, among other reasons, Dreyer was unable to get the actors he wanted. In many respects it caricatures his style.

Then between 1946 and 1954 came a number of shorts: *The Village Church*, the discarded *Water in the Country*, *They Caught the Ferry* (after Johannes V. Jensen), *Thorvaldsen*, *The Storstrøm Bridge*, and *A Palace Within a Palace*. One or two of these are characteristic of him, but it was not until 1955 that he returned to film-making as an art, in his screen version of *The Word,* a play by Kaj Munk. In this film about human suffering one senses a certain change in Dreyer's ideology. For the first time, he seems to be accepting a basically Christian faith. Dreyer personally rated this film highly, but it failed to avoid a certain formal rigidity. There was something about it that was statuesque and indeed almost solemn, making it less passionate than his other works. It came out best in the sequences where, on a basis of psychological realism, Dreyer, among other features, showed the effects of grief on his characters. But in its portrayal of the Christ-like Johannes it ended in chilly formalism.

But that was no reason why it should have taken nine years before Dreyer was able to make his next, and last, film, the astonishing *Gertrud,* based on a play by Hjalmar Söderberg. It caused a furor, dividing public and critics. Dreyer sought in *Gertrud* to give equal weight to dialogue and picture, and the film was accused of being theatrical. Uninfluenced in any way by younger filmmakers, Dreyer in *Gertrud* proved himself to be abreast of contemporary film trends in the endeavour to establish equilibrium between picture and word. Once again the principal character is a woman, but this time she does not succumb. Failing to realize the great, sovereign love, Gertrud withdraws into isolation. In this character Dreyer added yet another to his series of female portraits, and the last is not the least subtle or fascinating. Yet again he displayed his ability, equalled by few others, to expose spiritual conflicts in everything which constitutes film direction.

Gertrud was to be Dreyer's last work. He wanted to follow it up with a film based on the *Medea,* but above all he had visions of one about Jesus of Nazareth. When he died on March 20, 1968, he was absorbed in planning the film about Christ, his dream being perhaps nearer to fulfillment than it had ever been. A world was waiting for this film, which would have set the obvious seal on Carl Dreyer's artistic career, and it is a sad reflection that it might have been made had more people only realized that Dreyer was one of the greatest artists of our time.

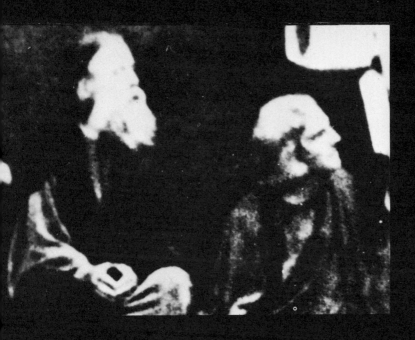

ILLUSTRATIONS

PAGES FROM SATAN'S BOOK (*Blade of Satans Bog*),
Nordisk Films Kompagne, 1919–21.
Used by permission of Anthology Film Archives.

PAGES FROM SATAN'S BOO
Dreyer's second film
traces the temptation of
man by Satan through
four ages. The first part
of the film,
"In Palestine," concerns
the passion of Christ.
Used by permission
of The Museum of Moder
Film Stills Archive.

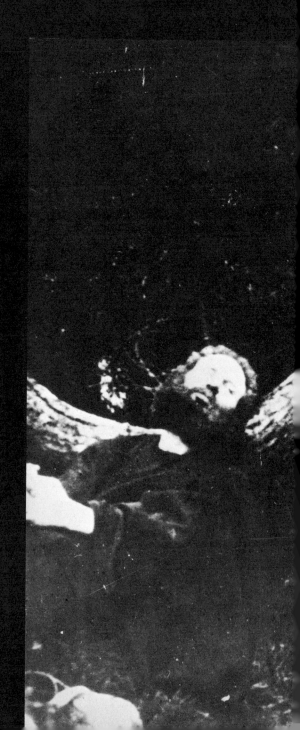

PAGES FROM SATAN'S BOOK.
Jesus, played by Halvard Hoff, in the Garden of Gethsemane.
Used by permission of Anthology Film Archives.

MICHAEL (*Mikaël*),
Decla Bioscop
Universum Film Aktien
Gesellschaft
Pommer Production,
1924. An adaptation
of a novel by
Herman Bang in which
Dreyer attempted
a film in the
manner of the German
Kammerspiele, or
intimate theatre. Used
by permission
of Anthology Film
Archives.

THE PARSON'S WIDOW (*Præsteenken*),
Svensk Filmindustri, Stockholm, 1920.
Used by permission of Anthology Film Archives.

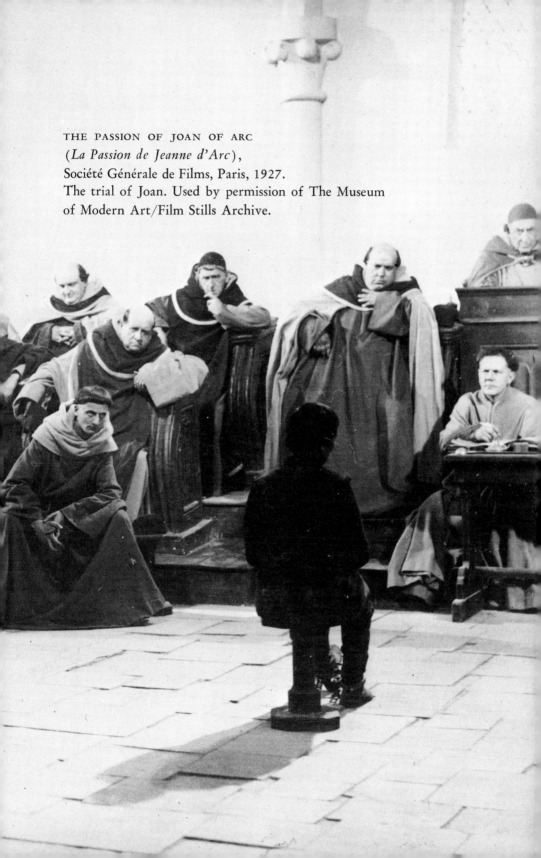

THE PASSION OF JOAN OF ARC
(*La Passion de Jeanne d'Arc*),
Société Générale de Films, Paris, 1927.
The trial of Joan. Used by permission of The Museum
of Modern Art/Film Stills Archive.

THE PASSION OF JOAN OF ARC.
Dreyer made wide use of low angle shots to suggest
the humility and innocence of Joan.
Used by permission of Anthology Film Archives.

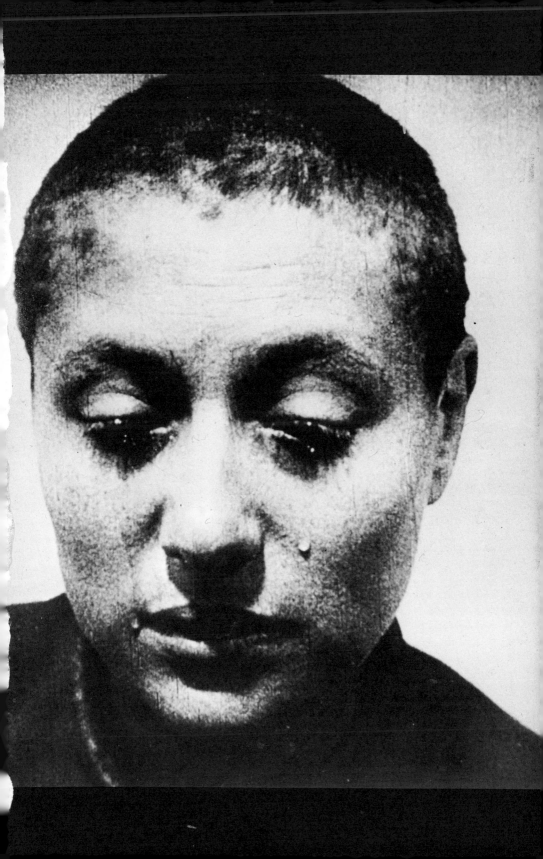

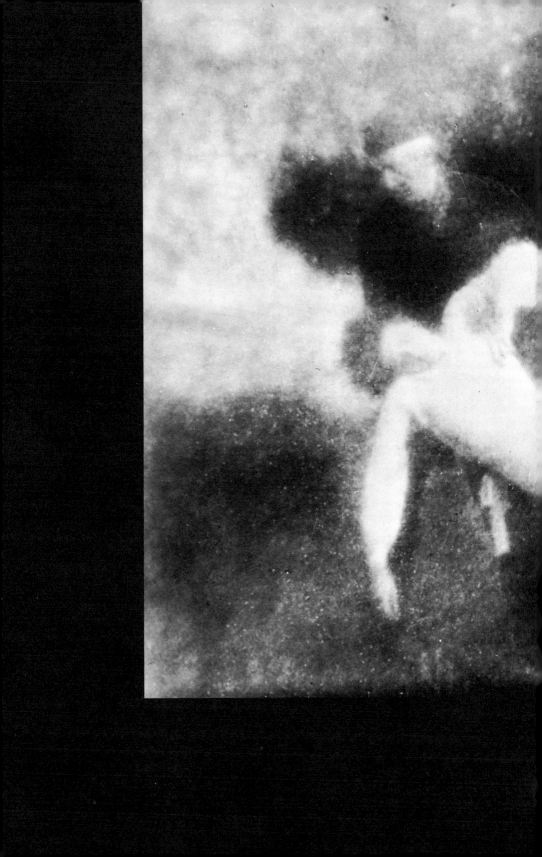

VAMPYR. Carl Theodor Dreyer Filmproduktion.
Paris-Berlin, 1932.
Used by permission of Anthology Film Archives.

VAMPYR.
Used by permission
of Anthology Film Archives.

VAMPYR.
The reaper at the ferry.
Used by permission
of Anthology Film Archives.

VAMPYR. Marc, played by
Jan Hieronimko,
imprisoned at the mill.
Used by permission
of Anthology Film Archives.

DAY OF WRATH (*Vredens Dag*),
Palladium Copenhagen-Tage Nielsen, 1943.
Anne, played by Lisbeth Movin.
Used by permission of The Museum of
Modern Art/Film Stills Archive.

THE WORD (*Ordet*),
Palladium, Copenhagen, 1954–55.
Johannes was played by Preben Lerdorff Rye
Used by permission of
The Museum of Modern Art/Film Stills Arch

THREE ESSAYS
BY CARL DREYER

Who Crucified Jesus?

I wrote the script for a film on Jesus in the United States at the suggestion of Mr. Blevins Davis in the late forties, but earlier I had already formed my own theories regarding the events which must have preceded the arrest of Jesus. Some days after the Germans occupied Denmark, it struck me that such a situation as we Danes were in was similar to that of the Jews in Judea in the days of the Roman Empire. The hatred we felt toward the Nazis, the Jews must have felt toward the Romans. It seemed to me that the capture, conviction, and death of Jesus was the result of a conflict between Jesus and the Romans.

Soon after my arrival in the United States, I came across a recently published book that agreed in substance with my own ideas. It was called *Who Crucified Jesus?* by Dr. Solomon Zeitlin, professor of Rabbinical studies at Dropsie College in Philadelphia, who was a Jewish scholar of international reputation.

Pontius Pilate, the Roman governor, was actually the ruler in Judea, but supposedly equal in authority, though appointed by

Pilate, was the high priest Caiaphas who was the effective leader of the Jewish population. Besides holding the highest religious office, Caiaphas was also the Jewish state's secular chief. He and the others in authority established a "wait-and-see" policy toward the Romans, a policy aimed at procuring for the population as tolerable conditions as possible by cooperating and negotiating peaceably with their Roman masters. The Romans, in order to pacify the Jews, granted them certain privileges such as religious freedom, municipal self-government, their own police and their own courts. In cases where the safety of the Romans was at stake, they reserved the right to pass sentence and execute punishment. This facade of self-government was similar to methods used by the Germans during their occupation of Denmark.

In their despair over this suppression, the Jews never gave up the hope that a Jewish kingdom would rise again when the Messiah, predicted by the prophets, would come to revenge Israel and chase the Romans from the land. Some maintained the courage to bear the Roman yoke in this hope, but there were others who did not bear their sufferings with patience and preferred to meet terror with terror. They united in a sect, the "Sicarii," and initiated an underground resistance movement against the Romans. Time and again their attempts at rebellion were crushed, but they did not give up. They also harassed those of their countrymen who cooperated with the Romans, among them some of the great landowners who let the Romans have their grain. The Sicarii maintained that such Jews—the "collaborationists" of that day—were traitors, and they burned or "liquidated" their crops.

Dr. Zeitlin notes the existence of another sect, the "Apocalyptic Pharisees," whose hopes for a revolution depended upon God's direct intervention. Probably, the Messiah they awaited was expected to be gifted with supernatural powers. Knowledge of the beliefs and activities of these two sects is necessary for any examination of the Roman attitude toward Jesus's activities. In Bethany, just on the outskirts of Jerusalem, Jesus awakened Lazarus from the dead. And in Jerusalem itself, Jesus cured a man who had been lame for thirty-eight years and restored the sight of a young man who had been born blind. The lame could walk and the blind could see: Was Jesus perhaps the Messiah with the super-natural powers that the Apocalyptic Pharisees were anticipating? The Romans kept a watchful eye both on the Sicarii and on the Apocalyptic Pharisees and regarded them equally as dangerous rebels, and members of both sects were crucified in great numbers.

Mark, Luke and John mention that Jesus, after his arrest in the garden of Gethsemane, was taken to the high priest's house and there put before "a council of elders and scribes." It is crucial to a proper understanding of the reasons for Jesus's crucifixion to determine what kind of council this was.

From old times, there existed a legislative council called the Great Sanhedrin which consisted of seventy-one members whose task was to interpret biblical law. Apart from this, another council, the Little Sanhedrin, composed of twenty-three members, had authority to judge in cases of crimes involving religious laws and also in moral crimes that exacted capital punishment, such as murder, incest, public profanation of the Sabbath, and blasphemy. The Little Sanhedrin met every day of the week except Saturday, and except on holidays and days which preceded them. While the Romans passed death sentences without scruple, the Jews were conscientiously humane in their court practice. They avoided the extreme penalty for as long as possible. A man could be acquitted the same day he was brought to trial, but he could not be sentenced to death before the following day. And even after the death sentence had been pronounced, the case could be taken up again if new information, regardless of its source, was presented in favor of the condemned man. So far went the Jewish judges' dread of executing an innocent man that when the condemned was taken to the place of execution a court officer headed the procession carry-ing upright a long stick on whose head was fastened a tablet in-scribed with the injunction that anyone who possessed information favorable to the prisoner should appear immediately before the council. If anybody reported, the execution was postponed and the case restudied. Since Jesus was crucified the day before Passover, it cannot have been the Little Sanhedrin to which Jesus was taken after his arrest, since the Little Sanhedrin did not meet before holidays. What sort of council was it, then, that Jesus was brought before? Dr. Zeitlin explains that in Judea there had long existed a political Sanhedrin, independent of the two religious Sanhedrins, whose responsibilities were to judge those who committed crimes against the state or its leaders. The members of this political Sanhedrin were appointed by the chief of state. During the Roman occupation, such civil cases were delivered over to the jurisdiction of the Romans. Since the high priest was responsible for social and political order in Judea, it was his duty to arrest those suspected of rebellious activities. The prisoner was then brought before the high priest and his advisory council—the political Sanhedrin. This council had no right to sentence the accused, only to hear him and examine witnesses. It was the Roman governor who passed sentence and had it executed.

In all known cases, as Dr. Zeitlin notes, the political council was only summoned after the arrest of a political criminal and did not meet with any stated regularity. Distinct from the procedural manner of the religious Sanhedrins, the political council could hold its meetings at any time of the day or night and in any place if circumstances required. Dr. Zeitlin concludes that it is to this political council Jesus was taken on the night of his capture. If so, then Jesus was considered a political criminal. The next question is, was there reason to suppose Jesus a rebel and an enemy to the state? Dr. Zeitlin reminds us that on his entry into Jerusalem, Jesus was cheered as "David's Son" and greeted with the cry: "Blessed be the kingdom of our father David, that cometh in the name of the Lord." (Mark 11:10.)

The old prophets who spoke in God's name had predicted that, sent by God, a man of David's family would some day come as a Messiah, and would declare himself king of the Jews.

Jesus was not only hailed as David's son, he was also greeted with shouts such as "Hosanna: Blessed is the King of Israel that cometh in the name of the Lord." (John 12:13.)

By allowing these epithets, Jesus provoked the Romans' suspicion of his being an accomplice of the revolutionary groups and his entry was in itself a direct challenge to Roman authority. Therefore, in their own lights, they were justified in demanding that Jesus be placed under their jurisdiction. Further, after his entry,

Jesus had cast the money changers from the temple courtyard. (Mark 11:15.) This was such a breach of social custom that both the Romans and the responsible Jewish authorities were filled with outrage; obviously it seemed as if it was the welfare of the Jewish people that Jesus was risking by his conduct.

According to Dr. Zeitlin, the high priest was obligated to have Jesus arrested, interrogated in the presence of the political council, and then—when Jesus confessed that he regarded himself as Messiah—delivered to Pontius Pilate.

I consider it possible that it was the Romans who demanded the arrest of Jesus, for the Romans, who commanded a well-organized "gestapo," were informed of all that went on in Judea, especially in Jerusalem during the Passover. In Denmark there was an analogous case during the Occupation when the Germans, on February 24, 1942, requested the arrest of Wilh. la Cour and had him transferred to their authority.

Caiaphas's remarks, cited in John, substantiate the fact that a particular political question was at stake: "Ye know nothing at all, nor consider that it is expedient for us, that one man should die for the people and that the whole nation perish not." The fretful, snappish tone seems to indicate that Caiaphas, even within the narrow political council, had met resistance to the handing over of Jesus from the advisors, who otherwise were puppets in his hand.

When Jesus was brought before Pilate the next morning, the first question the Roman governor put to him was: "Art thou the king of the Jews?" to which Jesus gave the evasive answer: "Thou sayest it." (John 15:2.)

In face of this, it seems obvious, as Dr. Zeitlin concludes, that Jesus was handed over to the Romans as a political criminal who had committed an offense against the Roman state by aspiring to become king of the Jews.

I had the pleasure of talking with Dr. Zeitlin after I had completed my manuscript. He read my manuscript and discussed it with me at length. We agreed on all points except one. In his book, Dr. Zeitlin is harsh on Caiaphas whom he describes as a "quisling." I don't think he was that. One may call him a collaborationist but definitely not a "quisling." There is, in my hum-

ble opinion, nothing that indicates that Caiaphas was not a conscientious man who had the people's welfare in his thoughts. He
was a realistic politician and, as such, considered it wisest for the
Jewish people to cooperate rather than face the loss of the little
freedom that was left them. For the Romans, religion was sub-
ordinate to the state; for the Jews, religion stood above the state
—religion was everything. And so I have gone my own way regarding the description of Caiaphas in my manuscript. But more
consequentially, I am deeply grateful to Dr. Zeitlin who has
achieved the goal he set himself: to refute the accusation against
the Jews of having murdered Jesus. This infamous charge was
stated for the first time during the first century after Jesus's death.
Anti-semitism is that old. We all know what this infamy has
brought the Jews in sorrow and tears, suffering and death.

The Roots of Anti-Semitism

The scrupulous and conscientious Nazi official Rudolf Höss was in 1941 called from Auschwitz to a meeting with Heinrich Himmler who informed him that "der Führer" had decided on a "final solution" of the Jewish question and that Himmler, for his part, had decided to entrust the execution of the plan to Höss.

With these instructions, Höss returned to Auschwitz and ordered four crematories, with furnaces and gas-chambers attached, from the Erfurt firm of Topf und Söhne for installation "soonest possible."

The four crematories were capable of burning 12,000 bodies a day so that it was possible to burn 4,380,000 bodies a year. However, from May to August, 1944, even these four furnaces could not satisfy the need, so certain shipments of Hungarian Jews had to be executed on open air pyres. In August of 1944, there were 24,000 cremations in a single day.

In his autobiography, Höss writes: "I would like to mention

that I, for my part, have never harbored any hateful feelings toward the Jews. To feel hatred is entirely alien to me."

When one's nausea has subsided, you take your head in your hands and ask: how did anti-semitism ever come into this world, after all? What is its origin, its background?

In order to find answers to these questions, we must go back 1900 years ago. Back to Golgotha. Here, too, Jews were done away with. One of them was the Jew, Jesus. For him, too, a "final solution" was found—at least the Romans thought so.

But Jesus had died on the cross as a political rebel. His followers spread his doctrine, and the little fraternal community developed into a sect called the Nazarenes. It was not a Christian sect but a Jewish one. Christianity as a theological concept did not yet exist. The members of the sect were all Jews who observed the Torah and complied with all the ceremonial precepts. Then some decisive events took place within the sect which determined its future. Seven Hellenistic Jews who had come to Jerusalem were admitted. One of them, Stephen, one day was accused of blasphemy by the Jewish council for proclaiming the divinity of Jesus and the betrayal of the temple leaders. Stephen was stoned to death outside the town, and present at this execution was a young tentmaker from Tarsus by the name of Saul. Given his impulsive temperament, it is likely that Saul was not a passive witness. On his way to the synagogues of Damascus to ferret out other disciples of Jesus, Saul suffered a "heavenly vision"—possibly the result of a psychological crisis of conscience regarding the stoning he had been witness to. Jesus appeared before him and said: "Saul, Saul why persecutest thou me?" Saul fell to the ground and was stricken blind. Only on the third day after did he regain his sight. A man of the Nazarene's sect, Ananais, opened his eyes and admonished him not to be against but for the new faith. After a great spiritual struggle Saul decided to join the Nazarenes.

At a very early moment, it seems to have been clear to Saul that if the Nazarenes were not to remain a small Jewish sect that would sooner or later disintegrate and crumble away for want of increase, they had to act with greater initiative. From where could they expect an influx if not among the heathens outside Palestine and, there, especially, within the borders of the extensive Roman Empire? But such a task could be solved only by a Hellenistic Jew who spoke Hebrew as well as Greek and who was familiar with the heathen peoples' attitude toward religion and ethics—a preacher and an agitator. Saul knew a man who was equal to the task—himself—and he was henceforth known as Paul. At the same time, he appointed himself an apostle. He was called to Antioch where his followers said they preferred not to be called Nazarenes any longer but to be called Christians. It is the first time we meet this designation. The Christian community decided sometime later to send Paul on a missionary journey to the surrounding heathen countries and Paul, thereby, had his highest hopes fulfilled. On his mission, it would be little wonder if Paul was not surprised at the large number of Jews he came across, for the majority of the Jewish people did not live in Palestine. There were in Palestine three million Jews and scattered abroad three and a half million, the vast majority of whom lived within the Roman Empire and its provinces in Europe, Asia Minor, Egypt and North Africa. These Jews had their own synagogues in most towns, and felt strongly attached to their faith, on the whole, and its religious center in the Temple of Jerusalem. Encouraged by their leaders in Jerusalem, these Jews were proselytizers and had made a considerable number of conversions among the heathens. Among the heathens, the prestige of the old gods and goddesses was on the decline. Together with this contempt for the gods, and the poverty of their worldly existence, the heathens longed for a new faith which gave hope of an afterlife.

The path was open for Paul and his new religion. He realized that Christianity's great opportunity was in the fact that it satisfied a crucial need of the time. The heathens were hungering for a new religion and preferably one whose daily rituals were not difficult. In its most exact form, the Jewish faith required the observance of no less than 613 commandments (which even Jews by birth had some difficulties observing). Paul simplified the matter by replacing the 613 commandments with the single requirement of believing in Jesus. Rules regarding circumcision and the dietary laws were dropped. For Christianity, Paul retained only two practices: baptism and communion.

The Jews who in their hearts had remained faithful to the ancestral religion were deeply offended at the loose moral manner with which Paul disposed of religious questions that to them were of the very greatest importance. Had not Jesus himself said: "Do not think that I have come to destroy the laws. I do not come to destroy but to fulfill"? But Paul swept away the law! Paul's behavior so awakened the righteous indignation of orthodox Jews that they united and drove him from their towns. Although Paul's new faith deviated more and more from the true Jewish doctrine, Paul still considered himself a Jew, something he was by birth and by conviction. It was Paul's opinion that the faith he was preaching was Judaism in a simplified form. He himself loyally and conscientiously obeys the ceremonial laws, but he does not demand such obedience of others, for he considers some laws absurd and others superfluous.

The Jewish historian Joseph Klausner says of the apostle, "Paul had transformed a little Jewish sect into a half-Jewish, half-Christian religion which spread over the whole world. He was the real founder of Christianity. It can safely be said: without Jesus no Paul. But it can be said with equal confidence: without Paul no Christian world-religion with a clearly developed and easily comprehensible theology."

That section in The Acts of the Apostles that deals with Paul is believed to have been written by the Greek-Christian, Luke, author of The Gospel According to St. Luke, a close friend of Paul. Its most striking and singular element is its hostile attitude toward the Jews. In at least twenty places, the Jews are mentioned in a hateful tone. According to this document, the Jews are the source of everything evil. They persecute the Christians and try to hurt them by slandering them before the Romans. Many things indicate that Paul has inspired Luke to these underhanded attacks on the Jews. If this is the case, we confront a most peculiar phenomenon, namely: "the anti-semitic Jew."

Some critics of the Bible have offered a logical explanation for this. Intuitively, Paul seizes on a great and revolutionary religious idea. Being an outstandingly effective agitator, he forges the base for this new religion. The heathens rally around him. One Christian community after another springs up. Soon he is at the center of a big web and needs only to pull the strands. Nevertheless, there are dangerous obstacles which could break the newly woven web. One is the orthodox Jews; the other is the Romans. Paul, of whom it was said that his "heart did not resemble his face," knows how to gain the confidence of the Romans and to allay their suspicion of the doctrine he is spreading. Paul does not point out that the Jesus the heathens are urged to worship is the one the Romans crucified years before for seditious activity. Jesus became an unknown man whose divine qualities appeared only when he rose from the dead. And it was not the Romans who had demanded the crucifixion, but the high priests and the scribes. This delusion, which exculpates the Romans and blames the Jews, is still active to this day. Fanatics of Paul's kind seldom have any scruples when it comes to promoting the cause for which they are fighting.

In its final form, The Acts of the Apostles is supposed to have been completed approximately in the year 95. The crucifixion took place in the year 30, and in the year 70 occurred the Destruction of the Temple when Titus demolished Jerusalem and the Jewish inhabitants were sold as slaves. When Paul's account gained a broad hearing, the Jews were in no position to offer any counterattack.

Without considering the consequences, Paul sowed the seeds of Christian anti-semitism, which during the early days of the Roman church would grow and spread like a dangerous weed. The tendency to fawn upon the Romans and to smear the Jews also appears in The Gospel According to St. John, which was written at the same time as The Acts of the Apostles and shows the same hostility toward the Jews. Two things are striking in a reading of this Gospel.

First of all, the word "Jew" is found more often there than in the three other Gospels. While the appellation appears five times in Luke and Matthew and six times in Mark, it figures in John seventy times. Next, John talks about the Jews as if he were talking about a foreign people—foreign to Jesus and foreign to himself, and always in a scornful, contemptuous way. The explanation is probably similar to the case of Paul—namely, the attempt to allay the fears and hostility of the Romans.

In his book *Jésus et Israel,* the French Jewish historian Jules Isaac (whose dedication page reads: "To my wife and my daughter/killed by the Germans/killed/simply because their name was Isaac.") details how Christendom has for centuries brought fertilizer to the ghastly weeds of anti-semitism.* A general outline of the earliest period yields the following:

SECOND CENTURY. *The holy Justin:* "Your circumcision is the mark of infamy with which omniscient providence has beforehand stamped you the murderers of Jesus and the prophets."

THIRD CENTURY. *The theologian and Bible interpreter, Origen:* "It is the Jews who nailed Jesus to the cross."

FOURTH CENTURY. *The church historian, Bishop of Caesarea:* "Thus the Jews were chastised as a punishment for their crime and their impiety."

The holy Ephrem calls the Jews "circumcised dogs."

Church-father Jerome stamps the Jews as "snakes in Judas's image" and solemnly promises them the Christians' hatred.

The holy John Chrysostom: "How can it be that believing Christians are not ashamed of having contact with those who have shed the blood of Jesus?"

FIFTH CENTURY. *The holy Augustine:* "The final hour has come for our Lord, Jesus! They hold him—the Jews. They insult him—the Jews. They bind him—the Jews. They crown him with thorns, they soil him with their spittle, they whip him, they shower him with scorn, they nail him to the cross, they plunge their lances into his flesh."

Right through the middle ages the Catholic Fathers sowed the

---

* *Editor's Note.* This book is now available in English: *Jesus and Israel,* by Jules Isaac. Translated by Sally Gran. Holt, Rinehart & Winston, 1971.

seeds of hatred for the Jews. Then the reformers enter the act. Luther declares that if he finds a pious Jew to baptise he will bring him out on the bridge over the Elbe, bind him, fasten a stone around his neck and throw him into the river with the words: "I baptise you in the name of Abraham"!

Luther can put his arm around the Catholic Fathers. Each and every one of them must bear the responsibility for the death of Anne Frank. But let us not thump our chest and believe that our own time is better. What do you think, for instance, of a little "legend" that Papini tells about a high-ranking Jewish Rabbi who goes to the Pope to make a deal with him. The Rabbi offers that a very great number of Jews will convert if the Church will, in return, strike the Passion Week from its calendar. In addition, the Rabbi offers a mountain of gold. The Pope answers with sublime dignity: "Do not force me to say that a Judas lives within every Jew. You sold Jesus for thirty pieces of silver and today you want to buy him back with some of the gold you have hoarded over the course of centuries through pillage and usury." This legend was composed in 1938.

Eight years later, Daniel Rops wrote in his holy tale about Jesus: "The Jews had shouted: 'Let his blood come over us and our children.' God in his righteousness heard them." And he continues: "The face of persecuted Israel fills history but it does not make us forget that other face, soiled with blood and spittle—this other face for which the Jews felt no pity."

Finally, in Herbert Pundik's book, *Israel 1948–1958*, occurs the following:

> On the 26th of June, 1947, the English Commander-in-chief in Palestine, Sir Evelyn Barker, sent out an army order in which he forbade the English troops to fraternize with the Jews in Palestine. The army order ended with the words: "I understand that these measures will create difficulties for the soldiers [but] they will punish the Jews exactly in the way that this race hates more than anything else: by aiming a blow against their pockets and showing them how much we detest them."

For nineteen hundred years the Jews have been held responsible for the death of Jesus and have been stamped murderers—Christ-killers. The curse has followed them, hatred has been preached against them, and they have been tortured and murdered in multitudes. This has to come to a stop. The Christians' aversion toward the Jews is foolish and illogical. Think of what the Christians have received from the Jews; above all, the faith in one God who is God of both Christian and Jew. Next, the idea that all human beings are equal to God. Christianity is a child of Judaism, and the New Testament has its roots in Jewish tradition. Christian eyes must be opened to the connection between Jewish faith and Christian faith and Jewish and Christian ethics. Only through mutual understanding, mutual respect and sympathy, only in this and not in anything else can one see a "final solution."

My Only Great Passion

Of his film *The Passion of Joan of Arc*, Dreyer said:

"In the film the English soldiers at the trial of Joan wear steel helmets and several critics resented that. But the truth is that fifteenth century soldiers actually wore steel helmets exactly like the ones English soldiers wore during the First World War. The same critics also made a fuss because one of the monks in the film wore horn-rimmed glasses which, in 1927 (when the film was made) were very much in fashion. But I could produce miniatures which show fifteenth-century people wearing horn-rimmed glasses. In the miniatures, we also found a scenic style that could suggest the era without overwhelming the drama. I followed the same principle in *Day of Wrath*, and I am also going to follow it in my film on Christ. Realism in itself is not art, but there must be harmony between the genuineness of feelings and the genuineness of things. I try to force reality into a form of simplification and abbreviation in order to reach what I call psychological realism."

The interviewer asked if Dreyer, despite the timeless quality in his films, was not strongly tied to the present and Dreyer answered:

"Concerning *Joan of Arc* and *Day of Wrath,* I can only say that one never knows what goes on in one's subconscious, but as for the proposed film on Christ there is certainly something to what you say. The first time I thought of the Gospels as material for a film was just after I had completed *Joan of Arc* and I was searching for a point of view that would be distinct from the traditional one. The German occupation of Denmark provided me with one. Ours must have been similar to the plight of the Jews in Palestine. For the Jews of the Roman times it was the Romans; we Danes had the Germans. For them there was Pilate; we had Renthe-Fink. The Jews had their underground movement—young patriotic Jews called 'Zealots' who attacked outlying Roman garrisons and set fire to Jewish collaborationists' houses and fields."

About "impartiality" in his films, Dreyer said:

". . . In both *Joan of Arc* and *Day of Wrath* I have consciously tried to remain impartial. The clergy in the two films did indeed condemn Joan and the harmless old witch to the stake, but it was not because they were evil and cruel. They were only caught up in the religious convictions of their times. When they tortured their victims in order to force a confession from them, it was because the confession insured the accused eternal life."

Concerning the public:

"Apart from the fact that I naturally take the trouble to organize my material so that the audience can easily grasp it, I must be honest and say that beyond that I don't have the public in my thoughts for one moment. I don't do anything to 'please' the public. I only think of working my way to a solution that satisfies my own artistic conscience. And I believe, you know, that this is the right way to work. In a couple of cases I had the experience of compromising my conception and it was only detrimental to me."

Why does Dreyer feel drawn to tragedy?

"Because I find it easier in tragedy to work in my own personality and my own outlook (on life)—to introduce this 'something' that, to use a tired phrase, people go home with."

Is there an intent in the film about Jesus?

"Yes, there is, insofar as I think it will aid in lessening the antagonism between Christian and Jew. For this reason, among others, I know that I want to let Jesus be shown as a Jew. The masses have a deeply rooted conception that Jesus was blond and Aryan. It is a good turn, I think, to see to it that this prejudice is stamped out."

Should the film director himself write the script?

"Ideally, the director should write his own manuscript. He first becomes a *creating* artist (as opposed to a *reproducing* one) in the deep sense only when he has written the manuscript himself. Then he is not only an attendant in the service of another vision. The manuscript has come into existence under the pressure of an inner drive to write just this film. And so he himself gives the film both content and form, he himself thereby insures its intimate dramatic and psychological coherence."

Finally, the interviewer asked: "What is film to you?" and Dreyer replied:

"My only great passion."

JESUS

A Film Manuscript

NARRATOR: *There was a man sent from God, whose name was John. He was not that Light, but was sent to bear witness of that Light, the true Light. He was in the World, but the World knew him not.* [John 1:6–10.]

At the River Jordan. The one called the Baptist recites a short prayer. A crowd gathers on the shore to listen intently to John the Baptist who addresses them. They are common people, simple folk, who have come to him with their needs. But among them are Pharisees and Sadducees, come out from Jerusalem to hear this strange man and his powerful preaching which has reached the farthest parts of the land. The movement which John and his disciples have led has increased in adherents daily.

Among the people is Jesus who is unknown but who draws attention to himself by his bearing, his calm, peaceful spirit, his face with its sensitive eyes.

John the Baptist stands upon a large rock. He says

The Kingdom of God is near and the day of judgment is at hand. Therefore, repent you because the axe is laid unto the root of the trees. Every tree, therefore, which brings not forth good fruit is hewn down and cast into the fire.

The Pharisees and the Sadducees exchange glances. Now is the time to ask the questions they have had in mind.

FIRST PHARISEE: *Who are you?*

JOHN THE BAPTIST: *I am not the Messiah.*

SECOND PHARISEE: *What then? Are you Eliah?*

JOHN THE BAPTIST: *I am not.*

THIRD PHARISEE: *Are you that Prophet? Which?*

JOHN THE BAPTIST: *No.*

FIRST SADDUCEE: *Who are you? That we may give an answer to them that sent us. What say you of yourself?*

SECOND SADDUCEE: *Why baptize you, if you be not that Messiah nor Eliah, neither that Prophet?*

JOHN THE BAPTIST: *I baptize with water; but there stands one among you whom you know not, who shall baptize you with the Holy Ghost and with fire.*

John the Baptist turns and looks toward Jesus, and the people follow his gaze. Jesus rises and leaves. Andrew and John, disciples of the Baptist, follow him, drawn by a power they feel but cannot understand. The voice of John the Baptist grows faint in the distance.

He it is, who coming after me is preferred before me, whose shoe's latchet I am not worthy to unloose. He that comes from Heaven is above all.

During the closing words the Pharisees and the Sadducees leave the crowd and go to their mules which rest contentedly under a tree. They discuss in low voices all they have seen and heard.

Jesus walks along the shore of the Lake of Gennesaret, a lovely spot. Small boys romp in its waters. Andrew and John walk behind Jesus. Jesus realizes that Andrew and John are following him, and he turns and says

What seek you?

For a moment the two are at a loss for words. Finally, Andrew speaks

Master, where dwell you?

With a quiet smile Jesus gives them an invitation

Come and see.

And they go together.

The Pharisees and Sadducees, in animated conversation, make their way homeward to Jerusalem astride their mules.

Along the shore of the lake Jesus, Andrew and John come upon a boat beached in the sand. Nearby a fisherman, Philip, repairs his nets. He looks up questioningly as the others approach. He has never seen Jesus before. John says

We have found the Messiah.

Jesus looks at him, and Philip, as though drawn by some unseen power, rises to his feet. For a moment the two stand face to face, and Philip knows he has found his Master. Andrew speaks.

Go, and tell the good news to Nathanael.

Philip smiles in a strange manner as he rushes off. Jesus looks after him with an approving glance.

As they continue their walk a peasant woman makes her way to the lake to wash her pots and dishes.

Philip finds Nathanael sitting in the shadow of a fig tree. He cannot be certain whether Nathanael is reading the book of the Law or simply dreaming.

PHILIP: *We have found him, of whom the Prophet did write.*
NATHANAEL: *Who is he?*
PHILIP: *Jesus . . .* (pause) *of Nazareth.*
NATHANAEL: *Of Nazareth? Can any good thing come out of Nazareth?*
PHILIP: *Come and see.*

With a doubtful expression, Nathanael gets up and follows Philip.

Jesus, Andrew and John come to a place on the shore where fishing boats are moored. Here they see Andrew's brother Simon, called Peter, and John's brother James cleaning their nets. Small boys have built a fire on the shore and are frying fish.

Andrew calls to his brother.

We have found the Messiah.

And he brings Peter to Jesus, who looks upon him and says

You are Simon, the son of Jonah.

Peter looks up surprised.

How do you know?

He is ready to question his brother, but Andrew shakes his head helplessly. Jesus then turns to Peter—and a bond is forged between them that is never to be broken.

Philip returns with Nathanael.

JESUS (seeing Nathanael): *Behold a Jew indeed, in whom is no guile.*

NATHANAEL: *Whence know you me?*

JESUS: *Before Philip called you I saw you under the fig tree.*

Nathanael (henceforth called Bartholomew) no longer doubts. He realizes that never before has he been in the presence of such a man. His words come slowly.

BARTHOLOMEW: *Now I believe you are the Son of God.*

JESUS: *You believe me because I said I saw you under a fig tree. You shall see greater things than those.*

These first disciples listen to him with wonder. It is clear to them that Jesus is the Messiah. They are drawn to him, and in his hands they willingly place their destiny.

Jesus, knowing what is in their hearts, speaks to them.

Follow me, from henceforth you shall catch men.

Eagerly they gather about him, listening to his words.

NARRATOR: *Now, as Jesus walked by the sea of Galilee his fame went through all the region round about, and many came in boats from the towns all around the lake to hear him preach.*

Jesus stands at the end of the pier. The disciples sit about in comfortable positions. Before him many ships have gathered, their masts jutting up like the trees in a young forest. The decks of the ships are crowded with men and boys who listen eagerly as Jesus speaks. They nod approvingly from time to time as he establishes his lessons by utilizing analogies from what is familiar to them.

JESUS: *Take heed what you hear. When you see a cloud rise out of the West, straightway you say, there comes a shower; and so it is. And when you see the southwind blow, you say, there will be heat, and it comes to pass. And when it is evening,*

you say, it will be fair weather, for the sky is red and lower-
ing. You can discern the face of the sky and of the earth;
then how is it that you do not discern this time? Even of
yourselves you can judge what is right. The time is fulfilled
and the Kingdom of God is at hand.
A VOICE: *What is the Kingdom of God?*

At this moment the overseer of the synagogue blows his horn
(the shofar) to announce the Sabbath. Jesus raises his right hand,
exhorting his companions to listen to the shofar which calls the
congregation to the House of God—to the Kingdom of God.

JESUS: *The time has come and the Kingdom of God is at hand.*
Therefore, repent you and obey the word of God.

NARRATOR: *And Jesus went about all Galilee and he taught on*
Sabbaths in their synagogues—being glorified of all.

The exterior of the synagogue. Two shepherds wrapped in
sheepskin cloaks arrive—a little late—before the synagogue. They
tether their flocks to a tree. The shepherds hasten into the entrance
hall of the synagogue. There in the center is the basin for washing
the hands. When the shepherds enter through the inner door the
voice of Jesus can be heard reading verses from the Prophets (and
its Targum after each three verses). Since the service is crowded,
the men have difficulty finding seats.
    The voice of Jesus is heard throughout. As he speaks the camera
moves through the listening crowd in the triple-aisled room toward
the south wall where the table with the scrolls is to be found. Before
it is a platform with reading stand and armchair. When Jesus comes
into view he is still standing at the desk but has just finished his
reading. He hands the scroll to the overseer who rolls it up and
carries it to the table with the scrolls. Jesus has seated himself in
the armchair and while still seated (as was the practice) he begins
to preach, his sermon based on the verses he has read.

JESUS: *Again you have heard that it has been said by them of*
old time, you shall not forswear yourself, but shall perform

*unto the Lord your oaths. But I say unto you, swear not at
all. Let your communication be, Yea, Yea; Nay, Nay; for
whatsoever is more than these comes of evil.*

As Jesus preaches, we see the faces of the congregation—the
aged with flowing white beards and beside them small boys. There
are rich and poor, and also women. All are astonished at the doctrine of Jesus, for he teaches with assured authority, unlike the
scribes. They look questioningly at one another. Is this a new
doctrine?

Seated between the table with the scrolls and the platform
from which Jesus is preaching are the Pharisees who face the congregation. They are listening sympathetically, interested in the
preacher's interpretation, even though their expressions from time
to time indicate that they are not entirely in agreement with him.

In the darkness of a side-aisle is a man known to all the town.
He is thought to be possessed of an evil spirit and his frequent fits
of rage lend credence to that opinion. In fact, he suffers from a
mental disease which shows itself in periodic bursts of hysteria. The
following scene depicts the ambivalent mind which characterizes
those afflicted. On the one hand, he is attracted by Jesus and wishes
to be healed; on the other, he is repelled and wants nothing to do
with him. The religious excitement is only the incidental cause of
his outbreak of rage.

Even though held by the preaching of Jesus, he is disturbed
by a feeling of unrest. Several times he looks toward the door, as
though he would like to leave. Perhaps he fears that he will have a
seizure, but the large audience makes it difficult for him to move
freely in any direction. His anxiety increases until he can control
himself no longer and he leaps to his feet, his eyes aflame with
excitement. He shouts

*Let us alone. What have we to do with you—you Jesus of
Nazareth? Are you come to destroy us? I know who you are.*

He beats the air violently. Those sitting nearby draw away from
him as he repeats again and again

I know who you are.

He becomes incoherent and starts to scream. Seized with a cramp, he falls to the floor. His lips covered with foam and his face distorted, he screams out time and again. Involuntarily, his arms are thrust back. His hands look stunted and his fingers are crooked like claws.

Jesus stops and steps from the platform. Quietly, he advances toward the wretched creature as the crowd makes way for him. When he reaches the afflicted man he bends over him, but the man creeps to the wall where he hides his face behind his arms and shouts

What have we to do with you, Jesus—you Son of God?

Jesus steps forward, seizing him with a firm grasp and speaking in a commanding voice to the evil spirit

Hold your peace, and come out of him.

But the sick man breaks free and with his face still distorted continues to shout

You Son of God . . . Son of God . . .

He tries to spit but the saliva gets no farther than the corners of his mouth. Then his eyes meet those of Jesus and he becomes calm. He wipes his chin with the back of his hand and then groans with a feeling of release. He looks with surprise at the people gathered about him. The spell is past. Moreover, he realizes that Jesus has healed him of his infirmity. At that moment the priest can be heard pronouncing the Aaronic benediction. Everyone faces the south wall and listens devoutly. After each verse the people reply Amen. Jesus and the man he has cured stand side by side.

After the benediction, Peter indicates to Jesus that he will go ahead to his house and wait for him there. He hurries away.

Meanwhile, the leaders of the synagogue, with some of the Pharisees, surround Jesus and the man. They look with curiosity and amazement upon the man once so afflicted and now healed and say among themselves

What word is this? For with what power he commands the unclean spirits, and they do obey him? [Luke 4:36.]

Jesus takes advantage of the confusion and, together with his disciples, slips away through a back door.

Peter has hurried away from the synagogue because his wife's mother is lying sick at home.

He reaches the large house where he lives with his wife, her mother and his brother, Andrew. On the doorpost is fastened the mezuzah. As a devout Jew, Peter touches the mezuzah and then kisses the fingertips which have touched the sacred object.

Peter walks on tiptoe when he enters the room where his mother-in-law is lying ill. His wife is watching at her bedside. One look at his wife is enough to tell him that there is no change for the better.

[The mother-in-law is ill with "the great fever." Greek physicians distinguished between the "great fever" and the "small fever." The first was accompanied by transitory delirious fancies like those found in cases of hysterics.]

Anxiously, Peter looks at his mother-in-law. The flush of the fever is in her cheeks and her lips are dry. She tosses restlessly in her bed, talking in her delirium about a fish that is going to eat a sheep.

Peter rouses her from her delirium. She looks about in bewildered fashion. She fixes a feverish glance upon Peter's face and then, overcome with ague, she falls back upon the bed, groaning and despairing of her condition. Tears crowd the eyes of Peter's wife. Peter tries to console her

Jesus will be here soon; he will make her whole.

But her weeping continues. Trying to encourage her, Peter tells of the miraculous cure he witnessed in the synagogue.

He has just cured a man of an evil spirit. You know Zadok, the demoniac? He commanded the unclean spirit to come out of him.

His wife is listening now. She looks at her husband through her tears.

THE WIFE: *And did he not hurt him?*
PETER: *No.*

His wife takes courage.

PETER: *I'll go and meet him.*

He leaves the room. Alternately, his mother-in-law groans and babbles incoherently in her delirium.

Outside the house. Jesus and his disciples arrive as Peter is leaving. Peter approaches Jesus and explains the situation.

My wife's mother is sick, Master. I know that if you will you can make her whole. . . .

Jesus puts his arm around him to comfort him.

Where is she?

Jesus and Peter enter the house, but not before Jesus has touched the mezuzah because he too is a devout Jew.

The room with the patient. Jesus and Peter enter. Peter's wife is about to leave, but Jesus motions to her to stay. The ill woman is still moaning in her delirium.

Jesus looks at her quietly and then goes to the head of the bed. Peter lends a hand and they lift the patient to an upright position. Jesus sits beside her while Peter and his wife see that she does not fall back upon the bed. It is obvious that the ill woman is suffering considerably. Her eyes have a glazed look and her throat is parched with thirst. Peter's wife gives her water.

Jesus takes her hand and succeeds in attracting and holding her attention. Peter bends over and begins speaking to her in a low earnest voice.

Fear not . . . you will be whole. . . .

There is a sudden alteration in the woman's condition. She breaks out with a heavy perspiration and beads of sweat run down her forehead and cheeks. Confidently, she fixes her eyes upon Jesus. Some strange healing power has passed from Jesus to the patient. Peter's wife wipes her mother's face several times with a napkin.

Finally, the gasping stops and the sick woman is breathing normally. She closes her eyes, and Jesus signals to Peter and his wife to lay her down in the bed so that she can rest. Almost instantly she falls into a deep sleep.

Peter's wife looks at Jesus gratefully and then leaves the room to make preparations for the evening meal. Jesus and Peter soon follow her. After they leave the room the mother-in-law suddenly awakes as from a long refreshing sleep. Feeling rested, she gets out of bed, dresses quickly and goes to her daughter in the kitchen who scarcely knows what to make of her mother's rapid recovery. A neighbor, who has dropped in to inquire about the patient, is startled and hurries to spread the news abroad.

Peter's mother-in-law returns to her household duties, and almost before the others realize it she is once again in full command of her home. Taking a tray of bread from her daughter's hands, she carries it into the room where Jesus and his disciples are awaiting their supper. A wine cup is on the table because it is customary to serve wine on Saturday evening. The men rejoice at the sight of the mother-in-law, but she gives all credit and praise to Jesus for his miraculous cure.

Suddenly the sound of the horn from the synagogue is heard marking the end of the Sabbath day. Every one arises, wine is poured into the cup, and Peter, as head of the household, pronounces the benediction.

After this, supper is served, and since it is customary to eat with the fingers they first have to be washed. Therefore, Peter's wife brings a basin and water jug and begins to pour water on the guests' hands.

Interrelated scenes show the neighbors spreading the news of the miraculous cure.

Other neighbors come to the door to visit the mother-in-law and to see Jesus. They ask if he is staying overnight and whether he is going to deliver another sermon that evening. Finally, Peter persuades them to leave, and he shuts and bars the door in order to make certain that Jesus and the disciples will not be disturbed again that night.

The news about Peter's mother-in-law spreads rapidly through the town and causes excited discussion in the synagogue. When the Sabbath is past people crowd to the house of Peter, some wanting to hear another sermon, others carrying with them sick relatives they hope Jesus will heal. They come from all directions, and each one has some particular need. A blind man is led by his daughter; a lame man is leaning upon the shoulders of two brothers; one man walks with the aid of sticks and another with crutches. A young mother brings her sick baby and a young girl her grandmother who has to stop at almost every step because of her coughing fits. A father and mother forcibly bring their imbecile daughter, hoping that Jesus will drive the evil spirit out of her as he did from the man in the synagogue.

It is not long before half the town has gathered in front of Peter's house and others continue to come in an endless train. The huge throng wait patiently for Jesus.

Inside the house, Peter and his guests have finished their meal. Andrew looks out the window.

The whole town is gathered at the door.

Peter and the others look at Jesus, wondering what he will do. Their faces show their satisfaction as he rises and moves toward the door.

Peter opens the door and comes out first. A wave of excite-

ment runs through the multitude as Jesus appears and indicates
that he is going to speak.

> *Come unto me, all you that labor and are heavy laden, and*
> *I will give you rest. Learn of me and you shall find rest unto*
> *your souls. Blessed are you that weep now; for you shall laugh.*

As Jesus speaks, the camera pans over the multitude. It shows
some scribes and Pharisees in front, as they were in the synagogue.
[It should be noticed that their attitude toward Jesus is not hostile.
To these people religious and theological problems were of the
greatest importance. The Judaism of that period encompassed so
many varying shades of theological thought that one more or less
did not make a great difference. Jesus's preachings are to them only
"something new" which has to be studied carefully. They therefore
listen attentively, desiring to be instructed in his doctrine.]

We see also a group of three men with earnest, resolute faces:
they are the revolutionaries. We have already seen them in the
synagogue. They too—but for other reasons—are listening to Jesus.
A patrol of Roman soldiers looks in to make sure the meeting is
not a political one. The three young men cast hateful looks after
the soldiers who move on with mocking grins upon their faces.
Nothing is going on except the preaching of one of those "crazy
religious fanatics."

Four men arrive carrying a lame man on a pallet. One is an
old man with a white beard. The other three are young men. The
old man seems to be the father of the sick man and the other three
are the latter's sons. They try to bring the lame man to Jesus but
cannot reach him because of the multitude. Some of the disciples
help the man to be placed safely at the feet of Jesus. One of the
sons tells of his father's illness.

> *This is my father. . . . He is taken with palsy. . . . Look,*
> *both his legs are lame.*

Another son uncovers the legs of the father and demonstrates
that the muscles are loose and flabby. He says

Look.

He takes a long needle and drives it into the calf of his father's leg. Philip addresses the lame man.

PHILIP: *You feel no pain?*
LAME MAN: *None at all.*

All are looking at Jesus in excitement: the disciples, the two sons, the aged father, and the third son who is peering through a hole in the roof. From the multitude no word is heard. There is a hush of expectation.

Jesus is looking with compassion at the invalid whose eyes never leave the face of the Master. Presently Jesus speaks with a gracious manner.

Man, your sins are forgiven.

At these words the Pharisees and the scribes look at one another and each knows the thought passing through the others' minds. Is not this blasphemy? Who can forgive sins but God alone? But Jesus too knows their thoughts, and he turns to them, asking

Why reason you those things in your hearts?

There is a long silence. The Pharisees and scribes do not answer as there is no particular reason why they should. According to their law God alone can forgive sins. No one can doubt or deny that fact. They feel that Jesus has gone too far and they are curious to see what he will do next.

Jesus continues, but there is no harshness in his tone

What reason you? Whether it is easier to say to the sick of the palsy: "Your sins be forgiven you"—or to say: "Arise and take up your bed and walk"?

There is another silence. The multitude looks first at Jesus and then at the Pharisees but without animosity toward either. The Pharisees are the respected leaders of the people, and the people realize that this is not a quarrel between men, but a theological discussion.

As the Pharisees do not answer, Jesus turns again to the sick man and says with a tone of authority

I say unto you—arise.

A tremor followed by a series of spasms runs through the body of the man, whose eyes are still fixed upon Jesus. The latter signals to the two sons, who lift their father out of bed. With their aid he gets to his feet. They would still assist him, but he sends them away and begins to walk alone, his confidence increasing with every step.

All the people, including the scribes and the Pharisees, are amazed. There are tears of joy in many eyes. Jesus speaks again to the man who has been healed.

Take up your bed and go your way into your house.

With a look of surprise the man takes up his bed, places it upon his shoulders, and walks away, followed by his sons and his old father. Expressions of joy are heard from all sides, and a voice from the crowd is heard shouting

In truth we have seen strange things today.

Jesus turns to the large crowd of sick people gathered in front of Peter's house, who are thronging about him.

The three young revolutionaries, impressed by the miracle they have witnessed, leave the place and are soon lost in the crowd. They are going to a secret meeting with other revolutionaries who have come from the towns around the lake.

The meeting place is on the seashore not far from Peter's house. We see an open shed with baskets, barrels, fishing nets, masts and other fishing equipment. There is little danger of being taken by surprise, but as an added safeguard a man is left on watch to warn against any Roman patrol that might come that way. The camera follows the three men on their way there.

NARRATOR: *The Pharisees tolerated the Romans as they waited for deliverance by God. But there were others who resolutely determined to throw off the Roman yoke as soon as possible. They were the revolutionaries, and they made up the underground movement of that day. They watched Jesus attentively, hoping to find in him the leader they needed.*

Those from nearby towns have already arrived. The three young revolutionaries we have already met. They are enthusiastic about what they have seen and heard, and they try to persuade the others to come with them and witness the miracles of Jesus.

FIRST REVOLUTIONARY: *You must come with us and see him.*
SECOND REVOLUTIONARY: *You must both see and hear him.*
FOURTH REVOLUTIONARY: *Whom?*
THIRD REVOLUTIONARY: *Jesus of Nazareth.*
FOURTH REVOLUTIONARY: *Oh! the preacher.*
FIRST REVOLUTIONARY: *Yes.*

The Fourth Revolutionary makes a gesture of disappointment.

FIFTH REVOLUTIONARY: *What manner of man is he?*
SECOND REVOLUTIONARY: *You never met a man like him.*
FIRST REVOLUTIONARY: *We have just seen him heal a man sick with the palsy.*
SIXTH REVOLUTIONARY: *No!*
THIRD REVOLUTIONARY: *Yes. And even unclean spirits obey him.*
SEVENTH REVOLUTIONARY: *Really?*
FIRST REVOLUTIONARY: *People say he is the Messiah.*

SECOND REVOLUTIONARY: *Listen, we have enough men; what we need is a leader.*
THIRD REVOLUTIONARY: *Yes, and he is the man.*
NINTH REVOLUTIONARY: *We'll accept no ruler except God.*

A warning whistle is heard from the man on watch, and he hurries up to the shed. They hide behind the barrels and the baskets. Through the shed the Roman patrol can be seen walking along the shore. But nothing arouses their suspicion, and they move on, turning away from the shore. The revolutionaries come out from their hiding and after making certain the patrol has left, they disperse in small groups, going to the house of Peter.

In front of Peter's house. Jesus, filled with compassion, moves about among the huge throng and heals many of those who are sick. Jesus moves with a certain radiant serenity. Upon his face can be seen an expression of gentle love and tender compassion. He goes from one to another, asking each individual in a low voice about the nature and symptoms of his illness. There is a certain excitement released in various ways in the different individuals who are sick. Some are taken with cramps, followed by immediate healing. Others fall into a sleep.

Friends and relatives gather about those who have been healed. Exclamations of joy are heard. An old woman expresses the thoughts of everyone as she says

Such power as his must surely be of God.

Then all the people join in singing a hymn.

As the scene ends we see one of those healed by Jesus walking away, happily swinging his crutches over his head.

The last scene of this sequence, acted in the evening light, is a long shot showing the multitude in the foreground and the house of Peter in the background. Without a change in the position of the camera the scene dissolves softly into another in morning light, showing exactly the same exterior, except that now it is deserted.

NARRATOR: *And in the morning Jesus went out and departed for a solitary place.*

Only Peter's wife, who is grinding flour, is seen outside the house. The creaking of the handmill is the only sound which is heard. We notice outside the house two stone troughs filled with water. They are used for the purification ritual.

Jesus comes out of the house. Peter's mother-in-law comes out to fetch the flour. Her daughter follows her back inside.

At the shore of the lake Jesus passes two fishermen who are tarring their boats. He shouts the Jewish greeting

Shalom.

And they answer back

Shalom.

Inside Peter's house. The mother-in-law and her daughter are preparing bread dough.

Jesus walks up a grass-covered slope, the other side of which is quite steep. After having passed the ridge of the slope, he disappears.

Outside Peter's house. Andrew is on his way to the roof by the outer staircase, carrying tools and materials needed to repair the hole that was made at the time of the healing of the lame man. Peter comes out, looking for Jesus. As he does not see him anywhere he approaches the outer staircase and asks Andrew

Where is Jesus?

Andrew shrugs his shoulders but suggests

Go and seek for him at the shore.

Peter nods and goes in the direction of the lake. Andrew begins working on the roof, kneading mud, sand and small stones into a cement.

Peter passes by two fishermen who are tarring their boats.

PETER: *I seek Jesus.*
FISHERMAN: *We saw him walking over there.*

They point in the direction of the grass-covered slope. Peter takes a step and then turns and asks

Are you going fishing?

One of the two makes a gesture toward the sky showing that he has no confidence in the weather. Then he adds

Better to lose time than to lose life.

Peter agrees and walks toward the slope.

Outside Peter's house. Andrew is spreading the mud cement and is filling up the hole in the roof.

Peter climbs the slope and sees Jesus, kneeling and absorbed in prayer, in the depression behind. Peter is greatly moved at this sight, and a power seems to transform the rough fisherman. A light appears to shine from within him, reflecting the new purity he has found. He moves away a short distance and rests on the grass waiting for Jesus.

Outside Peter's house. Andrew has finished spreading the mud cement and starts rolling it with a stone-roller.

Jesus comes back over the grassy slope and sees Peter, who explains his presence by saying

You were not in the house, so I came to look for you.

Jesus nods in appreciation and, still in the mood of devotion, the two men walk silently back to town.

Outside Peter's house. Andrew has finished working on the roof and is on his way down the staircase. He puts his tools in their place and washes his hands. At the same time Peter's wife and mother-in-law are setting the table outside the house, preparing the first meal of the day. Andrew approaches Peter's wife, showing her that he has torn the sleeve of his shirt. He says

Look.

She goes into the house and comes back with a needle, which is in a hollowed bone. She takes it out and begins to sew as Jesus and Peter arrive. They sit down and Peter's mother-in-law pours out goat's milk for them, and invites them to help themselves to bread, grapes and dates. As the mending of Andrew's sleeve is completed, several of the Pharisees who were there the night before come to the house. They are made welcome and invited to share in the meal. They accept, but before sitting down they approach the stone trough for the ritual handwashing. By means of a scoop, water is poured on the hands and allowed to run off outside the trough. Once this ceremony is completed, they sit down and begin eating.
[The succession of the situations of this scene progresses so rapidly that there will be no need of special and superfluous dialogue such as in the little courtesies of life.]
John and James arrive. They too are invited to share in the meal. They accept and begin eating at once without going through the ceremony of handwashing. One of the Pharisees, an old man (First Pharisee), speaks to John and James, and in his voice is a tinge of reprimand.

FIRST PHARISEE: You eat bread with unwashed hands?

John shrugs his shoulders.

THIRD PHARISEE: *The bread is a gift of God, and you profane it in his eyes if you do not receive it with clean hands.*

JAMES: *That is not written in the Law.*

FIRST PHARISEE: *But it is in the traditions. . . .*

JOHN (interrupting): *The traditions are not the Law.*

SECOND PHARISEE: *The traditions are given by God the same as the Law.*

JAMES: *The traditions are not of God, but of man.*

THIRD PHARISEE: *He who lightly esteems handwashing will perish from the earth.*

[There is no tension between those taking part in the conversation. It is only a friendly discussion setting forth the old and new points of view.]

The First Pharisee now turns to Jesus.

What say you? Why do your disciples eat bread with unwashed hands?

Jesus does not answer. Instead he looks at his hands as if he might find the answer there. Then he speaks

There is nothing from without a man that can enter into him and defile him.

He pauses. The Pharisees and the disciples listen attentively although they have difficulty in following his line of thought. He continues

But that which comes out of the heart, this defiles a man.

Jesus looks again at his hands, and then he gets up and enters the house. There is silence. The Pharisees are perplexed for they do not understand the profound meaning of the words of Jesus. In their eyes he is a maker of paradoxes and should not be taken too seriously.

The First Pharisee has been so absorbed in listening to Jesus that he has not noticed his departure. He is just about to speak when he realizes that Jesus has gone. His face shows that he is somewhat disturbed. But, collecting his thoughts, he turns to the other Pharisees and says

I think we too will have to go.

He rises. The Second Pharisee, seeing that the disciples are embarrassed at the situation, explains their hurried departure by saying

They are waiting for us at the synagogue.

Then they leave.

The four disciples, left alone, look at each other. Every time Jesus uproots some deep-seated custom or tradition, they are disturbed if not shocked. They cannot understand his apparently rude behavior toward the Pharisees, who had come as friends.

Peter breaks the silence.

Come.

All four enter the house.

[According to "the traditions of the Elders," handwashing before meals was a religious duty and the Pharisees had more regard for the tradition than for the Law. Some Pharisees were so scrupulous that they washed twice, before and after each meal. But beyond doubt there were many who did not obey the regulation so strictly. Each party to the discussion considered the question from his own point of view. The Pharisees looked upon it as a social, political and religious matter while Jesus thought of it in terms of the ethical and the spiritual. Both were right. Among the Pharisees two tendencies were dominant: the rigorous school of *Shammai* and the more liberal school of *Hillel*.]

Inside Peter's house his wife is mending some old clothes. Jesus is sitting beside her studying the way she is sewing a piece of *old* cloth on an *old* garment.

Peter and the three others enter the room. Peter speaks to Jesus.

The Pharisees were offended.

Jesus does not look or speak, thus indicating that there is nothing he can do about the matter.

JOHN: *They did not understand.*

John's tone suggests that neither he nor the others have understood the meaning of the words of Jesus any better than have the Pharisees. Jesus, therefore, looks up at them, asking

Are you also without understanding?

Their faces express their feelings. Jesus sighs. He will have to teach them step by step.

Do you not yet understand that whatsoever enters in at the mouth goes into the belly, and is cast out into the draught? But those things which proceed out of the mouth come forth from the heart, and they defile the man. For out of the heart proceed evil thoughts, murders, adulteries, fornications, thefts, false witness, blasphemies: these are the things which defile a man: but to eat with unwashed hands defiles not a man.

Now the disciples understand and their faces express their joy. They are at the same time ashamed and proud: ashamed because of their lack of confidence, and proud because they are his disciples. They do not *fully understand* but their intuition tells them that no mere man has ever spoken in such fashion before.

The three Pharisees arrive at the synagogue. Before entering, they talk about Jesus.

FIRST PHARISEE: *It is always the same way with him. I talk of the East and he talks of the West.*

SECOND PHARISEE: *Yes, and if I put a straightforward question to him . . .*

THIRD PHARISEE: *You get a vague reply.*

FIRST PHARISEE: *Or an evasive one.*

He makes a sign to his brothers to follow him into the synagogue.

Inside the synagogue. Outside we have heard a shrill-voiced boys' choir to whom the first lessons in the Holy Scriptures are given by the Overseer.

Entering the house of God, we see the boys sitting on the stone floor around the teacher, who is reciting one verse after another. They move their small bodies rhythmically according to the rhythm of the reading and to the time beaten by the teacher's stick, being taught the Law and the Prophets by repeating every verse over and over again.

The three Pharisees stop to listen to the children reading Ezekiel 36:26

A new heart also will I give you, and a new spirit will I put within you: and I will take away the stony heart out of your flesh, and I will give you a heart of flesh.

The teacher calls a halt. The Pharisees smile appreciatively. The Ruler of the Synagogue advances to meet them while the teacher speaks to the boys.

TEACHER: *Have I not told you that a man has 248 joints? And that what you learn here by heart cannot enter into your 248 joints if you do not speak loud? Have I not told you that?*

BOYS: *Yes.*

TEACHER: *Well then, let us start again with verse 25—and this time let us speak much louder.*

The teacher has the script roll on his knees, and while we are listening to the boys reciting the verses very loudly, we see in close-up the finger of the teacher gliding over the page, along the lines of Ezekiel 36:25

Then will I sprinkle clean water upon you, and ye shall be clean: from all your filthiness, and from all your idols, will I cleanse you.

The close-up of the page of the Book of Ezekiel dissolves softly into a scene of the customs house and the customs-gate of the town.

NARRATOR: *The Roman oppressors were sucking the lifeblood out of the Jews by imposing intolerable taxes. And they were being levied through the medium of Jewish tax collectors who were despised by their own people.*

The tax-collector Levi, who had been in the crowd in front of Peter's house, is sitting at his office, absorbed in thought. With him are two or three other Jewish customs officers. A group of Roman soldiers is on watch at the gate in order to lend authority if it is needed.

A peasant comes up to the gate leading a donkey laden with cauliflowers. One of the customs officers steps out and after inspecting the load fixes the duty fee. The peasant makes strong objections to his demands.

PEASANT: *Yesterday I only paid half that.*
CUSTOMS OFFICER: *Yesterday is not today.*
PEASANT: *But why the double? Why? Why?*
CUSTOMS OFFICER: *Pay—and don't waste my time.*
PEASANT: *No, I won't pay the double.*
CUSTOMS OFFICER: *You won't?*
PEASANT: *No!*

The customs officer turns to the soldiers, but the sergeant is already on his way. He needs only to let his presence become known in order to make the peasant pay. The sergeant returns to his soldiers. As the peasant leaves the gate, he cannot resist the temptation to spit after the customs officer.

Levi looks up and sees Jesus and his six disciples approaching the gate. Their appearance seems to be an answer to his prayers. He rises and goes to Jesus, falls to his knees before him and says

Good Master, have mercy on me.

Jesus helps him to his feet.

What would you have me do for you?

Levi looks around a little uneasily. He is embarrassed at speaking in such a way before the disciples, knowing the common prejudice of all Jews against the tax collectors. Understanding this, Jesus puts his arm about Levi and they find a quiet corner to talk. Levi speaks falteringly

When I heard you speaking I felt that you would help me to a better life.

Listening quietly, Jesus looks at him. Something about him, perhaps the light in his eyes, encourages Levi to continue

And I thought how blessed they are, whom you choose for your disciples—and that perhaps you would let me too be one of them.

Levi has finished speaking. Jesus examines his face closely. Then he speaks

Whosoever would be my disciple must forsake all . . . all.

Levi looks up and nods his acceptance.
Jesus rises, saying

Follow me.

Jesus and Levi (henceforth called Matthew) join the disciples waiting at the gate. They all go into the town. As soon as they have left the gate, a shepherd with a flock of sheep goes through the gate in the same direction. In the midst of the flock is a single black sheep.

The scene of the flock of sheep dissolves softly into the interior of the dining room in Matthew's house. He has invited Jesus and the disciples together with his fellow tax-gatherers—perhaps with the intention of giving them an opportunity to meet Jesus.

These men know themselves to be sinners, and they are accustomed to the contempt of the "honest" town people. But they appreciate the sympathetic attitude of Jesus and the fact that instead of despising them he tries to understand their problems and is anxious to forgive.

JESUS: *This merchant seeking good pearls—when he had found one pearl of great price—went and sold all that he had and bought it.*

TAX-GATHERER: *Again,* all *that he had.*

John and Peter, on some pretense, leave the room.

MATTHEW: *Oh, I understand. If I'll win the Kingdom of God I must forsake all else. That is what I am going to do.* (To Jesus) *I am ready to pay the price.*

Jesus smiles approvingly.

Three Pharisees stand at the street gate leading to the courtyard of Matthew's house. As it is the home of a rich person, there is a doorkeeper. The Pharisees are speaking to him. John and Peter appear in the courtyard.

FIRST PHARISEE: *Is it true that Jesus and his disciples are in there?*

DOORKEEPER: *Yes, there is a great party in his honor.*

FIRST PHARISEE: *Thank you.*

The First Pharisee looks at his two companions as if to say, you see, I was right. Then he sees John and Peter in the courtyard. He speaks to them.

FIRST PHARISEE: *How is it that Jesus eats and drinks with publicans?*

PETER: *He has made Matthew one of his disciples.*

SECOND PHARISEE: *Is that possible?*

THIRD PHARISEE: *I thought Jesus was one of ours.*

SECOND PHARISEE: *This is indeed an unheard of thing.*

JOHN: *What?*

SECOND PHARISEE: *That he is meddling with that kind of rabble.*

FIRST PHARISEE: *Does he not hate sin?*

PETER: *Certainly he does. But he does not hate sinners.*

FIRST PHARISEE: *You call those people sinners.*

THIRD PHARISEE: *I think I understand him. I too have received sinners at my own table to persuade them to lead a pious life.*

FIRST PHARISEE: *But you would not have been with them at their table? Or would you?*

THIRD PHARISEE: *Oh, no—never. And of course the sinner would have to take the first step.*

FIRST PHARISEE: *You see, that is the difference.*

JOHN: *Yes, that is the difference. You shun the sinner: he seeks him out.*

FIRST PHARISEE (shaking his head): *Seeking out sinners.*

SECOND PHARISEE: *Surely this is something new.*

THIRD PHARISEE: *Yes, indeed, it is a new thing, and we will have to give it grave consideration.*

Jesus, who has seen from the dining room his two disciples talking with the Pharisees, now approaches the group. The First Pharisee sees him.

FIRST PHARISEE: *There you are. We were just talking about you.*

THIRD PHARISEE: *We cannot understand. . . .*

Jesus looks questioningly.

SECOND PHARISEE: *We did not expect this of you . . . a religious teacher.*

Jesus now looks inquiringly at the First Pharisee.

FIRST PHARISEE: *You break bread with publicans and sinners.*

Jesus looks at them and nods pensively. Then he takes a seat on the bench in the midst of them and he says

They that be whole need not a physician, but they that are sick . . . for I am not come to call the righteous, but sinners to repentance. [Matthew 9:12–13.]

[There is no tension or excited rudeness. The Pharisees are surprised and shocked, but they are not hostile and neither is Jesus.]
During a scene shift, we hear

NARRATOR: *And Jesus spake a parable unto them, saying: A certain man had two sons . . .*

We see the father, a rich farmer, and his two sons in a room. The elder son, who is to inherit the farm when his father dies, is a stern-looking young man, a toiler, a slave to duty, stubborn and hard. The younger son is lighthearted and generous and full of the joy of life, but also giddy and weak. He is not bad but only unstable. The younger son has asked his father to give him now the portion of goods that will be his after his father's death. The father has promised to think it over. Now the father and his two sons have gathered together in order to discuss the matter.

FATHER: *You have not changed your mind?*
YOUNGER SON: *No, Father, I am bored to death by this manner of life.*
ELDER SON: *Start working, and stop dreaming—that's my advice to you.*

YOUNGER SON: *I tell you that farming holds no attraction for me.*

ELDER SON: *Why? It does for me.*

YOUNGER SON: *With you it is different. Some day the farm will be yours. Then I will have to move out. Better to leave now and start my own life.*

The father lays his hands on the shoulders of the younger son.

FATHER: *You are certain that you wish to leave?*

YOUNGER SON: *I am certain.*

FATHER: *You shall have your own way.*

ELDER SON: *Fool.*

FATHER: *No, your brother is no child. He is old enough to decide for himself.* (To the younger son, pointing to the heap of money on the table) *Here is your third.*

YOUNGER SON: *Thank you, Father.*

He collects the money hurriedly, putting it into a small chest. The father looks at him with an expression of sadness in his eyes.

[WIPE TO THE NEXT SCENE.]

At the gate to the farm, the young man is about to take leave of his father and elder brother. The latter is cool, and there is a smirk upon his face. The father embraces his son warmly and before letting him go takes a gold ring from one of his fingers and places it on the hand of the young man. The latter makes his departure. The father looks after him until he disappears around a bend in the road. His eyes are filled with tears. The elder son shakes his head in disgust as the two go back to the farm.

[WIPE TO THE NEXT SCENE.]

The road. The younger son is seen from behind, traveling on his journey. The road divides the picture vertically in two equal parts. This scene dissolves softly into a street in an oriental city, such as Damascus. The street divides the picture into two parts —just like the road. In the street the awnings throw a shade pattern onto the pavement.

In the crowd we notice the younger son who has just arrived. We follow him around a corner. He enters a barbershop and explains to the barber how he wishes his hair cut.

Take away the beard and cut my hair in the Greek fashion.

The barber starts to work, using scissors, knife, comb and curling-iron.

The barbershop faces a small square where a girl can be seen sitting under a tree. She starts playing on a flute. Her eyes are encircled with black, and her cheeks and her lips are rouged. There is an exchange of smiles between the young man and the girl who continues playing on her flute. When he leaves the barbershop they go off together.

[WIPE TO THE NEXT SCENE.]

The prostitute and the young man enter a tavern of a rather sordid type. By winking at the innkeeper, the girl makes him understand that she has a sucker in tow. The innkeeper therefore outdoes himself in politeness, and the young man is flattered. The girl orders wine and snails for food. They are served at once. While they sit at the table the young man apologizes for being ignorant of the Greek language. The girl promises to teach him, and they begin their first lesson at once, using fingers and sign language and laughing cheerfully. The innkeeper, seeing this, joins in the laughter and recommends the girl to the young man by saying

She is a good girl—and her heart is in the right place.

A street seller enters the tavern and approaches the young couple. He has jewelry set in gold for sale. The girl is eager for an armlet, and the boy buys her two of them, one for each arm. She is deliriously happy as she teaches him to eat snails with a pin-edged spoon. The lesson in snail eating causes them both to laugh uproariously.

[WIPE TO THE NEXT SCENE.]

A lane. Moonshine. The girl moves ahead of the young man. She slips suddenly into a house, dragging the young man along with her.

[WIPE TO THE NEXT SCENE.]

A very short scene at the girl's house. In a ray of moonlight we see only the man's back, and the naked arms of the girl twining round his neck.

[WIPE TO THE NEXT SCENE.]

The same. Again in a ray of moonlight we see only her naked arm lifting up his arm into the light. She takes the golden ring which his father gave him when he was leaving home off his finger.

[WIPE TO THE NEXT SCENE.]

The tavern. The young man enters and timidly approaches the innkeeper.

YOUNG MAN: *Could I get some food on credit?*
INNKEEPER: *No, I never give credit.*
YOUNG MAN: *Could you lend me five drachmas?*
INNKEEPER: *No.*
YOUNG MAN: *Two drachmas?*
INNKEEPER (brutally): *No begging is allowed here. Leave. Quickly.*

The innkeeper drives the young man out of the tavern.

[WIPE TO THE NEXT SCENE.]

Outside the girl's house. It is night. The young man knocks at the door. He is now dressed in his old clothes. He knocks again.

GIRL: *Who is it?*
YOUNG MAN: *Open the door.*
GIRL: *No. What do you want?*
YOUNG MAN: *I have no money and nowhere to sleep.*
GIRL: *What is that to me?*

YOUNG MAN: *I know you have money.*
GIRL: *Go away now. I am done with you. Go away.*

He leaves.

[WIPE TO THE NEXT SCENE.]

A square in the city with a huge stone in the center on which stand the slaves who are to be sold. Here also day laborers gather looking for work. Among these is the young man. A peasant who has come to town in order to find a helper stops in front of him, inspecting him closely as if he were a cow or a horse.

PEASANT: *Do you know anything of farming?*
YOUNG MAN: *My father is a farmer.*
PEASANT: *Where?*
YOUNG MAN (evasively): *Far from here.*

The peasant, realizing that the young man has had a quarrel with his father, does not press him for a further explanation but invites him to come with him to his farm.

[WIPE TO THE NEXT SCENE.]

The peasant makes the boy tend his swine. He, a Jew, has become a swine keeper for a heathen peasant. During the day the herd of swine search for food in the field. At night they are kept in the hog pen where the swine keeper must sleep too. As there is a famine in the land the food for the swine is sometimes better than the food for their keeper. To appease his hunger the son often has to eat the carob-beans which are given the swine for food.

One evening, while sitting in the hog-sty among the swine, he remembers the happy evenings in his father's home, with all the servants gathered with the family for supper. Then he recalls his parting from his father. He weeps silently and then breaks down as great sobs shake his body. He bites into his coat so that no one will hear his weeping. Suddenly he comes to himself and makes up his mind. He rises, opens the door and goes out.

[WIPE TO THE NEXT SCENE.]

The boy on the road—on his way home in his rags, like a tramp.

[WIPE TO THE NEXT SCENE.]

The father is out in the field, watching the plow drivers make one furrow after another. Now and then he glances toward the road. Day after day he has kept watch, but it has always been in vain. But it is as though his eyesight has been especially sharpened for today because he is able to recognize his son at a great distance even though he is dressed in rags. The father runs to meet him, and then embraces his son tenderly. And his son says

Father, I have sinned and I am no longer worthy to be called your son.

But the father does not listen. He cannot cease kissing him and embracing him. There is not an angry word or any suggestion of reproach. We see only the great heart of a loving father.

As they are approaching the house, the father calls his servants, saying:

Bring hither the fatted calf, and kill it; and let us eat and be merry. [Luke 15:23.]

[WIPE TO THE NEXT SCENE.]

The feast taking place outside the house is in full course. The younger son is seated next to his father in the place of honor. He has on new clothes and on his feet new sandals. And now the father puts a golden ring on his finger. Everyone is filled with joy, and laughter echoes through the air, accompanied by song and music. At some distance from the men's party the girls and young women from the farm are enjoying their folk dances.

At this moment the elder son arrives. He has been out in the fields and is late. Surprised at hearing the songs and music, he calls one of the servants.

ELDER SON: *What do these things mean?*
SERVANT: *Your brother has come back.*

ELDER SON: *How did he look?*

SERVANT: *Miserable. Very poor indeed. Dressed in rags.*

ELDER SON: *Then what is all this?*

SERVANT: *Your father has killed the fatted calf.*

ELDER SON: *Why?*

SERVANT: *Because he has received him home again safe and sound.*

The elder son's face is filled with anger.

SERVANT: *Are you not coming to meet your brother?*

ELDER SON: *No.*

The servant goes to the father and tells of his conversation with the elder brother.

SERVANT: *Your son has come in from the fields.*

FATHER: *Is he not coming here to bid his brother welcome?*

SERVANT: *I asked him to come, but he said he would not.*

The father is disturbed and goes to the elder son.

FATHER: *Why do you not come and meet your brother?*

ELDER SON: *Father, lo, all these many years I have served you, neither transgressed I at any time your commandments: and yet you never gave me a kid, that I might make merry with my friends.*

FATHER: *You never asked me.*

ELDER SON (pretending not to hear): *But as this your son was come who has devoured your living with harlots you have killed for him the fatted calf.*

The father looks at the son for a long moment and then answers mildly

Son, you are ever with me, and all that I have is yours. It was meet that we should make merry, and be glad; for this your brother was dead, and is alive again, and was lost, and is found.

The father waits. For a moment father and son stand face to face. Then, on a sudden impulse, the son turns and goes his way out into the fields. The father looks after him with a sad expression. Then he returns to the feast.

While the elder son is crossing the fields many thoughts crowd his mind, chief of which is that he has been wronged. He is vexed and offended that his father is giving such a party for his good-for-nothing brother who has disgraced the family. He feels that he has been deceived because his father apparently prefers this fool to himself. One might well conclude that his father had only one son, the one for whom the family homestead was not good enough. But even though his father has lost his head, he, the elder son, would retain his senses and keep things moving in proper fashion.

NARRATOR: *Jesus concluded: More joy shall be in Heaven over one sinner who repents than over ninety-nine just persons who need no repentance.*

The elder son sits down on a stone fence. Behind him, some distance away, is a shepherd with a flock of sheep. The shepherd hails him

Shalom.

But the elder son does not hear him.

In the distance is heard the song and music from the farm, but this sound dies away little by little and is replaced by the sound of the reed pipe which the shepherd is playing to divert himself.

By means of a semicircular pan we follow the shepherd and his sheep and we leave the elder son. Then we see Jesus and his disciples. We stay with them and the shepherd and his sheep leave the picture.

Jesus is sitting on the stump of a tree surrounded by six of his disciples: Andrew, John and his brother James, Philip, Bartholomew (Nathanael) and Matthew. They are waiting for Peter, who presently arrives, accompanied by five other new disciples chosen by Jesus. These are Thomas, James (Jacob), the son of Alphaeus (Alphai), Thaddaeus (Taddai), Simon the Canaanite (sometimes called Zelotes or the Zealot), and Judas ish Querijoth (from the town Querijoth), usually called Judas Iscariot.

[All of them apparently have been drawn from the middle class, who at the time of Christ were particularly interested in spiritual and religious matters. They were very different in character and temper. The most remarkable of them was certainly Peter, great-hearted, staunch in his loyalty to Jesus, strong and weak at the same time, but profoundly sincere. His brother Andrew was as sincere as Peter and was more calm and gentle. John and James were hasty and violent and therefore were called "Sons of Thunder." Thomas was skeptical and cautious, but also straight and courageous. Bartholomew had once been a skeptic but was now a faithful believer in Jesus. Of Judas we will speak later.]

As Peter approaches Jesus, Jesus introduces the new disciples one by one, and each in turn kisses him as a sign of love and respect.

THOMAS: *I will follow you wherever you go.*
JUDAS: *I, too, will follow you wherever you go.*

Jesus then speaks to James, the son of Alphaeus.

JESUS: *Follow me.*
JAMES: *Let me go first and bid those who dwell in my house farewell.*

But Jesus says to him

No man having put his hand to the plough, and looking back, is fit for the Kingdom of God.

James, the son of Alphaeus, smiles, signifying his loyalty, and kisses Jesus.

Then Jesus turns to Simon the Canaanite.

JESUS: *Follow me.*

SIMON: *Let me first go and bury my father.*

JESUS: *Let the dead bury their dead; but go you and preach the Kingdom of God.*

Simon the Canaanite nods assent and kisses Jesus. Then Thaddaeus approaches Jesus.

THADDAEUS: *I will follow you wherever you go.*

He kisses Jesus. Jesus rises. The disciples gather about him, and together with Jesus they continue on their way, talking as they walk along.

From far away the sound of the sheep-bells is heard, and the shepherds speaking familiarly to the sheep in a strange rhythmic language that is somewhat akin to the sounds made by the animals themselves.

While they are walking, Jesus points at the meadow which is filled with flowers of wondrous colors.

JESUS: *Consider the lilies of the field, how they grow. They toil not, neither do they spin.*

The disciples look at the flowers.

JESUS: *Therefore, take no thought of how you shall be clothed, for your heavenly Father knows you have need of all these things. But seek you first the Kingdom of God, and all these things shall be added unto you.*

Jesus and the disciples continue their walk through a village. Their way leads them beside a stone wall. They can see a farmhouse inside the wall. From within the house is heard a woman's sweet voice, singing softly and lulling a baby to sleep. Not far from the house is a hay barn.

Jesus and his disciples stop to listen to the woman's voice. Then Jesus speaks to Peter

*Go and tell them that we will spend the night at their house,
in the hay barn.*

While Peter enters the house, Jesus and the others go to the
barn, where the disciples lie down.

Peter meets the young farmer who, with oriental hospitality,
bids Jesus and his disciples welcome. He and his wife make preparations for a meal.

In the barn the disciples have made themselves at home. Without drawing attention to himself, Jesus leaves, and it is only after
Peter returns that they notice his absence. Peter says

He has gone to pray.

One of the disciples looks through the crossbars at the back
of the barn and sees Jesus praying in a lonely place. All the disciples are filled with awe because of the loveliness of his countenance;
they long to be able to pray in the same manner.

The farmer announces a simple meal: milk, bread, figs and
dates. The disciples have just finished eating when Jesus comes
back. He tastes a cup of milk and then the farmer bids them good
night. As soon as he has retired, Peter approaches Jesus, saying

Teach us to pray.

Jesus nods, then the disciples gather around him. And he
speaks to them

*When you pray, when you have shut your door, pray to your
Father, who is in secret, and your Father, who sees in secret,
shall reward you openly. After this manner therefore pray
you.*

*Our Father which art in Heaven,
hallowed be thy name.
Thy Kingdom come.
Thy will be done in earth, as it is in Heaven.*

Give us this day our daily bread.
And forgive us our debts, as we forgive our debtors.
And lead us not into temptation,
but deliver us from evil:
For thine is the kingdom, and the power, and the
glory, for ever.
Amen. [Matthew 6:9–13.]

As Jesus gives them each article of the prayer the disciples repeat the words after him.

After "Amen" there is a devout silence. Then Jesus rises and wishes them good night; and they all go to their rest.

Without any camera movement, this scene in evening light dissolves softly into the hay barn in the morning. Jesus and the disciples awake and rise.

[WIPE TO THE NEXT SCENE.]

In the courtyard of the farm. The disciples are up and washing their hands and faces. While some are washing, others carry water in buckets from the farm well.

The road outside the farm. Three donkey-drawn carriages, laden with limestone from a nearby pit, pass by. The stones are intended for a new building being erected on the outskirts of the nearby town.

The farm. Having finished washing, Jesus and his disciples sit down at a table which the farmer and his wife have set for them in the courtyard. Placed before them is butter, milk, cheese and large baskets of bread. Before eating, one of the disciples says grace.

The three carriages pass by and we hear the drivers curse and shout.

Jesus and his disciples leave the farm as the farmer and his wife bid them farewell.

The three carriages arrive at the new building. A dozen people are working there. The walls have already reached a considerable height. The builder himself is standing on the top of the building, singing in order to keep up the spirits of the masons and their helpers. Then the builder shouts to the drivers to unload the stones. Then he resumes his singing. The masons are busily occupied with their work. Solid planks are placed from the ground to the upper part of the building, and the workmen use these in carrying up the necessary material: stones, water, mortar, etc. There is also the noise of the chisels of the stonecutters. Beside the building is a lime pit.

The new building is situated at the junction of two roads, one running south and the other west.

One of the workmen suddenly notices a procession coming from the south. At its head are some of the "elders" from the nearby town and with them the commander of the garrison, leading his horse by the bridle. He is not a Roman, this part of the country being outside the Roman military territory. He is a gentile and a commander of the mercenaries in the service of King Herod Antipas.

At a respectable distance the procession is followed by a crowd.

A boy, sent ahead for reconnoitering by one of the elders, comes back hurriedly, announcing that Jesus and his disciples are coming on the west road. The elders confer with one another and with the commander and they decide that the elders shall meet Jesus at the junction. All the laborers on the new building have ceased working and singing and are gazing at what is happening in the street.

One of the elders speaks to Jesus.

FIRST ELDER: *Do you see that man there?*

Jesus looks in the direction of the commander.

SECOND ELDER: *He is the commander of our town.*

Jesus nods.

FIRST ELDER: *He has a servant who is very dear to him and who is sick and about to die.*

Jesus looks inquiringly at the elder.

SECOND ELDER: *He wishes you to help him in his hour of need.*

THIRD ELDER: *He is worthy of being helped for he loves our nation and he has built our synagogue.*

FIRST ELDER: *Can he come and see you?*

JESUS: *Yes.*

The elders beckon to the commander.

COMMANDER: *My servant lies at home sick of palsy and grievously tormented.*

Jesus looks at him quickly and then he speaks

I will come and heal him.

The commander looks greatly relieved but says

I am not worthy that you should come under my roof: but speak the word only and my servant shall be healed. For I am a man under authority, having soldiers under me. I say to this man: go, and he goes: and to another: come, and he comes: and to any servant: do this, and he does it.

Jesus seems amazed at this, and looking around at the elders and the disciples, he says

Verily, I say unto you, I have not found so great faith, no, not in Israel.

Then Jesus turns to the commander, saying

Go your way, according to your faith, so will it be done unto you.

The commander is hesitant and looks questioningly at Jesus. Then Jesus repeats

Go your way. Your servant lives.

Then the commander believes, and mounting his horse, he rides away.

Meanwhile a crowd has gathered round Jesus, and from all sides they beseech him to speak to them, calling him

Lord, Lord. Come up here and teach us.

Jesus walks up one of the inclined planks. With the new building in the background, he faces the crowd and begins to speak

Why call you me Lord, and do not the things which I say. Therefore, whosoever hears these sayings of mine, and does them, I will liken him unto a wise man, which built his house upon a rock: And the rain descended, and the floods came, and the winds blew, and beat upon that house; and it fell not: for it was founded upon a rock. And everyone that hears these sayings of mine, and does them not, shall be likened unto a foolish man, which built his house upon the sand: And the rains descended and the floods came, and the winds blew, and beat upon that house; and it fell: and great was the fall of it. Therefore, not every man that says unto me: Lord, Lord, shall enter into the Kingdom of Heaven; but he that does the will of my Father which is in Heaven.

When Jesus finishes speaking, the people are astonished. As he comes down from the building many seek to touch him, for the power of divine virtue emanates from him. But the disciples hold them back.

Just as Jesus and his disciples are leaving the place, the Ruler of the Synagogue of the town, by name Taitus, comes to meet him. When he sees him he beseeches him

My little daughter lies at the point of death: I pray you, come and lay your hands on her, that she may be healed, and she shall live.

Jesus goes with him, and many people follow him and throng about him.

In some interspersed scenes we have seen the commander on horseback making his way home. At his arrival the servants, beside themselves with joy, meet him.

COMMANDER: *How is he?*
SERVANTS: *He lives.*

The commander hurries into the sick-room of his servant, who is sitting up in bed and eating with a good appetite. The commander inquires of the other servants

When did he begin getting well?

The servants explain

He took a turn for the better only a short while ago.

The roof of a poor house. Hens and chickens are running about. A woman is sitting on the floor, protected against the sun by a tent cloth. Stalks of hay are spread on trays for drying. A handloom is set up in a corner. Her daughter is on her way up the outer staircase with a cup of milk for the mother. After delivering the milk she sits down at the handloom and starts weaving. The picture is centered on the mother, who sips her milk.

NARRATOR: *A certain woman which was twelve years diseased with an issue of blood and had spent all her living upon physicians neither could be healed of any, was nothing bettered, but rather grew worse. When she heard of Jesus she said within herself: If I may but touch his garment, I shall be whole.*

The voices of the crowd are heard. The daughter rises and runs to the parapet of the roof, looking in the direction of the noise, and then shouts at the mother

That must be Jesus. . . . Yes, Mother, it is Jesus.

The mother listens with excitement. Then she calls the daughter

Come and help me.

The daughter helps her to her feet and then helps her down the staircase. Once in the street the woman runs unaided, making her way into the crowd surrounding Jesus. She comes into the press behind Jesus and succeeds in touching the hem of his garment—and she feels in her body that she is healed.

But Jesus, immediately knowing in himself that virtue has emanated from him, turns about, saying

Who touched me?

He looks questioningly at those behind him but no one answers. Peter and those with him shake their heads. They do not understand what he means.

PETER: *You see the multitude throng about and pressing you and you say: who touched me?*

JESUS: *Somebody has touched me, for I perceive that virtue is gone out of me.*

And Jesus looks around to see who has done this thing. When the woman realizes that hiding is useless, she comes forward fearfully and tells him all the truth.

WOMAN: *It was I who touched you—and I have been healed.*

Jesus looks at her with compassion.

JESUS: *Be of good comfort. Your faith has made you whole.*

The woman takes her leave and runs most of the way home.

While Jesus is speaking to the woman, a servant comes to the Ruler of the Synagogue with a message.

SERVANT: *Your daughter is dead. Why trouble you the Master any further?*

But when Jesus hears this, he speaks to the Ruler of the Synagogue

Be not afraid, only believe, and she shall be whole.

Jesus's intention in saying this is to encourage the father and inspire him with faith and hope, removing all fear and doubt. He succeeds, and the father believes implicitly in Jesus and in his power as a healer.

Jesus comes to the Ruler's house. In the courtyard just inside the gate he meets the minstrels with flutes and the mourning women. He speaks to them with authority

Give place.

He and his disciples enter the courtyard and he speaks again to the minstrels and the wailing women

Why make you this ado? The girl is not dead.

Surprised, they stop playing and wailing and look inquiringly at the Ruler, who gives them to understand that they are not needed and that he will send for them if necessary. In the meantime Jesus gives his disciples instructions to close the gate after the minstrels and not to let anybody in.

Then he chooses Peter, John and James to follow him into the house, leaving the others at the gate to prevent unbelievers from entering the house. Judas is vexed because he has not been chosen to go with Jesus, but Andrew makes him understand that Jesus's orders must be obeyed.

Jesus enters the sick room. The twelve-year-old daughter is lying in her bed, apparently dead. At the side of the bed is the mother, weeping silently. She looks up when Jesus and her husband enter. The room is filled with relatives and friends, mostly women who, according to common custom, have been summoned in order to be present at the moment of death.

Some of them have taken off their head-coverings. Others have covered the lower part of the face to the upper lip. As a sign of mourning they are all sitting or lying on the floor, having taken off their sandals. Some of them lay a hand on their head. They are unrestrained in their mourning, and their eyes are washed with tears. Wails of woe are heard.

Woe, woe my sister, woe is me.

When Jesus comes in he sees how they weep for the girl, and he says

Weep not, she is not dead but sleeps.

Knowing that she is dead, they shake their heads and some of them smile in disbelief.

Jesus sends them out of the room, and they go into the court-yard and stay with the disciples.

The father and mother do not understand why their relatives and friends who have come to pay their respects to their daughter are put out of the room, but they do not interfere. They commit themselves to God—and to Jesus. The father goes to the bed and puts his hand under the cover and touches his daughter's feet. They are cold as ice. He and his wife look at one another but, placing their faith in Jesus, join in a silent prayer.

Jesus's purpose in sending away the relatives and friends is to create a positive atmosphere of faith, hope and confidence by eliminating the negative influence of mourning and every tendency toward doubt and disbelief. For this same reason only his three most faithful disciples are admitted to the sick-room, together with the father and mother. His task is to revive the spirit of the lifeless girl by affecting her still accessible subconscious mind.

For a time, silence fills the room.

As soon as Jesus feels that he has the girl's subconscious mind under his control, he puts his exceptional and mysterious power of suggestion into force. He approaches the bed, takes her hand, which is still cold, and speaks to her

JESUS: *Talitha cumi.* (Damsel, I say unto you, arise.)   [Mark 5:41.]

Those in the room are watching intently and excitedly. Now all of them look at the girl, and her spirit actually returns to her. She moves, opens her eyes, then she rises and walks. "And they were astonished with a great astonishment." (Mark 5:42.)

The mother embraces her daughter. Jesus says to her

Give her something to eat.

The mother hurries out to find some food for the girl. The father kisses and caresses his daughter. The mother comes back with some fruit which the girl eats. Jesus takes the father aside, cautioning him not to speak to anybody of what has just taken place.

See that no man shall know of this.

[Jesus always impressed upon the people he helped the importance of not speaking to anybody of their miraculous healing. For a person who has been healed by the power of suggestion often meets with doubt and disbelief which undermines his faith, so that the psychological causes of the disease return.]

Jesus and his disciples take leave of the girl and her mother. The father accompanies them to the gate. The relatives gather around them asking many questions.

VOICES: *Has she come to life again? Is she alive?*
FATHER: *Yes, she is alive.*
JESUS: *I told you that she was not dead but slept.*

Then Jesus and the three disciples join the others at the gate and go on their way.

The sick room. The daughter, while eating the fruit, is exhaustively questioned by her mother.

MOTHER: *We thought you were dead.*
DAUGHTER: *I know.*
MOTHER (surprised): *How do you know?*
DAUGHTER: *I heard the doctor say so.*
MOTHER (astonished): *You say you heard the doctor say it?*
DAUGHTER: *Yes, mother.*
MOTHER: *And you were not surprised?*
DAUGHTER: *No.*
MOTHER: *Or alarmed?*
DAUGHTER: *No.*
MOTHER (after a pause): *Did you also hear the weeping and the wailing?*
DAUGHTER: *I know all that went on.*
MOTHER: *Also that we were preparing for your burial?*
DAUGHTER: *Yes.*
MOTHER: *Why didn't you rise? Why didn't you cry out?*
DAUGHTER: *I couldn't move or say a word.*

The mother shakes her head, wondering if this has all been a dream.

From the courtyard of the Ruler's house a side door leads to the street. The relatives leave the house through this door. The camera is placed in the street, facing this exit. The Ruler of the Synagogue stands in the door seeing the relatives off. They go to the right while the camera, placed on a truck, moves to the left, passing people walking and shopping. Among the people we notice a couple of young girls standing in front of a shop. Two Roman soldiers try to flirt with the girls, who only scold them and make them feel sheepish. The camera turns a corner and stops in front of an open gate leading into the house of a wealthy man who is a banker and a merchant. With the camera we move into the court-yard, passing the janitor at the gate. To the right is the banker's private office and next to this a room packed with clerks. The camera approaches the banker's private office.

NARRATOR: *A wealthy man who carried on many different busi-nesses decided to take account of his servants.*

The banker's private office. The banker is sitting with the manager of his office beside him. He is a cultured man who seems humane and tolerant. The manager of the office also appears to be of a sympathetic disposition. Before the banker stands a man ap-parently in poor circumstances, probably a tenant.

TENANT: *You know the harvest failed.*
BANKER: *Yes, I know.*
TENANT: *It's the first time I have been behind.*
BANKER: *Yes, I know that too. Well, I will give you three months longer to pay. Will that be sufficient?*
TENANT: *Yes, thank you.*

The manager leads the tenant into the main office and at the same time opens the door for the next debtor, who has been sum-moned.

NARRATOR: *And a man was brought unto him who owed him ten thousand denarii.*

The steward who enters is a dubious character. During the following conversation the banker looks at his papers.

BANKER: *You owe me a considerable amount, do you not?*
STEWARD: *Yes, sir.*
BANKER: *Ten thousand denarii?*

STEWARD: *Yes, sir. You see . . .*

BANKER: *I see that you have not made any of the promised pay-ments.* (Pause) *Why not?*

STEWARD: *I have had losses.*

BANKER: *Losses? How?*

STEWARD (hesitating): *I have speculated.*

BANKER: *Speculated? Behind my back and with my money—money I have given you for a better purpose? How much have you lost?*

STEWARD: *Every penny.*

BANKER: *But you must have something of value.*

STEWARD: *Nothing.*

BANKER: *Your house?*

STEWARD: *Is given in mortgage.*

BANKER: *The jewels of your wife?*

STEWARD: *Sold.*

The banker rises, trying to stifle his anger and indignation.

BANKER: *Do you know what you are? A rascal and a scoundrel.*

STEWARD: *I acted for the best. Have patience with me.*

BANKER: *No.*

STEWARD: *I will pay you back. I will give you half of my earnings until all I owe is repaid.*

BANKER: *No, no. I am done with you.* (To the office manager) *Will you see to it that this man, his wife and his children are taken to the slave stone and sold?*

STEWARD: *You have not the heart to do that?*

BANKER: *Yes, I have. You are a dishonest and unscrupulous man.*

The steward pleads with great humility.

STEWARD: *Take pity on me—if not for my own sake, then for the sake of my wife and children.*

The office manager takes the banker aside and speaks to him in a low voice, apparently saying something in favor of the wife.

The banker, moved with compassion, turns again to the steward and says

> *Well, for the sake of your wife and children I will have mercy on you and forgive you the debt.*

The steward's face lights up with joy. He expresses his thanks and then hurries out of the banker's office. One would imagine he would feel grateful for being spared from slavery. But not so. Outside he discovers a fellow servant, who is in his debt for only a hundred denarii. He approaches him quickly, shouting.

STEWARD: *What about the hundred denarii you owe me?*
SERVANT: *I am sorry, but I have not the money.*
STEWARD: *Why not? It was due a month ago.*
SERVANT: *My wife has been ill.*
STEWARD: *What is that to me? I need the money now.*

The steward lays hold of him. The servant begs him to have mercy.

SERVANT: *Have patience with me, and I will pay you all.*
STEWARD (harshly): *No.*
SERVANT: *Take pity on me; if not for my sake, then for the sake of my wife who is ill.*
STEWARD (inflexibly): *I said no.*

The steward calls his two slaves who have been waiting and says to them

> *Take him to the prison till he has paid his debt.*

The other servants have crowded together. They are indignant and offended at the steward because of his heartless behavior, and they raise their voices and make strong objections to what he is doing.

At this moment the banker and his office manager appear. They notice the noise and ask some slaves what is going on.

FIRST SLAVE: *It is the steward—he has sent Joseph to prison.*
BANKER: *Why?*
SECOND SLAVE: *Joseph owes him a hundred denarii.*
BANKER: *And for that sum he is sending him to prison?*
FIRST SLAVE: *He who himself has been pardoned for much more!*

The banker turns to his manager.

BANKER: *Call him into my office.*

The banker retires to his office, and a few moments later the manager appears and behind him the steward and several slaves. The banker is now thoroughly angry and has made up his mind. This unrighteousness merits punishment for the ungodly steward. As soon as he enters the office the banker speaks to him

> *You are a bad and wicked man. I forgave you all your debt. Should not you also have had compassion on your fellow servant, even as I had pity on you?*

And turning to the office manager he continues

> *Deliver him to the tormentors.*

The slaves lay hold of him and the closely guarded steward is led into the street from the courtyard and carried off to prison.

The camera, placed on a truck in the street, faces the gate of the banker's house. At first it follows the movements of the steward but leaves him when he and his guards turn a corner. Moving along the street the camera picks up some Pharisees, and we notice how people rise and bow to them, except for the artisans who are allowed to remain seated. The camera stops before a wine shop and we enter. There are four or five girls, prostitutes, sitting around and drinking with some companions. Their eyelids are daubed with black, their hands jewel-laden, and their fingernails colored by henna. Their hair is anointed. One of the girls even has golden ornaments fixed

in her nostrils. The girls and their friends are gay and jubilant;
some are exceedingly drunk. One of the girls, however, does not
take part in the merrymaking. Her name is Ruth and she sits
staring moodily into space. One of the young men tries to tickle
her, only to be pushed away, and another also receives the same
treatment. One of the girls indicates to the young men that they
are to leave Ruth alone. As the Pharisees pass by, this girl remembers a story she has heard recently and she begins telling it.

FIRST GIRL: *A girl, you know . . . a girl like one of us, was in
love with a young student, soon to become a scribe. But he did
not care for her.*
SECOND GIRL: *Why not?*
FIRST GIRL: *He said she was "unclean." She was hurt and decided
to avenge herself on him. Can you imagine what she did?*
THE OTHERS: *No, no. What did she do? Tell us.*
FIRST GIRL: *She stole his prayer-straps and went to the synagogue
and showed them to the elders and said: "Look, for lack of
money he gave me these."*
THE OTHERS: *Well—and what happened?*
FIRST GIRL: *He denied it, but the elders would not believe him.*
THIRD GIRL: *And then?*
FIRST GIRL: *Then he went up to the roof and jumped off.*
THE OTHERS: *And died?*
FIRST GIRL: *And died.*
SECOND GIRL: *Poor fellow.*
FIRST GIRL: *Poor? I do not know. The scribes and the Pharisees
too are always so hard upon us, are they not?*

General approbation.
Absorbed in her own thoughts, Ruth has not listened to all
this. The girl is weary of a life spent in drink and sin. She would
like to begin a new and better life, but does not know how to go
about it. She is lonesome and unhappy and longs for some depend-
able support to which she can cling. Tears come into her eyes.
Suddenly she rises and leaves the wineshop. The other girls look
after her, shaking their heads. They know from their own experi-

ence how she feels. In order to break the silence another girl starts telling a story.

At the square near the prison Jesus speaks to the multitude. The Pharisees we have seen in the street are present. They do not miss any opportunity to study Jesus and to listen to his teaching. We also recognize the young revolutionaries who attended the first meetings.

JESUS: *Give and it shall be given unto you, for with the same measure that you mete withal it shall be measured to you again. Ask, and it shall be given you. Seek, and you shall find. Knock, and it shall be opened unto you. For every one that asks receives. And he that seeks finds. And to him that knocks it shall be opened.*

While Jesus speaks, the girl named Ruth has walked into the square. She listens to the words of Jesus and her spirits revive. A couple of old men try to restrain her: one of them says

This is not for girls like you.

Determined, Ruth presses forward until she finds a place where she can clearly see and hear the preacher.

JESUS: *And I will speak this parable to you: a certain man had a fig tree planted in his vineyard, and he came and sought fruit thereon and found none. Then he said unto the dresser of his vineyard, behold these three years I come seeking fruit on this fig tree, and I find none. Cut it down, why cumbers it the ground? And he answering him said unto him: Lord, let it alone this year also, till I shall dig about it, dung it, and if it bear fruit, well, and if not, then after that you shall cut it down.*

The Pharisees look at each other and shake their heads. Again Jesus has shocked them. One of them, named Simon, speaks

It is dinner time. I will go and bid Jesus come and eat bread with us.

The suggestion meets with general approval, another proof of the good feeling existing between Jesus and the Pharisees.

While the other Pharisees go on ahead, Simon makes his way through the crowd to Jesus, to whom he says

Master, I have prepared a dinner for some friends and we desire that you would sit at meat with us.

Jesus accepts the invitation, takes leaves of his disciples and goes to the house of Simon the Pharisee.

Ruth has been standing nearby. A great change has come over her. There is still a feeling of heavy pressure upon her, but the words of Jesus have inspired her with new hope and confidence. If only she could receive his forgiveness. But how should she approach him? Hoping that some opportunity will arise, she follows Jesus and Simon the Pharisee at a respectful distance.

For a few moments we follow the group of revolutionaries leaving the meeting. Because of the danger of spies they choose their words carefully. But it is easy to tell they have been greatly impressed by the words of Jesus.

FIRST REVOLUTIONARY: *He gets more and more followers.*
SECOND REVOLUTIONARY: *And he makes people listen.*
THIRD REVOLUTIONARY: *And inspires them.*
FOURTH REVOLUTIONARY: *Yes, words, words. But what we need is action.*
SECOND REVOLUTIONARY: *Quickly.*

They decide to summon a meeting of the revolutionaries for this same afternoon.

Simon the Pharisee's luxurious house. The Pharisees are just arriving from the meeting. Slaves and servants attend them. They take off their sandals, wash their feet, and anoint their heads. While this is going on, they are excitedly discussing the preaching of Jesus.

The dining room. Ruth has slipped unnoticed through the maze of servants and entered the dining room. The Pharisees are disturbed at seeing this woman of bad repute, for it is unseemly for a woman to approach men at table, and almost unheard of for such a girl to enter the house of a Pharisee.

She goes to stand at the side of Jesus. At first she is discouraged by the disapproving glances of the Pharisees. Then her eyes meet those of Jesus, and she is comforted. For a moment she is at a loss for words. Then she begins to cry and the hot tears trickle down her cheeks. She feels depressed and unclean in the presence of Jesus. Finally two words pass her lips.

RUTH: *Forgive me.*

She falls at the feet of Jesus, wetting them with her tears and kissing them passionately. She looks for a cloth with which she can wipe his feet, but as she does not find anything suitable she gathers her dishevelled hair into her hand and wipes away the tears. From out a fold of her garment she takes an alabaster box of ointment with which she anoints his feet. No words are spoken during this scene. The Pharisees are amazed though silent witnesses.

Simon does not say anything but in his own mind he is certain that Jesus cannot be a Prophet, because if he were he would know who and what manner of woman this is. Jesus reads his thoughts.

JESUS (kindly): *Simon, I have something to say to you.*
SIMON: *Master, say on.*
JESUS: *There was a certain creditor who had two debtors. One owed five hundred pence and the other fifty. And when they had nothing to pay, he frankly forgave them both. Tell me, therefore, which of them will love him most?*

Simon understands the purpose of the question, but he has no choice—he must give the answer Jesus expects.

SIMON: *I suppose that he to whom he forgave most.*
JESUS: *You have judged rightly.*

Jesus turns to the girl, motioning her to rise and saying to Simon

> *This woman saw that I entered your house. You gave me no water for my feet, but she has washed my feet with tears and wiped them with her hair. You gave me no kiss, but this woman has not ceased to kiss my feet. My head with oil you did not anoint, but this woman has anointed my feet with ointment. Wherefore I say unto you: her sins, which are many, are forgiven for she loves much, but to whom little is forgiven, the same loves little.*

And Jesus turns to the girl once more and says

> *Your sins are forgiven.*

Ruth tries to utter some words of thankfulness but her lips are trembling and tears of joy stream down her face. Jesus continues

> *Your faith has saved you. Go in peace.*

With an angelic smile to Jesus the girl leaves the room.
The Pharisees shake their heads. Once again Jesus has forgiven sins. Who does he believe he is? It is evident that a breach between Jesus and the Pharisees is developing.

We see just a glimpse of the girl in the street. Her poise and self-confident movement evidence the self-respect she has regained.

The secret meeting of the revolutionaries takes place in an abandoned corn mill. The walls are coated with the white corn dust that also covers the floor. The phantomlike querns have not been in use for a long time.

FIRST REVOLUTIONARY: *I believe in him. I believe he is the Messiah we are waiting for.*

SECOND REVOLUTIONARY: *So do I.*

THIRD REVOLUTIONARY: *If he would only proclaim himself our leader.*

FOURTH REVOLUTIONARY: *Is he a leader?*

FIFTH REVOLUTIONARY: *I am afraid he is not. His plan is not like our plan.*

SIXTH REVOLUTIONARY: *Has he a plan?*

SEVENTH REVOLUTIONARY: *He has no plan.*

FIRST REVOLUTIONARY: *Then, what about his miracles?*

THIRD REVOLUTIONARY: *Today he has raised one from the dead.*

SECOND REVOLUTIONARY: *I believe he is the Son of God.*

Ruth has decided to return to her parents, who live on the family farm some distance from the town. She returns to the farm late in the afternoon. Her mother is alone in the house. She is astonished to see the daughter whom she had considered lost forever. Their eyes meet, but neither speaks. Then the girl goes to a corner of the room. Without saying a word she discards all of her jewelry: necklaces, armlets, anklets and the finger-rings. The mother, who cannot take her eyes off her daughter, finally breaks the silence.

MOTHER: *Have you come back?*

RUTH: *Yes, mother.*

MOTHER: *To stay here with us?*

RUTH: *Yes, mother.*

At this moment Ruth's sister approaches the house. Her mother joyously calls out.

MOTHER: *Your sister is here.*

SISTER: *Ruth?*

MOTHER: *Who else?*

The sister approaches Ruth, who avoids her kisses.

RUTH: *Will you help me to a bath?*
SISTER: *Of course I will.*

The mother, exceedingly happy, nods approvingly.

MOTHER: *You know it is the Sabbath?*
RUTH: *Yes, mother.*
MOTHER: *I will go and tell father.*

She leaves the house.

The two sisters enter a room in an outhouse. Here is a pit which, when filled with water, is used by the women for the ritual bath which is taken after menstruation or when for some other reason they have become "unclean." The two sisters start filling the pit with water.

The mother finds the father in the field and tells him the good news. He is as happy as his wife, who hurries back to the house in order to prepare the Sabbath meal.

Scenes of the bathing are interspersed with those of the mother preparing the Sabbath feast. The father returns from the field. He greets his daughter and welcomes her back home. It is all very simple and without sentimentality, according to Oriental manners. Then they gather around the table and wait for sunset. The mother, thanking God, lights the candle. The father pronounces the Proverb of Solomon, the homage to the good wife

> *Rejoice with the wife of thy youth. Let her be as the loving hind and pleasant roe, let her breasts satisfy thee at all times, and be thou ravished always with her love.*

Ruth is asked to say grace. After the father has broken the bread, they sit down and begin to eat.

The scene dissolves softly into the interior of the synagogue. We hear voices. The camera approaches Jesus, who sits in the chair of the preacher. To his right are his disciples; to his left the Pharisees and some scribes. The synagogue is filled with people. In the crowd we notice the revolutionaries.

Jesus has just begun a discussion with the Pharisees. So many false Messiahs have made their claims in recent years that the Pharisees have good cause to question his divine mission. Therefore, they question Jesus.

SECOND PHARISEE: *What sign can you show us that we may see and believe you?*

FOURTH PHARISEE: *Our fathers did eat manna in the desert; as it is written.*

SECOND PHARISEE: *Moses gave them bread from heaven to eat.*

THIRD PHARISEE: *What can you do?*

Jesus has been smiling as he listens to the Pharisees. He shakes his head indulgently.

JESUS: *Moses gave you not that bread from Heaven. But my Father gives you the true bread from Heaven.*

The Pharisees look at each other. To their uncomprehending minds the words of Jesus are just another paradox.

Jesus realizes that the Pharisees have not understood his words.

JESUS: *The true bread of God is he which comes down from Heaven and gives life unto the world.*

One of the Pharisees, entering into the spirit of what Jesus is saying, makes a request.

FIFTH PHARISEE: *Then give us this true bread.*

Jesus answers, but this time he does not address the Pharisees but the congregation.

JESUS: *I am the bread of life. He that comes to me shall never hunger; and he that believes in me shall never thirst. For I came down from Heaven, not to do mine own will, but the will of Him that sent me. And this is the will of my Father, that sent me, that everyone who sees the Son, and believes in him, may have everlasting life, and I will raise him up at the last day.*

The people listen attentively but the Pharisees whisper among themselves. The camera approaches the Pharisees, and one of them speaks a bit louder than the others.

THIRD PHARISEE: *How is it that he can say he came down from Heaven?*

Jesus turns toward the Pharisees.

JESUS: *Murmur not among yourselves.*

Again Jesus addresses the congregation.

JESUS: *I say unto you: He that believes in me has everlasting life. I am that bread of life.*

The people are ready to believe in Jesus, but the faces of the Pharisees show that they are not convinced. One of them (Sixth Pharisee), who till now has kept quiet, breaks the silence. An old man who rests on crutches, he has a long white beard and white hair and a sharp face. His deep-set eyes look fanatically at Jesus as he shouts

How know you letters, having never learned?

The other Pharisees tell him to be silent. They do not wish the discussion to fall to the level of merely attacking personalities. Jesus answers quietly and with restraint, respecting the extreme old age of the man.

My doctrine is not mine, but His who sent me.

The old fanatic would have answered again but the other Pharisees persuade him to keep quiet.

JESUS: *I will ask you one thing; is it lawful on the Sabbath day to do good or to do evil—to save life or to destroy it?*

Once again Jesus has put so subtle a question to the Pharisees that they are unable to give an immediate answer, for if they answer according to the letter of the Law the people will accuse them of hardheartedness. Therefore they keep silent and say nothing.

Jesus speaks again. He addresses the Pharisees.

JESUS: *What man shall there be among you that shall have one sheep and if it fall into a pit on the Sabbath day will he not lay hold on it and lift it out? How much then is a man better than a sheep? Therefore it is lawful to do well on the Sabbath days.*

The Pharisees step back and Jesus does not have any chance to reply because a priest has already gone to the platform pronouncing the Aaronic benediction.

After the benediction the congregation leaves the synagogue. The people talk of Jesus. Some say that he is a good man, while others say that the Pharisees are right to question him. The Pharisees gather in a corner to discuss the measures which will have to be taken concerning Jesus.

FIFTH PHARISEE: *Come and let us talk matters over. It cannot go on in that way.*

THE OTHERS: *He uses the Law to destroy the Law, and he uses the Prophets to destroy the traditions.*

FIFTH PHARISEE: *We have patiently tolerated his wild sayings but he is now going too far.*

SIXTH PHARISEE: *Let him speak.*

FIFTH PHARISEE: *No, we will not let him speak. Now we will speak.*

SECOND PHARISEE: *You are right. His teaching is an insult to our Law and to our traditions.*

FIRST PHARISEE: *And a danger to our faith.*

FIFTH PHARISEE: *If his doctrine gains ground among the population, all that we have built up will fall down.*

FOURTH PHARISEE: *More than that—we must keep aloof from
him and warn people against him. Let us go out and see what
he is about. Come.*

They leave the synagogue.

People have gathered on the steps of the synagogue and on
the square in front of it. Some have come with the sick. Jesus
moves among them, comforting them. When the Pharisees leave
the synagogue, Jesus is talking with a man who has been deaf and
dumb for years. The Pharisees draw near.

The sick man's wife explains to Jesus the reason her husband
has come.

WIFE: *He is deaf, and he has an impediment in his speech. If you
put your hand on him, he will be healed.*

The sick man stammers out some unintelligible sounds, but his
eyes plead with an eloquence he is unable to articulate.

The sick man's wife demonstrates how deaf he is by beating
together two pieces of wood, making a sound like a shot. The man
does not move.

Jesus separates the sick man from the crowd, especially from
the hostile influence of the Pharisees. Only the wife is allowed to
follow when Jesus guides him to a place where they can be un-
disturbed. Here Jesus makes him sit down. His eyes look into the
eyes of the sick man. Then he puts his fingers into his ears and
touches his tongue. And looking up to Heaven, he says to him

Ephphatha. (The Aramaic word for "Be opened.")

The eyes of the sick man have all this time been staring fixedly
at the face of Jesus. Now a change takes place. His face becomes
deathly pale. He falls into a swoon so that his wife has to aid him.
After a few seconds he is taken with a violent fit of convulsions,

so that his wife must make use of all her strength to keep him from falling. He conveys to them that he is suffering from terrible pains in the head, particularly in his ears. He turns his head from side to side, and he does this so quickly that it is not possible to distinguish the distorted features of his face. The wife would drag him away but he makes signs to her to stay. Suddenly the convulsions cease. For a while he sits with a downcast look. Then he raises his head and looks about as if listening to some distant music. His wife looks at him with astonishment.

WIFE: *Can you hear now?*

The man only nods as if he does not wish to be disturbed.

WIFE: *Can you speak too?*

The man does not answer at once. He looks at Jesus, smiling gratefully, and then he catches the hem of Jesus's cloak, kissing it. Only then does he turn to his wife and answer her question.

MAN: *I am healed.*

He rises and goes back to the square in front of the synagogue where he is besieged by the multitude asking him all manner of questions.

When Jesus returns the crowd gathers around him, astonished beyond measure. Jesus turns toward the Pharisees, speaking with a force and energy similar to that of the Prophets of old.

JESUS: *But I say unto you, that every idle word you speak, you shall give account thereof in the day of judgment, because he that is not with me, is against me, and he that gathers not with me, scatters.*

Doubtless he has carried the day. The crowd is with him. When the fanatical old man (Sixth Pharisee) raises his voice again, the position of the Pharisees is only weakened.

SIXTH PHARISEE: *You dare to teach us who read the divine books every day! You should cease your abominable doings and not deceive the people with your reckless speech.*

The other Pharisees do their best to stop the old man, but he resists them until he has finished what he has to say. Then he leaves the square—the sound of his crutches against the stones of the pavement can be heard for some time.

The Pharisees, even though they have suffered a setback, are not disposed to yield. One of them steps forward.

SECOND PHARISEE: *Once more we ask you to show us a sign that we may see and believe you.*

JESUS: *I say unto you: there shall be no sign given unto this generation.*

He tries to make his way through the crowd, but they cling to him and will not let him pass. Yet he would have a final word for the Pharisees. Raising his hand, he says loudly

Heed the words of the Prophet Isaiah: Behold my servant whom I have chosen.

He goes away with his disciples.

The crowd, impressed by the strength and force of Jesus, does not leave but continues discussing and debating the sayings of Jesus and the miraculous healing of the deaf mute. The dispute with the Pharisees is also discussed. Some side with Jesus while others side with the Pharisees.

Among those who side with Jesus we notice a group of revolutionaries, who whisper among themselves.

SECOND REVOLUTIONARY: *You see—he has great power over the people.*

FOURTH REVOLUTIONARY: *Yes, he was like another man today.*

FIRST REVOLUTIONARY: *That is what I said; he is a born leader.*

THIRD REVOLUTIONARY: *A man of action.*

FIFTH REVOLUTIONARY: *If we could only get him on our side.*
SECOND REVOLUTIONARY: *If? We shall.*
FOURTH REVOLUTIONARY: *And if he refuses?*
FIRST REVOLUTIONARY: *We will urge him. Come.*
FIFTH REVOLUTIONARY: *Now? At once?*
SECOND REVOLUTIONARY: *Why not?*

In order not to attract attention they move slowly and singly in the same direction as Jesus.

Jesus and his twelve disciples arrive at Peter's house. Peter carefully locks the door. Inside, there are other followers who have considered themselves as disciples although they have not belonged to the inner circle. They are disturbed because of the preaching of Jesus and are murmuring among themselves.

FIRST BELIEVER: *That was a hard saying.*
SECOND BELIEVER: *Who could hear it without being offended?*

When Jesus hears them murmuring in this fashion he turns to them.

JESUS: *Did it offend you?*
THIRD BELIEVER: *It offended the Pharisees.*
JESUS: *But did it offend you?*

They do not answer. Jesus continues

What if you shall see the Son of Man ascend up where he was before?

Again they do not answer, but the words of Jesus appear blasphemous to them.

JESUS: *The words that I speak unto you, they are the spirit, and they are life. But there are some of you that believe not. How is it that you have no faith?*

Jesus turns his face away. Those to whom he has spoken feel offended because of his rebuke, and with scowling faces they start to leave the room, some of them shaking their heads.

Jesus realizes that he is facing a crisis. He wishes to know how those closest to him feel. Therefore he decides to put "the twelve" to a test and let them make their choice. Have they faith or are they too beginning to waver?

He says to them

Will you also go away?

Peter looks about, studying the faces of the other disciples. Then he answers

Master, to whom shall we go? We believe you have the words of eternal life.

Again Peter looks about to see if the others are with him. All of them nod assent. Only Judas is hesitant in giving his approval.

Outside the house a crowd of the common people who trust in Jesus have gathered. In their center is the group of revolutionaries. They begin to shout, insisting that Jesus show himself. Jesus is seated and he indicates to Peter that he is to go out to them.

While Peter is outside, the other disciples, curious to know what is going on, approach the half-open door. Peter returns and, after locking the door carefully, turns to Jesus and says

They wish to make you their leader.

The other disciples are watching the face of Jesus closely. All of them have been dreaming, to some extent, of an earthly kingdom in which they would hold prominent positions.

Jesus does not answer and Peter continues

They believe God has sent you to free Israel from the Romans.

The face of Jesus bears a troubled look. He realizes that his mission has been a failure. No one, not even his disciples, understands his teaching: that the Kingdom of God is a spiritual kingdom. He also realizes the danger he is facing if his activity as a religious' teacher and preacher unites him with a political party known to be hostile to the Romans.

With an expression of sad resignation Jesus studies the faces about him. Then Peter speaks, this time with a smile

They said that if you would not heed their demand they would come and take you by force to make you a king.

The word "king" causes Jesus to put aside the many thoughts that have been racing through his mind and forces him to give attention to the needs of the moment. He gets to his feet and speaks with authority.

JESUS: *Let us go away to a solitary place where we can have peace.*
PETER: *Where?*
JESUS: *To the other side of the lake.*

Puzzled, the disciples look at him. They do not understand his reasons for refusing the offer, and they follow him reluctantly. Secretly, they all leave the house and go down to the shore, board a boat and set out for the other side of the lake.

Outside Peter's house. A Roman patrol, making its rounds, suspects the crowd of holding a political meeting, and the sergeant orders his soldiers to form a guard around the place. At the sight of the Roman soldiers the revolutionaries slip away, and then the other people disperse.

Some revolutionaries and a part of the crowd, looking for Jesus and his disciples, go to the shore and see the boat some distance away. Many run along the shore, following the boat as it moves out of sight around a point, though they are unseen by the men on board. The revolutionaries, however, continue to follow the shore path.

When the boat has rounded the point, Jesus directs the disciples to enter the bay and go ashore. They are some distance from the shore when they see the crowd of people coming out from the town. As the boat nears the shore, the crowd sets up a great shout.

VOICES: *Do not go away yet. Do not leave us. We have come all this way for your sake.*

Jesus is moved with compassion for the people and he says to the disciples

They are as sheep having no shepherd.

Addressing the crowd ashore, he cries

What will you that I shall do unto you?

From the shore a voice out of the crowd is heard.

We have come to question you on a certain matter.

Jesus tells Peter to have the boat brought to shore. Shortly, they are within a few feet of the shore and one of the disciples casts anchor. The boat now lies with its broadside toward the shore and Jesus stands in the stern where he can be both seen and heard.

The people ashore sit on the grass or on some stone blocks. A young revolutionary stands on one of the blocks.

FIRST REVOLUTIONARY: *Jesus, we believe in you. Your words are divine and you are working mighty miracles. You are working by word and authority and through some invisible power. We believe that you are sent by God to accomplish many things. We want you to be our leader and to use your power to free us from the hands of the Romans and then to become our king, the King of the Jews.*

VOICES: *Yes, we will make you a king, our king.*

Jesus does not answer. All the disciples look at him expectantly.

SECOND REVOLUTIONARY: *Are you the Messiah? If you are, tell us in plain words.*

Jesus does not answer.

THIRD REVOLUTIONARY: *Are you the king we are waiting for?*

Finally Jesus decides to answer.

JESUS: *I have come to establish the Kingdom of God on earth.*
FIRST VOICE: *You have said that the Kingdom of God is near. Why do you then hide here in Galilee?*
THIRD VOICE: *Why do you not go to Jerusalem?*
SECOND VOICE: *Why do you keep it secret?*
FIRST VOICE: *Yes, why? Show yourself to the world.*
JESUS: *My time is not yet come.*
FOURTH VOICE: *How long shall we be left in doubt?*

These short remarks follow rapidly one after the other. There is a brief silence.

FOURTH REVOLUTIONARY: *When will the Kingdom of God come?*
JESUS: *The Kingdom of God comes not with observation. The Kingdom of God is within you.*
FIFTH REVOLUTIONARY: *Will you make us free?*
JESUS: *If you continue in my word, you shall know the truth, and the truth shall make you free.*
SIXTH REVOLUTIONARY: *We do not understand what you mean.*

The more Jesus speaks the more confused the people become.

JESUS: *You have heard that it has been said, you shall love your neighbor and hate your enemy. But I say unto you: love your*

*enemies, bless them that curse you, do good to them that hate
you, and pray for them who despitefully use you and persecute you.*

Some people in the crowd are laughing disdainfully.

FIFTH VOICE (ironically): *Shall we love also the Romans?*

Jesus refuses to notice the irony.

JESUS: *You have heard that it has been said: an eye for an eye,
and a tooth for a tooth. But I say unto you: that you resist
not evil. And if anyone forces you to go one mile, go with
him two miles.*
SIXTH VOICE: *If he is a Roman, as well?*

Jesus continues in a calm manner.

JESUS: *And whosoever shall smite you on your right cheek turn
to him the other also.*

Already many are starting to leave because his words have
dashed their hopes for a leader to free Israel. To those who remain,
Jesus says

*All things whatsoever you would that men should do to you,
do you even so to them: for this is the Law and the Prophets.*

Jesus makes signs to the disciples to weigh anchor. From the shore
there comes a last shout.

SECOND REVOLUTIONARY: *Are you he who should come, the
promised one, or have we to look for another?*

There is no answer from those in the boat. The disciples give
themselves to their task, and with strong strokes send the boat
through the water.

FOURTH REVOLUTIONARY (to Second Revolutionary): *Our lost leader.*

The crowd that had arrived with great expectations is bitterly disappointed. In gloomy silence the people stare in the direction of the boat. Then, with much grumbling, they return to the town.

But the disappointment is no less among the disciples, who feel that Jesus's popularity has received a serious blow. Their departure seems to them more like a flight. The happy days in Galilee when Jesus was met with love and confidence on every side have come to an end and a time of doubt and anxiety is waiting for the Prophet and his disciples.

We leave the boat with the dejected disciples, and the camera pans to another boat with two fishermen standing up and rowing in time with their singing. One leads off in the singing. After so many measures he stops and the other takes up the refrain.

The scene of Jesus and his disciples sailing away dissolves softly into a close-up of the Sabbath lamp in the synagogue of Nazareth. We see the lamp being lighted.

[SCENE SHIFT]

NARRATOR: *And Jesus went to his own country, and he came to Nazareth where he had been brought up, and as his custom was he went to the synagogue on the Sabbath day.*

The scene with the Sabbath lamp dissolves softly into a scene at the front of the synagogue. People are waiting for Jesus. We see fathers with their young sons. A boy of twelve talks to a group of old men with long beards. They listen attentively to him, answering his questions and correcting him when he is wrong.

When Jesus and his disciples arrive, he sees among the people a woman who is bent over. She is led to the synagogue by her daughter. She has suffered eighteen years from this crippling infirmity. Jesus takes pity on her. He approaches her and speaks in an encouraging tone

Woman, you are loosed from your infirmity.

The woman does not immediately comprehend his meaning. Therefore Jesus repeats

You are delivered from your plague.

Saying this, he lays his hands on her, and wonderful things begin to happen. The woman regains her strength and at the same time the full control of her limbs. To the surprise of herself and all the people around, she is able to straighten herself up. She is transfixed by joy, overwhelmed with tears and emotion.

The woman wishes to thank Jesus but does not find an opportunity of doing so because the Ruler of the Synagogue, who has just come out of the sanctuary and has witnessed the healing, speaks up in a friendly tone of mild reproach

There are six days of work: in them therefore come and be healed, and not on the Sabbath day.

The woman looks to Jesus for help. He gives her a comforting smile and answers the Ruler.

JESUS: *Ought not this woman whom Satan has bound these eighteen years be loosed from this bond?*
RULER: *Yes, but not on the Sabbath. Her infirmity could be borne one more day.*
JESUS (after a pause): *You hypocrites.*

The Ruler is a man of calm mind who speaks quietly, conscious of having the Law on his side. On the other hand, the voice of Jesus has in it a sharpness we have not heard before.

The poor woman who has been healed does not know what to say.

Some of the people agree with the Ruler, whom they know to be a pious and good man; others are impressed by the miraculous healing of the woman.

Jesus, after his last words to the Ruler, turns and enters the synagogue. His disciples follow. This scene dissolves into a close-up

of the table with the scrolls. We see the hands of the overseer draw
the curtain aside and take out a script-roll. It is that of the Prophet
Isaiah. While the Law had a "roller" at both ends, the rolls of the
Prophets had a "roller" only at one end, so that the reader had to
roll it back again to the beginning after the lecture.

Soft dissolve into the interior of the synagogue. In the beginning only the platform with the pulpit and the chair for the
preacher is shown. Jesus receives from the overseer the script-roll
of Isaiah. He opens it, rolls it out to chapter 61, and reads verse 1.

JESUS: *The Spirit of the Lord God is upon me; because the Lord
hath anointed me to preach good tidings unto the meek; he
hath sent me to bind up the brokenhearted, to proclaim liberty
to the captives, and the opening of the prison to them that
are bound.*

He puts down the roll and then seats himself. The eyes of all those
in the synagogue are fastened on him. A hush of expectancy runs
through the room. Then Jesus speaks precisely

This day is this scripture fulfilled in your ears.

While the people wonder at his words, the Pharisees turn to
each other and shake their heads. Jesus looks at them, and then he
opens the roll of Isaiah again and reads

*He hath blinded their eyes, and hardened their hearts, that
they should not see with their eyes, nor understand with their
hearts and be converted.*

Jesus hands the roll to the overseer. Then he rises. There is
a tension in the atmosphere, as the feeling is general that Jesus is
likely to create a controversy. Again Jesus speaks

*He that believes in me, believes not in me but in him that
sent me. And he that sees me, sees him that sent me.*

The congregation look at each other: what does he mean? But Jesus continues unaffected

For I have not spoken of myself: but of the Father which sent me; he gave me a commandment, which I should say, and what I should speak.

If Jesus was met with indifference before he entered the synagogue, he is now becoming the object of contempt. What is the meaning of this boasting?

Among the crowd we notice a group of devout Jews, ascetics, who are shocked at the sayings of Jesus. They are his brothers. The most fanatical of them is Jacob, a very short man. Their mother is with them; she cannot restrain her tears. Her two daughters try to comfort her.

There is a short silence after the last words of Jesus. Then a man in the congregation rises, and after him another, and then yet another. The storm is about to burst.

FIRST MAN: *You have said you came down from Heaven. We will ask your mother how that happened.*
SECOND MAN: *She is sitting over there.*
THIRD MAN: *Look, she is weeping. She is ashamed on your behalf.*
FOURTH MAN: *You should have stayed at home like your brothers.*
FIFTH MAN: *And left the preaching to the preachers.*
SECOND MAN: *And the healing to the doctors.*
FIRST MAN: *If you are a doctor, then heal yourself.*
FOURTH MAN: *You need a doctor yourself.*
SIXTH MAN: *But a good one.*

Jesus stands silently while the insults are showered upon him. The last remarks are drowned in a wave of scornful laughter and after that there is a pause. The people are angry and some curse him.

What entitles him to act as a religious teacher and Prophet? He is mad, there can be no doubt of it. The whole congregation cries out indignantly. They curse him as they howl and stamp the floor. For a while a riot develops, but the noise quiets down for a moment as the voice of Jesus is heard crying

I say unto you: no Prophet is accepted in his own country.

Again there is a furious outbreak of which Jesus appears to take little notice. He leaves the platform quietly. It is clear to him that here in his native town not only the Pharisees but also the common people are against him. They are all outraged because of his work and his claims, and they follow him out, heaping upon him scorn and abuse.

Outside the synagogue a great crowd gathers about him threateningly.

SEVENTH MAN: *You say you have not come to destroy the Law, but that is just what you do.*
EIGHTH MAN: *You blasphemer.*
FIFTH MAN: *A false Prophet, that's what you are.*

To one side stands a small group—the mother of Jesus and his brothers and sisters. The mother and sisters are weeping. The Ruler approaches them in order to give comfort.

RULER: *He is beside himself.*
JACOB (hardhearted): *He is mad.*
JESUS'S MOTHER: *If we only could lay hold of him.*

The second brother, who has tried to force his way through the crowd, comes back.

SECOND BROTHER: *I cannot get near him for the press of the crowd.*
RULER: *Wait. Let me try.*

The Ruler approaches the crowd surrounding Jesus, and it gives way before him; then he gets close to him.

RULER: *Behold, your mother and your brethren seek you.*

JESUS: *Who is my mother, or my brethren?*

He looks at his disciples who are with him.

JESUS: *Behold my mother and my brethren. For whosoever shall do the will of God, the same is my brother, and my sister, and mother.*

The Ruler looks at Jesus in bewilderment and then returns to the mother, who cannot control her tears. Her two daughters look after her. But Jacob, the elder brother, cannot restrain his anger. He points at Jesus and shouts

That's the way with you, defiant, willful, and as always, it is I, I, I. Now I say unto you: be gone as soon as possible, you are no longer one of ours.

Voices from the crowd are heard.

Yes, go, go. Away with you.

The people take Jesus's words literally. They are shocked at his apparent heartlessness and shake their fists at him.

A man from the crowd climbs up on a rock and shouts

There will be no peace in this town as long as this man is among us.

But Jesus is already on his way out of town, followed by the disciples. The crowd hastens after him.

The road skirts a ravine. The disciples are busy talking to people, trying to make them listen to reason and explaining how the words of Jesus are to be understood. Jesus walks a little apart from his followers. Suddenly he finds himself surrounded by violent fanatics. He is standing alone with his back to the ravine. Apparently, his attackers plan to encircle him and cast him headlong over the edge. People are shouting.

VOICE: *Go to your death—you blasphemer.*
ANOTHER VOICE: *Yes, stone him.*

The attackers pick up stones beside the road and are about to hurl them at him, but Jesus does not move. Unflinching, he stands with his arms outstretched, facing the men. His calmness causes the crowd to become silent, and one by one the men drop their stones. Fearlessly, Jesus moves toward his attackers whilst they retire: there is a deathlike silence. He passes through the midst of them, continuing on his way with his disciples following.

A wide stretch of water whose surface is splintered by heavy drops of rain. Flashes of lightning inflame the surface. Thunder is heard.

Then follows a sequence of rapidly changing scenes. There is a Palestinian torrential downpour. Strong whirlwinds beat violently against the trees and houses. Puddles fill the roads. Floods of water are rushing away heaps of earth causing earth-slides; the waters flow into the valleys and inundate the fields. And all this is accompanied by claps of thunder and lightning flashes.

NARRATOR: *Jesus had stirred up a storm. Despised by his family, and in open fight against the Pharisees, he withdrew from the Jews and turned to the Gentiles. And so we meet him some time later in the heathen town of Caesarea Philippi. The earliest name of the town was Paneas, so called because a sanctuary for the Greek god Pan was erected on the rocks near the town.*

The thunderstorm sequence dissolves softly into a scene showing the statue of Pan in a niche hewn into rock. By means of a wide pan and trucking shot we move from Pan to Jesus and his disciples standing near the rock.

Because of adversity, the character of Jesus has changed, especially with regard to his belief in his own divine authority. There is a new accent in his voice. His disciples have remained faithful, and their love and loyalty strengthen his own belief in himself.

Jesus fixes on an insistent idea. He remembers the words from the shore reaching him in the boat: "Are you he that should come, the promised one?" Thinking the question over again and again, he asks himself if he might not be that one. And the disciples do their best to nurture the thought. Little by little Jesus sees himself in a new light: might he not be the chosen one, the Messiah? He has a foreboding of the mission to which he is called.

Jesus is sitting alone, pondering. At some distance the disciples, speaking in low voices, discuss the problem of who Jesus is and what is his mission on earth.

JOHN: *The question is—what is Jesus to himself?*
BARTHOLOMEW: *What is he to us?*
THOMAS: *To me, a Prophet.*
MATTHEW: *More than a Prophet.*
PETER: *God's Son. The Messiah.*
ANDREW: *John the Baptist said it.*
THADDAEUS: *And then all his miracles.*
JUDAS: *But why keep it secret?*

Jesus has risen and is approaching. Peter tells the disciples to be quiet. Jesus sits among the disciples. Suddenly he asks them a question

Whom do the people say I am?

The disciples look at each other, momentarily embarrassed. The face of Jesus does not disclose his thoughts. He just listens.

JAMES: *Some say Elijah.*
THOMAS: *And some Jeremiah.*
JOHN: *Some even say that one of the old Prophets is risen again.*

Jesus nods but says nothing. He appears to be giving thought to what his disciples are saying. He must have noticed particularly that no one has said he is the Messiah. Perhaps he is also considering how many of the Prophets have been killed in the past.

Jesus's first question was intended only to draw them out. Now he comes to his real objective. After a pause he looks at them intently, and then he asks

But whom say you that I am?

The disciples are silent for some moments. They wonder if Jesus has been aware of what they have just been discussing.
As usual Peter speaks for the disciples

We believe in you and are certain that you are the Messiah.

The others nod approvingly.
Jesus, deeply moved and pleased, looks at Peter and says

Blessed are you, Peter, for this has been revealed to you by my Father who is in Heaven.

Then, addressing all the disciples, he adds

But I say unto you that you shall tell no man that I am the Messiah.

It is a great disappointment for the disciples to be forbidden again to proclaim Jesus the Messiah. They do not understand why it must be kept secret. Judas shakes his head. Jesus speaks to them

I have something to say unto you. I am the Messiah. And I know my destiny.

The disciples become tense and look inquiringly at Jesus.

JESUS: *It was foretold by Isaiah.*
JOHN (surprised): *Isaiah?*

Bartholomew, who knows the Law and the Prophets by heart, answers for Jesus, quoting Isaiah 53:5.

He was wounded for our transgressions, he was bruised for our iniquities: the chastisement of our peace was upon him; and with his stripes we are healed.

Jesus nods, adding with an expression of sadness

I too shall suffer greatly . . .

A great anxiety possesses the disciples as Jesus continues

And be killed.

All this sounds exceedingly strange to the disciples.

ANDREW: *Why must you go through all these things?*
JESUS: *To prepare the way for the Kingdom of God.*
JAMES, SON OF ALPHAEUS: *Where will you suffer in this fashion?*
JESUS: *In Jerusalem.*

And he rises and says with great emphasis

But I shall rise again from the grave as the true Messiah.

Lovingly he embraces the whole group of disciples. Then he turns away and walks toward a fountain in the nearby rock. Here, he crouches down and drinks the water.

Meanwhile the disciples quietly discuss the meaning of his words. His prediction of his suffering is in every respect strange and unthinkable to them. It was contrary to all the exalted expectations which the Jews generally associated with the coming of the Messiah. They try in their own minds to resolve the paradox of a suffering Messiah, but it is too much for them.

JUDAS: *This is madness.*
SIMON THE CANAANITE: *What?*
JUDAS: *To go to Jerusalem.*
THADDAEUS: *Even in his native town he was in danger.*

THOMAS: *How then will it be in Jerusalem?*

MATTHEW: *He will immediately come into conflict with the Pharisees.*

PHILIP: *And then with the Sadducees.*

BARTHOLOMEW: *And sooner or later with the Romans.*

JAMES: *In Jerusalem he will be in more danger than in any other place.*

JOHN: *It is hopeless, an act of desperation.*

There is a short pause. Then Andrew, as spokesman for the other disciples, speaks to his brother

Peter, try and persuade him to act differently.

After hesitating for a moment Peter agrees and goes to Jesus. The other disciples watch him intently.

PETER: *Master, you must abandon this idea of suffering and death.*

Jesus raises his head to listen.

PETER: *Be it far from you, this shall not be unto you. You are not to undergo any suffering; you are the Messiah the people are waiting for.*

Now Jesus rises and turns around to look at him. In a tone of authority, such as might have been used by one of the old Prophets, he says

Get you behind me, Satan, you are an offence to me, for you savor not the things that be of God, but those that be of man.

Peter realizes that he has been unwise in seeming to prefer an all-conquering Messiah to a suffering Messiah. In humiliation he bows his head.

Jesus has made it clear that he has chosen the way of grief

and suffering. He knows that death probably awaits him if he goes to Jerusalem, but fear cannot shake his determination.

Followed by Peter, he returns to the other disciples. He wants them to understand perfectly and to be rid of all foolish dreams, all false expectations and all misinterpretations of the Kingdom of God. If they wish to be his disciples, they must suffer with him. Therefore, he speaks to them solemnly

If any man would come after me, let him deny himself and follow me. For whosoever will save his life shall lose it, and whosoever will lose his life for my sake, the same shall save it. For what is a man profited, if he shall gain the whole world, and lose his own soul?

The disciples, their faces revealing their serious frame of mind, listen to Jesus. It is a hard truth they are being taught. But all of them are fully committed to Jesus and they are ready to follow him wherever he leads.

In a milder tone Jesus continues

I shall tell you of a truth, there be some standing here, which shall not taste of death, till they see the Kingdom of God. [Luke 9:27.]

The disciples understand the words of Jesus to a certain point, but they cannot yet understand their profound meaning.

Jesus indicates that they are to rise and go on. The road Jesus and his disciples travel on, leaving Caesarea Philippi, forks at a certain point. One branch runs northeast toward Mount Hermon, the other to a neighboring village northwest of Caesarea Philippi. They follow the road toward Mount Hermon.

Jesus and his disciples arrive in the vicinity of Mount Hermon. According to a plan they have decided upon, Jesus takes Peter, John, and James and goes up into the mountain to pray, leaving the others to wait for them at the foot of the mountain.

Jesus and the three disciples on their way up to the mountain. They climb to the top of the mountain. While Jesus, as is his custom, goes apart to pray, the disciples lie down under a tree to rest. After the long climb they are tired and heavy with sleep.

The mountain. At some distance from the sleeping disciples Jesus is standing with his face turned toward Jerusalem and praying. His eyes are fixed as on a vision in the distance.

The disciples are sleeping. Suddenly a brilliant light shines upon their faces. They awake and see Jesus in his transfiguration. His garments are incredibly white. His face too is changed and shining from a great inner light. The disciples are filled with wonder and amazement. They do not know whether they are dreaming or if they are really looking at Jesus.

With considerable excitement they watch as a white cloud passes between them and Jesus. When it has moved away, they see two men standing with Jesus who appear to them to be Moses and the Prophet Elijah. At this sight the disciples become afraid and cling to each other.

MOSES: *Verily you are the only Son of God and chosen to establish His Kingdom on Earth.*

ELIJAH: *And strength will be given unto you for all that is to come.*

To the disciples it appears that Moses and Elijah are about to leave. The bewildered Peter thinks suddenly that maybe they can be persuaded to stay. Partly rising, he speaks to Jesus

Master, it is good for us to be here: and let us make three tabernacles; one for you, and one for Moses, and one for Elijah.

There is no answer. A bright cloud covers Jesus, Moses and Elijah, and they are hidden from the disciples. Out of the cloud comes a voice.

GOD THE FATHER: *This is my beloved Son in whom I am well pleased: Hear ye Him.*

When the disciples hear the voice of the Almighty speaking directly to them, they are frightened and fall on the ground.

After the voice is heard, there is a silence. The disciples are afraid to lift up their faces. Finally they hear the voice of Jesus.

Fear not.

Then the disciples raise their heads. The cloud has drifted off and they see no man save only Jesus. He approaches them, saying

Arise.

When he reaches the disciples, he addresses them once more.

You shall tell no man of the things you have seen.

Jesus continues speaking as they descend the mountain, but his words are not audible.

[SCENE SHIFT]

NARRATOR: *Then Jesus came to a city of Samaria, near to the parcel of ground that Jacob gave to his son Joseph; and there was a well.*

According to tradition the patriarch Jacob had hewn this well out of the rock. It was a cistern containing rain water, placed in the shade of some trees.

After a long day's walk Jesus has sat down to rest. The disciples have gone to town to buy some food. Along the path from the village comes a young woman carrying a water jar on her head. She goes to the well and gives a hasty glance at Jesus.

She has brought with her a bucket for drawing up the water. While she is lowering the bucket Jesus speaks to her.

Give me to drink.

A faint smile crosses the face of the young woman. Was it not humiliating for him, a Jew, to ask something of her, a Samaritan woman? And she answers

How is it that you, being a Jew, ask a drink of me—a woman of Samaria?

Jesus looks at her in silence, and then he answers

If you know the gift of God and who it is that says to you: give me to drink, you would have asked of him, and he would have given you living water.

[The term "living water" is a play on words. "Living water" is a Jewish expression for spring water and distinguishes it from cistern water.]

Ironically, the woman asks

You have nothing to draw with, and the well is deep: from whence then have you that living water?

Jesus answers quietly

Whosoever drinks of this water shall thirst again. But whosoever drinks of the water that I shall give him shall never thirst. But the water that I shall give him shall be in him a well of water springing up into everlasting life.

The woman is taken aback. Instinctively she feels that there is a profound meaning behind the words of Jesus that she is unable to define. Therefore, her answer comes hesitatingly.

Give me this water, that I thirst not, neither come hither to draw water.

Jesus, wishing to turn the conversation in another direction, uses his clairvoyant power and surprises the woman by saying

Go, call your husband, and come here.

Disconcerted, the woman is silent for a while.

WOMAN (in a low voice): *I have no husband.*

JESUS: *You have well said: "I have no husband." For you have had five husbands. And he whom you now have is not your husband. In that said you truly.*

The woman looks at Jesus, speechless with astonishment. Then she says, not without a certain admiration

I perceive that you are a Prophet.

There is a short pause. The woman sits down on the parapet, and in an effort to get away from an unpleasant topic she changes the subject.

Our fathers worshipped in this mountain, and you say that in Jerusalem is the place where men ought to worship.

Jesus appreciates what she is saying and answers her kindly.

Woman, believe me, the hour comes when you shall neither in this mountain, nor yet at Jerusalem, worship the Father; when the true worshippers shall worship the Father in spirit and in truth: for the Father seeks such to worship Him. God is a spirit, and they that worship him must worship him in spirit and in truth.

[These words of Jesus were not new. They had their origins in the Prophets. Jeremiah, for instance, had predicted that the time would come when all peoples would have the law of God written on their hearts.]

The woman is deeply interested in the words of Jesus but they are beyond her. She rises and picks up the bucket, saying

I know that the Messiah comes. When he is come, he will tell us all things.

To this Jesus answers simply

I that speak unto you am he.

The woman is about to lift up her water jar, but hearing these words of Jesus she puts it down again. Once more she is speechless with astonishment. At this moment the disciples return with the food in bundles and baskets. They marvel to see Jesus speaking with a woman belonging to a people despised by the Jews. But they do not say anything.

The woman, on the other hand, feels their coldness. Perhaps she is ashamed to be seen talking to a stranger. She leaves her water jar behind and goes to the village. On her way she meets some men and tells them that she has met the Messiah and that he has told her about everything she has ever done.

In the meantime the disciples have unpacked the food and parceled it out. Some of them rest in the shade of the trees, some on the parapet.

Now we have a shot inside the well from below, toward the sky, and after that another shot inside the well from above toward the surface of the water, reflecting the parapet with Jesus and several disciples sitting on it, among them John.

John invites Jesus to take some of the food.

JOHN:　*Master, eat.*
JESUS:　*I have meat to eat that you know not of. My meat is to do the will of him that sent me, and to finish his work.* [John 4:31–34.]

This scene reflected in the surface of the water dissolves softly into a close-up of a dagger chest. We see the hand of a young man remove a short dagger.

NARRATOR: *Apparently the Jewish people groaned in silence under the yoke of their Roman oppressors, but beneath the surface smouldered the hatred that resulted in numerous guerrilla attacks and in continuing revolts.*

The camera follows the dagger as it is lifted. The camera glides backward at the same time. Finally we see the whole room. The young man holding the dagger has risen from his bed and is trying to leave the room without making any noise. His father is sleeping in the same room. He awakes from his sleep and is surprised to see his son about to leave.

The son is a young, fanatical patriot, belonging to the most aggressive faction of the revolutionaries—the "Sicarii," so called after the name of the short dagger, "sica."

FATHER (whispering): *Is it tonight?*
SON: *Yes.*

The father rises too. He blesses his son, saying

Be careful.

The son nods, smiling confidently, and then slips away. Keeping the door ajar, the father watches his son disappear into the darkness.

[WIPE TO THE NEXT SCENE.]

A lonely ravine where the revolutionaries meet. The young man from the preceding scene arrives. The leader is delivering an address to the thirty or forty young men who have gathered about him.

Long ago, men, we determined not to serve the Romans nor to submit to any slavery; therefore let us willingly accept the punishment that awaits us if we are to fall into Roman hands alive. For my part I had rather be dead if I cannot be free.

The leader makes a sign for them to be silent, and then he continues.

LEADER: *Everybody knows what he has to do?*
VOICES: *Yes, yes.*
LEADER: *Nobody is in doubt?*
VOICES: *No, no.*
LEADER: *Well, then let us get to work.*

The meeting is adjourned and the conspirators leave.

[WIPE TO THE NEXT SCENE.]

A mountain pass. The same night. A wooden bridge crossing a ravine.

This bridge is of strategic importance to the Roman army, and they keep watch over it day and night. Men are stationed at each end of the bridge. On one side is a tent for the officer of the watch. Suddenly the bridge is overrun by the Jewish guerrillas. For a few moments fierce fighting takes place which results in the killing of all the Romans except the officer in charge, and also some of the Jews. Some fall on the bridge, some on the rocks at either end, some of them are flung into the deep. When the fighting is over and the Jews have picked up their dead, the bridge is set on fire. Then they leave, taking the Roman officer with them.

Without camera movement the scene dissolves softly into the bridge at the very moment when, consumed by fire, it falls into the ravine. It is time for the watch to be relieved and fresh troops arrive. On the rocks near the bridge they find one of the Jewish insurrectionists forgotten by his companions. The Roman soldiers kick at him and discover that he is not dead. They pick him up. He might be useful during the investigation.

[WIPE TO THE NEXT SCENE.]

A Roman torture chamber. The young Jew whom the Roman soldiers have picked up at the bridge is being interrogated. He sits, the upper part of his body stripped, on a low stool. Two executioners hold his outstretched hands firmly while the examiner, seated in front of him, is questioning him.

Who were the others? Tell me some of their names. One of them? Who is your leader?

The prisoner has not betrayed any secret. The examiner, irritated by the prisoner's stubbornness, signals to a third executioner who stands behind the prisoner holding a flaming torch. He applies the torch to the back of the young Jew who lets out a piercing cry.

[WIPE TO THE NEXT SCENE.]

The interior of the first scene of this sequence. The same young man and his father are asleep. In the distance, the muted thuds of spiked sandals. The father awakens first. He sits up and listens. He knows only too well what this night sound means. Now he hears the distant sound of a sword's hilt hammering on a nearby door. A rough voice is heard shouting words of command. He hears weeping and wailing. There is a short pause during which the sound of marching is heard again, then hammering upon another door and the commanding voice. Now the young man also awakens. It is clear to him at once what is happening. He rises. His father also rises and embraces his son. The soldiers are approaching. The father holds the son closely. There is no question but that the soldiers are coming to their house; they are knocking now. With a look of determination the son embraces his father, smiles courageously, and opens the door. The soldiers seize him and bind him. For a moment the father stands in the door looking after his son through eyes blinded with tears. Then he shuts the door. A plaintive weeping is heard through the door.

[WIPE TO THE NEXT SCENE.]

An underground vault in a Roman fortress. Seven or eight of the insurrectionists, among them their leader, are bound fast in stocks, waiting for judgment and death.

LEADER: *We have acted as men, and we will die as men. We are not afraid to die. Life without liberty is not worth having. Do any of you think it is?*
OTHERS: *No, no.*

The leader turns to one of his companions, saying

You, Rabbi, pray for us.

The Rabbi offers a prayer. The others answer

Amen.

Then the leader starts singing a lively, joyous Jewish hymn and the others join in. Some non-Jewish prisoners listen with surprise. The song continues during the following three scenes, little by little fading away.

[WIPE TO THE NEXT SCENE.]

On a hill outside the town: the place of execution. Seven or eight crosses are raised and the insurrectionists are nailed to the crosses. The crosses are evenly spaced and form a curved line. Vultures circle above the crosses. Two or three slaves are seen cleaning the place of the remains of the last gang of crucified revolutionaries.

[WIPE TO THE NEXT SCENE.]

A single cross close-up. A pan from the foot of the cross to the top with the vultures circling above.

A large heap of human bones and skulls—reminding one of the Russian painter Vasily Vereshchagin's famous painting. Human remains are seen landing on the heap, thrown there by the slaves— now off scene—who have been cleaning up. This scene is the last scene of the insurrectionist sequence.

Soft dissolve into a village marketplace. We can hear the sound of flutes. At first we see just a few girls dancing gracefully, then the camera glides backwards and we see other girls and boys playing flutes. They are playing at "weddings." The camera pans to the opposite corner of the marketplace where Jesus sits surrounded by his disciples. Though he has only just arrived, people are already gathering to hear his teaching. Most of them are women. Some approach Jesus with their children for him to touch them. His disciples try to drive them away.

Do not bother the Master. Leave your children at home. They have no understanding.

When Jesus sees this, he rebukes the disciples.

Suffer the little children to come unto me, forbid them not: for of such is the Kingdom of God.

He lays his hand upon the children pushed forward by their mothers to receive his blessing. He takes the other small children in his arms and lays his hand upon them and blesses them.

Meanwhile, subdued sounds of the young boys and girls are heard in the background.

More people gather around Jesus and some Pharisees have come to dispute with him.

FIRST PHARISEE: *Is it lawful for a man to put away his wife?*

Jesus turns questioningly to the Pharisee, as though not fully understanding him. The other Pharisees join in.

SECOND PHARISEE: *Can he send her out of the house . . . ?*
THIRD PHARISEE: *If he finds some unseemly thing in her?*
JESUS: *What did Moses command you?*
SECOND PHARISEE: *Moses suffers us to write a bill of divorcement and send her away.*

Jesus nods and looks meaningfully at the Pharisees as if to ask: Yes, and do you know why Moses did that? Aloud, he says

For the hardness of your heart he suffered you to put away your wives. But from the beginning it was not so.

Now the Pharisees fail to understand Jesus, and look at him perplexed. Jesus continues

Have you not read that from the beginning when God created the world, he created man and woman as male and female?

Bartholomew, proud of his knowledge of the Scriptures, is happy to display it and quotes Genesis 24:2.

Therefore shall a man leave his father and his mother, and shall cleave unto his wife: and they shall be one flesh.

Jesus nods, adding

So they are no longer two but one flesh.

But the Pharisees still refuse to accept his arguments.

FIRST PHARISEE: *That is true enough with "one flesh," but if the man no longer cares for his wife, what then?*
SECOND PHARISEE: *Or if he has found a woman he likes better?*
FOURTH PHARISEE: *In that case man and wife are no longer "one flesh."*
THIRD PHARISEE: *Is it not better then that they separate?*
FOURTH PHARISEE: *And that the man be permitted to divorce his wife?*

These speeches follow rapidly. Jesus listens, and when they have finished, he answers.

JESUS: *What God has joined together, no man shall put asunder.*
SECOND PHARISEE: *According to the Law the man is allowed to send off his wife at will.*

Jesus rises and speaks with such authority that the Pharisees are discouraged from further questioning.

And I say unto you: whosoever shall put away his wife, except it be for fornication, and shall marry another, commits adultery: and whosoever marries her which is put away does commit adultery too.

Among those present are many women and they are pleased by this interpretation of the Law. One of the women says to him

Blessed is the womb that bore you, and the breasts that you have sucked.

With a side glance at the Pharisees Jesus says

Rather blessed are they that hear the word of God, and keep it.

The camera returns to the little boys and girls who are playing "weddings" and the scene ends with one boy and several girls dancing. The sound of flutes, which has been subdued, becomes louder.

The final shot of the children playing "weddings" dissolves softly into a very short close-up of the top of a pomegranate tree in blossom. This dissolves into a scene showing a path through a field outside the village. The sound of the flutes is heard in the background, but almost imperceptibly the flutes are replaced by a distant choir of little children singing the same tune and in the same rhythm. At both sides of the path pomegranate trees grow wild.

A young farmer walks along the path, leading his camel. From the other direction comes a girl, a pitcher filled with water on her shoulder. They greet each other as they pass. Their names are Miriam and Joseph. When they have passed each other the young man turns around and calls the girl, who also turns around. She is a virgin and very fair to look upon. She holds her veil in her teeth so that we can barely see her nose and eyes through the narrow slit.

They stand facing each other. Then Joseph speaks.

Let me, I pray you, drink a little water from your pitcher.

Miriam sets down her pitcher and gives him a drink. There is a moment of embarrassment and then he speaks again.

JOSEPH:　*Whose daughter are you? Tell me.*
MIRIAM:　*I am the daughter of Jotham, the son of Amalek.*
JOSEPH:　*What is your name?*
MIRIAM:　*Miriam.*

He repeats her name, liltingly. It is easy to see that he likes it.

She returns the pitcher to her shoulder and is about to leave when he speaks again

JOSEPH: *When shall we meet again?*
MIRIAM: *Ask my father.*
JOSEPH: *I will.*

She continues on her way home without looking back. He rejoins his camel but continues to look after her. The camel is laden with sheepskins. On impulse, he takes out a beautiful white skin, and runs after the girl, calling her name. She turns and waits for him. When he reaches her he shows her the skin, saying

This is for you.

After a short pause, he rolls up the skin and puts it under her arm, saying

You are very beautiful.

She turns around again and starts out once more for her home. He returns to his camel and taking it by the bridle begins leading it in the opposite direction.

Soft dissolve into a short shot picturing some beautiful branches from the top of a pomegranate tree in full bloom, dissolving softly again into the interior of Miriam's father's house.

Joseph has come to ask for Miriam in marriage. He is talking to her father and mother.

You must be honest with me: do you, or do you not, believe that God himself showed me your daughter and gave me the sign that I should make her my wife?

The father looks at him and then at his wife and says

All things proceed from God.

The mother nods approvingly, adding

MOTHER: *We cannot tell you yes or no.*
FATHER: *We will call her and let her speak for herself.*

The mother again nods approvingly and calls the daughter, who enters. She and Joseph greet each other. Then the father asks his daughter

Will you marry this man?

With a calm voice and without change of expression Miriam answers

I will.

Joseph takes a step forward and puts a gold bracelet on each of Miriam's wrists and an earring in her ear. Her father and mother bless her.

The scene dissolves softly into another close-up of the blooming branches of the fruit tree, which dissolves softly into a room in Miriam's father's house.

The blooming young bride, Miriam, is waiting for her bridegroom. She sits on a dais like a princess on a throne, looking rather uneasy in her bridal garments, which cover her from head to toe. On her arms are armlets. From the bridegroom she has received gold and silver coins and some of these coins are fastened on her headkerchief, while others have been strung together to form a heavy necklace.

The door has been shut to prevent curious friends and neighbors from entering the room. When someone knocks, the two sisters turn them away, saying

She is not ready yet.

Another knock at the door. One of the sisters asks who it is and then turns to the mother, saying

It is Sarah and the other girls. They would like to see Miriam before they go to meet the bridegroom.

The mother gives her consent. With the door ajar, ten girls holding lamps slip into the room. With cries of joy and admiration they fuss about the patient bride and touch her garments and jewelry. Their curiosity satisfied, they light their lamps and leave the room, laughing and talking.

The mother and sisters fasten the bride's veil and put the room in order for the wedding reception.

The ten bridesmaids are on their way to meet the bridegroom. All the virgins carry lamps. The lamps consist of a small oval vessel with a spout for the wick at one end and a handle at the other. On the under side of the container is a hole so that the lamp can be fixed on a long wooden pole and borne aloft.

The bride's chamber. Miriam still sitting on her dais. The mother has a few stitches to make on the wedding gown. In a plaintive, childish voice the bride says

I am hungry.

One of the sisters gives her a piece of bread while the other raises her veil.

The bridesmaids stop at a crossroad. Sarah, the eldest, says

We had better wait here.

Near the crossing is a watchtower in a vineyard. The roof of the tower is covered with leaves. The lower part is open and enables the bridesmaids to rest in the shade.

NARRATOR: *And Jesus likened the Kingdom of Heaven unto the ten virgins who took their lamps and went forth to meet the bridegroom. Five of them were wise, and five were foolish.*

They that were foolish took their lamps, and took no oil with them. But the wise took oil in their vessels with their lamps.

The ten virgins make themselves comfortable in the shade of the watchtower. But the five wise virgins decide to trim their lamps before resting. They talk among themselves.

FIRST BRIDESMAID: *I think I will fill my lamp now.*

SIXTH BRIDESMAID (surprised): *Have you some extra oil with you?*

FIRST BRIDESMAID: *Of course I have.*

SECOND BRIDESMAID: *So have I.*

THIRD BRIDESMAID: *It was the prudent thing to do.*

SEVENTH BRIDESMAID: *I have no extra oil.*

EIGHTH BRIDESMAID: *Nor have I.*

NINTH BRIDESMAID: *Oh, it will not be long.*

TENTH BRIDESMAID: *I hope not.*

The five wise virgins fill their lamps and they all sit. The lamps have been removed from their poles and placed on a board above their heads. It is late and they begin to yawn.

The girls relax and soon they are dozing. A faint murmur of song from the bridal house mingles with the distant music and song which accompanies the approaching bridegroom and his followers.

The procession of the bridegroom on the road. Surrounded by friends, Joseph rides a richly bedecked camel. All carry lamps or torches. Passersby have joined the train and the whole procession is shouting, singing and playing musical instruments. The women are waving their hands.

The bridal chamber. Miriam sits alone, covered by her thick veil. Joseph enters, followed by her father and mother, who remain in the background. In close-up Joseph greets Miriam and tries to peer through the veil as he speaks to her.

JOSEPH: *Thou hast dove's eyes.*

MIRIAM: *Thy neck is like the tower of David.*

JOSEPH: *Thy teeth are like a flock of sheep.*
MIRIAM: *Thy hair is like a raven's.*
JOSEPH: *Beautiful is thy face and sweet is thy voice, milk and honey are under thy tongue.*

They know they are quoting the Song of Solomon, and they say these words simply, without sentimentality—indeed, even with a hint of humor and self-irony.

The five foolish virgins arrive at the bride's home with unlit lamps. They find the door locked. They knock. The father comes to the door and calls

FATHER: *Who is there?*
SIXTH BRIDESMAID: *We are your daughter's bridesmaids.*
ALL THE BRIDESMAIDS: *Open the door! Let us in!*
FATHER: *I do not know you.*

The scene is interrupted by the voice of Jesus.

Watch, therefore; for ye know neither the day nor the hour.

A hill not far from a village. We hear in the distance the noise of a wooden rattle. Although no one appears, we hear the voices of husky men shouting

Unclean, unclean.

The sounds draw near and then ten miserably dressed creatures appear, carrying earthen jars, pots, and mugs, which they place on the crest of the hillside. They continue shouting

Unclean, unclean.

After putting down their possessions, the men retreat behind the hillside and are again hidden.

Three or four women carrying vessels with food and pitchers of water appear. They place the food in the jars, pots and mugs, after which they hurry away.

The men reappear from behind the hill. They are lepers. They sit down to eat the food their relatives have brought and the camera examines their faces closely.

Their skin is dry and glistening, studded with white specks. Some are disfigured by clustered boils as large as peas or hazelnuts. The tip of one man's nose has been corroded to the bone. Another has lips that have swelled. Another is bleary-eyed and a fourth almost toothless. Others have stiff and crooked fingers and toes. Their bodies tremble and shake violently.

[These wretched men were banished and forced to live outside the towns and villages. They were required to stay at a six-foot distance from others or farther than a hundred feet if the wind blew in the direction of those they approached. According to Leviticus, lepers wore mourning—for themselves. They were considered the living dead.]

While the ten lepers are eating, their leader rises and shades his eyes to stare at a group of men approaching in the distance.

SECOND LEPER: *What is it?*
FIRST LEPER: *Is not that Jesus?*
THIRD LEPER: *The Prophet?*
FIRST LEPER: *Yes.*
FOURTH LEPER: *Surely it is.*
FIRST LEPER: He *could make us clean.*
FIFTH LEPER: *If he would, yes.*
FIRST LEPER: *If we believe, he will.*
SIXTH LEPER: I *believe.*
SEVENTH LEPER: I *too have faith in him.*
NINTH LEPER: *So have I.*
EIGHTH LEPER: *Let us go and ask him.*
TENTH LEPER: *Yes, come.*

They cross the crest of the hillside and approach Jesus and his disciples. But they do not forget to use the rattle and they shout

Unclean, unclean.

They fall to the ground and the leader says

Jesus, Master, have mercy upon us.

The disciples draw away from the lepers, but when they see Jesus step forward they know that a miracle will be performed.

The lepers rise to their knees, their faces lit with hope and expectation. Jesus speaks to them while they carefully maintain the distance ordained by the Law.

JESUS: *Go your way, and show yourself to the priests, and offer for your cleansing those things which Moses commanded.*

The lepers rise, at first a little uncertainly. Then they do as he bids them and go toward the village. So great is their faith in Jesus that they leave before they are certain that they have been healed.

Jesus and his disciples look after them with compassion, and then as they are starting on their way themselves James asks

How or by what sin has this come to them?

Jesus shakes his head.

JESUS: *Think* you *that these men are sinners above all men because they suffer such things?*
BARTHOLOMEW: *There is another old saying that "not the serpents kill but the sin."*
JESUS: *I tell you: nay. They are not sinners above all men.*

Jesus and his disciples continue on their way.

We follow the lepers to the priests. They stop at a pool of stagnant water, fall on their knees and bend forward to look at the reflection. We see the faces in the water and not a trace of the horrible disease remains. The lepers are beside themselves with excitement, and they laugh and weep at the same time, stretching their hands toward Heaven.

One of them, a Samaritan, rises quickly, turns and runs back toward the hill. Surprised, the others watch him. Then one of them, filling his hands with water, says

NINTH LEPER: *I will wash my face.*
SECOND LEPER: *Not yet.*
NINTH LEPER: *Why not?*
EIGHTH LEPER: *It is forbidden.*
SECOND LEPER: *Until the priests have pronounced you clean.*

They rise and go toward the village. Some village men throw stones at them and shout

Get you gone, you godless sinners.

But the lepers speak to the villagers. The huskiness has left their voices.

SECOND LEPER: *Leave us in peace.*
THIRD LEPER: *We are clean.*
FOURTH LEPER: *Look at our faces.*
FIFTH LEPER: *Listen to our voices.*
TENTH LEPER: *Jesus has healed us.*
FIRST LEPER: *Go and call the priests.*

The villagers see that the lepers speak the truth and they stop throwing stones. Some of them go to the village and call the priests.

The Samaritan has left the others to express his gratitude to Jesus. He runs back to the hillside and, finding Jesus and his disciples, falls at the feet of Jesus

I have come to give you thanks . . . for health and healing . . . for help in hopeless need.

Jesus is moved at the sight of this man who has delayed his meeting with the priests and his family for *his* sake. Jesus says

Arise, and go your way. Your faith has made you whole.

The Samaritan rises, and hurries back to join the others and show himself to the priests. Jesus looks inquiringly at his disciples and asks

Were there not ten cleansed? Where are the other nine?

The disciples are unable to give any answer.

In intercalated scenes we have seen a dozen priests and as many Levites come out of the village to meet the nine lepers and prepare the ceremony by which the lepers may regain their position in the community.

Now the Samaritan appears, at the same time as a pigeon-dealer with ten small pigeon cages. The Samaritan is treated in the same way as the others.

The nine lepers and the Samaritan, sitting in a row, the upper parts of their bodies naked, have their hair and beards shaved off. The priests pass from one to the other giving each a careful examination to verify that they really are healed. A young priest draws the attention of an older priest to a white speck on the crown of the head of one of the lepers, and asks

What is that?

The old priest studies the white speck and then he says

That is nothing, it is an old leprosy.

Another old priest takes this opportunity to teach the young priest. He points at the speck and enlarges upon the explanation of the other old priest.

Look, there has been raw flesh, but "if the raw flesh turn again and be changed unto white then he is clean."

Then begins the cleansing ceremony. Earthen water vessels are placed on the ground. Pieces of cedar wood, scarlet sage, and hyssop are put into the water. Now one of the older priests approaches the first of the lepers. A Levite, with one of the cages in his hands, takes out a pigeon and hands it to the priest, who kills it. We see only the drops of blood drip into the water. The priest sprinkles the water seven times upon the leper. The Levite hands another pigeon out of the cage to the priest, who dips it in the water and then lets it go free.

The last scene of this sequence is a close-up of the upstretched hands of the priest at the moment when he frees the pigeon. By means of a left to right pan, the camera glides to the hands of the priest at the moment when he looses his pigeon—and so on down the row, as a pigeon is let loose after each man is cleansed.

The sideways pan of the birds being let loose dissolves softly into a close-up of a young man running with a flaming torch in his hands. We follow him and the close-up turns slowly into a long shot which shows him throwing the burning torch into a fire on top of a hill. By means of a wide pan we see other hills and on top of each one a great fire is burning.

[SCENE SHIFT]

NARRATOR: *On one day, when fires were lit on all the hills and all the mountains to call the pilgrims to Jerusalem for the Passover, it came to pass that a certain man named Lazarus, whom Jesus loved, became deathly ill. He was a native of Bethany, outside Jerusalem, where he lived together with his father and two sisters, Martha and Mary.*

The scene on the hills dissolves softly into a room in Lazarus's house.

Lazarus's father was a Levite. Lazarus himself was a scribe who had established a fine reputation. Many synagogues ordered copies of the Law and the Prophets from him. His elder sisters, Mary and Martha, were needleworkers and made garments for the priests.

Though the family were friends of Jesus, they were also on good terms with the local religious authorities and the people of Bethany.

Lazarus is lying in bed at the point of death. He is so ravaged by fever that almost all life appears to have left him. Only his fingers move incessantly, and from time to time he utters unintelligible sounds. His old, white-bearded father moves about restlessly in the room while the sisters take turns caring for the patient.

Neighbors enter quietly. In whispers they inquire of Mary about Lazarus's health, but the silent shake of her head tells them that her brother is considered beyond recovery. That is . . .

Mary has a sudden impulse. She approaches her sister and speaks in a low voice. Martha seems to approve the suggestion and leaves the room. Mary goes back to the sick-bed and wipes the face of Lazarus.

In the courtyard. Martha calls a man-servant and speaks to him

Go and find Jesus and tell him: "He whom you love is sick."

The servant repeats the words

"He whom you love is sick."

He sets out at once after filling his bag with some food. Martha returns to the sick-room.

The sick-room. Martha enters, followed by a physician. The sisters watch him anxiously as he prepares a drug for the sick man. As is the custom, the physician, in handing the remedy to the patient, pronounces the words

Arise from your fever.

But there is no change in Lazarus's condition. It is as if the Angel of Death is already standing at the head of the sick-bed.

[WIPE TO THE NEXT SCENE.]

Morning. A farmer and his wife are traveling along the road leading to Jerusalem, the Holy City. The man, unburdened in any way, is riding on a donkey. His wife walks behind carrying a large basket on her head. They meet the servant from the house of Lazarus, who stops them and asks

Have you seen or heard anything of Jesus of Nazareth?

The farmer points in the direction from which he has come.

FARMER: *He is somewhere behind us.*
SERVANT: *How far?*
FARMER: *If you are quick you may soon catch up with him.*

The servant thanks the farmer and moves on rapidly.

[WIPE TO THE NEXT SCENE.]

Lazarus's sick-room. He has just drawn his last breath. The physician, feeling his pulse, declares that he has been delivered from his sufferings and has entered into the joy of the Lord. He moves to one side and makes room for the old father, whose duty it is to render the last offices to his dead son. With tears in his eyes, the father bends over the son and kisses him for the last time. Then he closes the eyes and mouth of the dead. Martha lights an oil-lamp which, according to Jewish custom, must be kept burning for seven days and nights, symbolizing the immortality of the human soul. Mary has fallen down on her knees and, throwing out her hands, she cries hysterically

Woe is me, woe is my brother.

The physician leaves the room. Relatives, friends, and neighbors have gathered at the door to express their sympathy. The physician answers the question in their eyes by invoking the traditional words

Weep with them, all you who are bitter of heart.

One by one the relatives and friends enter the death-room. Mary is beside herself with grief and Martha is trying to console her. Locked in each other's arms, the sisters weep together. The newcomers first speak comfortingly to the father and then to the sisters.

FIRST RELATIVE: *May the Lord of Consolations comfort you.*
SECOND RELATIVE: *Remember that in death the two worlds meet and kiss.*

Heartbroken, Mary wails.

[WIPE TO THE NEXT SCENE.]

The servant from Lazarus's house, on his way across the desert that lies between Jerusalem and Jericho. Some camels are being driven along the road. The servant asks the drivers

Have you seen or heard anything of Jesus of Nazareth? Do you know where he is?

One of the camel-drivers points across the wilderness.

CAMEL-DRIVER: *Over there, beyond that hill.*
SERVANT: *The first one?*
CAMEL-DRIVER: *No, the next one.*
SERVANT: *Thank you.*

He hurries away.

[WIPE TO THE NEXT SCENE.]

Outside Lazarus's house. The body of the dead has been washed, anointed, wrapped in the finest linen, and laid in a wicker bier bordered with myrtle. The face is turned up and the hands are folded on the breast.

Present are the old father, the two weeping sisters, and a great number of relatives, friends, and neighbors. The Leader of the Synagogue delivers the funeral oration.

> *In truth he was a Saint. But in the sight of God the death of his Saints is precious. He welcomes the souls of the pure and just—awaiting their coming as new brides, with delight. And with delight the ministering angels rejoice over their coming to abide among them. Therefore, weep you for the mourners, not for him who is lost. He has found his rest. And now: let us bring him to the cave and lay him to rest.*

At the end of the oration the male relatives and friends lift the bier upon their shoulders and carry it to the tomb. The mourners sing the "Elegy."

[WIPE TO THE NEXT SCENE.]

The funeral procession on its way to the tomb—"the house of silence." The men carrying the casket do not wear shoes.

At the head of the procession is the Leader who delivered the oration. After him come the father, Mary, Martha, and the immediate family. Then comes the casket, which is followed by the hired mourners. At the rear is a great crowd so organized that the men and women are separated. The funeral elegy from the preceding scene is heard again accompanied by flutes and cymbals.

Some men quarrying stones by the roadside stop working and stand reverently until the procession has passed.

[WIPE TO THE NEXT SCENE.]

The procession has arrived at the "house of silence."

The same song and music can still be heard, and it continues through the three following scenes.

Lazarus is laid in the family tomb. It is rock-hewn, consisting of a vault with niches for the bodies along the sides. Besides the vault there is a small anteroom from which a corridor leads to the

outside. The opening to the tomb is covered by a heavy circular
stone that can be rolled aside. The mourners walk by the casket
chanting over the deceased "Depart in Peace." Young men of the
immediate family lift the body and carry it into the tomb, followed
by the father.

[WIPE TO THE NEXT SCENE.]

The interior of the vault. The young men have laid the body
in the niche and have withdrawn, leaving the father alone with
his beloved son. As he tries to keep back his tears, the old man
covers the face of the dead with a cloth, the last favor from a
father's hand.

[WIPE TO THE NEXT SCENE.]

Outside the tomb. The father comes out, walking backward
so as not to turn his back to the dead.

His daughters come to his side. Some young men roll the
circular stone into place so that it covers the entrance. The camera
approaches and the scene ends in a close-up of the stone.

The song, the music and the wailing are fading away, and the
scene dissolves softly into a rocky deserted landscape where Jesus
sits surrounded by his disciples and a few Pharisees. A short distance away is another small group of Pharisees and lawyers. Apparently, both groups have halted here on their way to Jerusalem.
Jesus has not yet made any final decision as to whether he will
spend the Passover in Jerusalem or stay in the desert where he is
safer.

A lawyer approaches Jesus and asks him

Master, what shall I do to inherit eternal life?

There is no ulterior motive in his asking this question. Jesus
receives the question in good faith, and being experienced in the
art of dialectics he answers with a question

What is written in the Law?

The lawyer, already on the defensive, quotes from Deuteronomy.

Thou shalt love the Lord thy God with all thine heart, and with all thy soul, and with all thy might.

Jesus nods encouragingly as if to say: and what more? The lawyer thinks for a moment and then continues, this time quoting Leviticus.

Thou shalt love thy neighbor as thyself.

Jesus nods approvingly and answers by quoting another text from the same book.

This do and you shall live eternally.

The lawyer, recognizing how good Jesus is at this sort of discussion, wishes to make it clear that he, for his part, will not accept a superficial solution of a problem of such great importance. A precise definition of "neighbor" is needed. Leviticus says: "Thou shalt not avenge, nor bear any grudge against the children of thy people, but thou shalt love thy neighbor as thyself." According to this a "neighbor" could only be an Israelite. Therefore he asks Jesus the very simple question

Who is my neighbor?

Jesus thinks for a moment and then decides that the best way to make the matter clear is by use of a parable.

The transition from reality to the parable is carried out as follows: Jesus and his disciples are seen standing at a place just south of the road that runs across the desert from Jericho to Jerusalem.

Now the camera makes a 120 degree turn, from the group of Jesus and his disciples to the road.

NARRATOR: *And Jesus spoke a parable of a certain man who went down from Jerusalem to Jericho, and fell among thieves. . . .*

The country between Jericho and Jerusalem is a rocky desert with a gloomy and sinister look. The road between the two towns is tortuous, at times running along the edge of steep precipices and at other times at the foot of rocky walls. It thus lent itself to sudden attacks by robbers who hid in the innumerable caves in the trackless mountains. Though the road was dangerous for travelers, it was used a great deal because it was the only road between Jericho and Jerusalem. At the time of Christ it was named the "red" or the "bloody" way. Halfway between Jerusalem and Jericho there was an inn which gave a night's shelter to people and animals. This inn had a courtyard surrounded by a high wall. Inside the wall were roof-covered colonnades. Here men, women, and children slept together while the animals spent the night in the middle of the open courtyard, around rock-hewn water cisterns. In addition to the colonnades there were a few rooms for travelers of some means. There was only one gate in the wall.

Assuming that Jerusalem is behind the camera, we see the "certain man," probably a Jewish merchant, leading his heavily loaded donkey along the road. Suddenly the road is overrun with armed robbers coming down from the rocky slopes. Taken by surprise, the merchant is overpowered, robbed, and stripped naked. Some of the robbers take the donkey, pulling it after them up into the mountains. Others fall upon the merchant, stabbing him with their daggers. Then they hurry away leaving him half dead.

[WIPE TO THE NEXT SCENE.]

NARRATOR: *By chance there came down a certain priest.*

The priest, coming from the Holy City, is probably returning to his native town after having completed his turn of duty in the Temple. Seeing a man apparently dead he passes by quickly. He was forbidden to touch a dead body because this would make him unclean for seven days. Thus was the Jewish Law.

[WIPE TO THE NEXT SCENE.]

NARRATOR: *Likewise a Levite, when he was at the place . . .*

A Levite comes from Jerusalem. He too passes by.

[WIPE TO THE NEXT SCENE.]

NARRATOR: *But a certain Samaritan, as he journeyed, came, and when he saw him, he had compassion on him . . .*

The Samaritan, too, comes from Jerusalem. He rides a donkey. As soon as he becomes aware of what has happened, he gets off the donkey and hurries to the helpless man. He has pity on him and begins to help him. In order to disinfect the wounds he cleans them with wine. In order to heal them and to relieve the pain he rubs them with oil. After that, he bandages the wounds and then lifts the poor man onto his donkey and starts out for the nearby inn.

[WIPE TO THE NEXT SCENE.]

NARRATOR: *And he brought the man to the inn and took care of him . . .*

We see the Samaritan arriving at the inn where he is well received. Obviously he is a frequent visitor. The innkeeper helps the Samaritan carry the wounded merchant to a room where he is placed upon a couch.

[WIPE TO THE NEXT SCENE.]

NARRATOR: *And on the morrow when the Samaritan departed he took out two denarii and gave them to the host . . .*

We see the Samaritan the next morning, about to make his departure, speaking to the innkeeper in the room where the wounded man is lying in a deep sleep.

Handing the innkeeper two coins and glancing at the patient, he says

Take care of him; and whatsoever you spend more, when I come again, I will repay you.

[WIPE TO THE NEXT SCENE.]

The Samaritan leaves the inn and rides away along the same road on which the merchant had been attacked the day before.

This is the end of the parable. By means of a wide pan we return to Jesus surrounded by his disciples and the lawyer. Jesus asks this question

Which now of these three, think you, was neighbor unto him that fell among thieves?

The lawyer's first impulse is to answer: "The Samaritan." But he hesitates because, being a Jew and a lawyer, he has always felt harsh toward the Samaritans. And his animosity is so great that the word "Samaritan" cannot pass his lips. Finally he answers

He that showed mercy on him.

To this Jesus replies

Go, and do you likewise.

[Jesus taught that any man of any faith and of any race may be your neighbor—*it is the heart that imports*. These thoughts were not only new for that age: they were revolutionary and contrary to Jewish faith, and it was not surprising that pious Jews opposed them.]

After Jesus's last remark, the lawyer and the Pharisees withdraw and join their own group and go on their way.

The servant sent by Martha of Bethany with the message for Jesus arrives. Respectfully approaching the group around Jesus, he makes a sign to one of the disciples that he has a message for Jesus. The disciple draws the attention of Jesus to the servant, and Jesus goes to him. The disciples, filled with curiosity, rise and follow Jesus. The servant, after the usual greetings, says

Martha has sent me with a message. This is what she told me to say unto you . . .

The servant pauses like a schoolboy about to recite a lesson learned by heart. Then he speaks.

He whom you love is sick.

Jesus nods earnestly. It is as if this message has confirmed a premonition. He says to the disciples

Let us go to Bethany.

The disciples are startled. To go to Bethany, close to Jerusalem, would be extremely dangerous, for Jesus would be in danger of being at the mercy of his enemies—the religious authorities. The disciples show their anxiety.

JOHN: *To Bethany?*
JAMES: *To Jerusalem?*

Jesus nods assent.

PETER: *Are you really determined to go to Jerusalem?*

Jesus answers affirmatively.

BARTHOLOMEW: *Now, at Passover time?*
JESUS (quietly): *Yes, now.*
PETER: *Are you aware of the danger?*
MATTHEW: *Of late they sought to stone you.*

Jesus, looking very serious, says after a short pause

I must go. Our friend Lazarus sleeps, and I may awake him out of his sleep.

Jesus is speaking of Lazarus's death but the disciples "thought that he had spoken of taking of rest in sleep." (John 11:13.) Therefore Peter says

But if he sleeps he shall do well.

They still have scruples about the wisdom of going to the Holy City. Philip adds

And there is no need for us to go up to Jerusalem just now.

Then Jesus decides to speak to them plainly.

JESUS: *Lazarus is dead.*

The disciples are silent for a while, standing as though struck dumb, because all of them love Lazarus. But they also love Jesus and are deeply concerned about the danger. For this reason John once more attempts to make Jesus abandon his plan.

JOHN: *If Lazarus is already dead and cannot be saved—why then go to Bethany and Jerusalem?*

Absentmindedly Jesus listens to what John is saying, for he is concerned with other thoughts and ideas. He says

Yes, Lazarus is dead. And I am glad for your sake that I was not there, in order that you may believe.

After a short pause he repeats

Lazarus is dead. Nevertheless let us go unto him.

The meaning of these words is beyond the comprehension of the disciples. Peter speaks urgently to Jesus

Then you are still determined to go to Jerusalem?

Jesus nods assent.

JOHN: *In spite of the danger?*

With a slight tremor in his voice Jesus answers

It cannot be that a Prophet die outside of Jerusalem.

The disciples look at each other, disturbed because of the danger threatening their beloved teacher. It is Thomas who acts as spokesman for all of them.

Since it is to be so, let us also go that we may die with him.

All of them agree and they flock round Jesus, listening attentively to his words. We follow as Jesus and the disciples make their departure.

JESUS: *Are there not twelve hours in the day? If any man walks in the day, he stumbles not, because he sees the light of this world. But if a man walks in the night, he stumbles, because there is no light in him.*

In close-up, we see Jesus and several disciples clinging to him and listening intently. The angle is cut in a way that leaves the right upper corner free.

Soft dissolve to an oil lamp in the right upper corner. To the left we see the face of Martha wet with tears; then her hands as she refills the lamp. She leaves the scene.

A dissolve softly into the dead Lazarus lying in the tomb. This time the dissolve from the preceding shot is not complete. We see a superimposition of the close-up of the lamp (in the right upper corner) and the niche (with the head of Lazarus in the left lower corner).

The superimposition dissolves softly into the oil lamp only. As soon as the dissolve is completed the camera glides backward until it encompasses the whole room in which Lazarus died.

The mourning lasts thirty days but only the first three days were a time of deep mourning. Silence prevails, interrupted only by the sighs and the weeping of the immediate relatives who are seated on the floor. During these first three days the mourners do not eat or drink. Among the mourners we see Mary, her father, and a few others.

The practical Martha has again taken up her housework. She enters the room with a few dried figs which she offers to Mary, who refuses them. She weeps inconsolably. Martha, falling to her knees, tries to comfort her dazed sister. Weeping, Mary says

Oh, if . . . if . . . if . . .

Martha embraces her.

MARTHA: *If what?*
MARY: *If Jesus had been appealed to in time . . .*

Lifting up her tear-filled face Mary continues.

MARY: *Our brother would still be alive.*
MARTHA: *How could we know it would be the death of him? Be quiet now, it will do no good to weep any more.*

Some neighbors now enter the room to console the sisters.

[WIPE TO THE NEXT SCENE.]

Martha enters the kitchen and looks to see what work needs to be done. As she walks to the door, her attention is attracted by a group of men entering the village. She wipes the tears from her eyes and is able to make out who the men are: Jesus and his disciples and at the head of the group her servant. She runs to meet Jesus.

As soon as Jesus catches sight of Martha he moves quickly to meet her. Martha cannot restrain her tears, and Jesus does his best to comfort her and makes her sit down, saying

Do not weep.

Martha, sobbing, tells him what has happened.

Lazarus is dead.

Jesus only nods. He knows it. Martha continues

If you had been here my brother would not have died.

In a quiet reassuring voice Jesus answers

Your brother shall rise again.

Martha cannot interpret his words literally.

MARTHA: *I know that he shall rise again in the resurrection at the last day.*
JESUS (after a pause): *Martha . . .*

There is in the voice of Jesus a strange note which makes her lift her head and look at him in surprise. Jesus continues

I am the resurrection and the life: whosoever lives and believes in me shall never die.

Martha stares at him, moved by the tremendous thing he is saying. Now Jesus asks her

Believe you this?

Martha, almost overcome by the words and manner of Jesus, answers weakly

Yes, I believe.

And after a pause she adds

I believe that you are the Messiah which should come into the world.

She rises, still looking at Jesus, and says

I'll go and tell Mary . . .

She leaves the place and Jesus sits down, waiting for Mary.

[WIPE TO THE NEXT SCENE.]

The mourning-room. Mary is sitting in the same place as before. Other neighbors have entered the room. Martha appears. She quietly approaches her sister and tells her in a whisper that Jesus waits outside. Mary leaves the room with Martha, and the other mourners look after them in surprise and ask questions of each other.

FIRST MOURNER: *Why did Mary rise so hastily?*
SECOND MOURNER: *Where did she go?*
THIRD MOURNER: *Certainly to the grave to weep.*
FATHER: *Let us also go to the grave.*

The mourners, headed by the father of Lazarus, leave the room.

[WIPE TO THE NEXT SCENE.]

Jesus is still in the place where Martha met him. When Mary arrives, she falls at his feet weeping, and says

If you had been here, my brother would not have died.

Tears of despair blind her eyes. Seeing the tears also of the mourners and Martha and their father, Jesus is filled with compassion. He asks them

Where have you laid him?

The father answers

Come and see.

Jesus follows him.

[WIPE TO THE NEXT SCENE.]

At the tomb. The crowd which has gathered near the tomb is kept at a distance by the disciples. We notice a group of Pharisees and scribes, one of whom speaks.

FIRST SCRIBE: *Could not this man, which opened the eyes of the blind, have caused that even this man should not have died?*

Jesus stands before the entrance to the tomb. Between him and the tomb are the father, the two sisters, and other relatives of the immediate family. [The angles of this scene are cut in a way that makes them as much as possible similar to the angles of the funeral scene.] This time there is no music, no song, not even any wailing—just a heavy, oppressive silence. All look at Jesus, who stands calm and motionless. To his disciples it is clear that he is concentrating all his psychic power, thus preparing for the great task he has undertaken. The silence is broken by Jesus.

JESUS: *Take away the stone.*

Some young men from among the relatives approach the stone, but the impulsive Martha makes a sign for them to wait and then she turns to Jesus.

MARTHA: *Master, he has been dead four days.*

It is not clear to her what Jesus intends, and she is seized with fear. Now that her brother is dead she wishes him to rest in peace. But Jesus rebukes her.

Said I not unto you, that if you would believe, you should see the Glory of God?

She hangs her head in humility and Jesus makes a sign to the two young men to remove the stone.

Jesus is seen again concentrating his psychic powers. His eyes close and tears run down his cheeks. Some people in the crowd whisper

Behold, how he loved him.

The stone has been rolled aside. A wave of expectation runs through the crowd. Jesus does not move, does not speak. Then he lifts up his eyes and speaks in a low voice.

Father, I thank you that you heard me.

There is another silence, then Jesus cries loudly

Lazarus, come forth.

All who are present hold their breath in fearful excitement. After a few seconds a white shape is seen moving slowly in the corridor leading out from the anteroom. It is Lazarus wrapped in his grave-clothes with the cloth in his hand. Jesus turns to Martha and Mary and says

Loose him, and let him go.

Martha hurries to Lazarus's aid, looses his clothes, and embraces him, but Mary is awestruck and clings to her father.

The Pharisees and the scribes mutter among themselves.

FIRST PHARISEE: *Surely, these works are not of God.*
SECOND PHARISEE: *Certainly not.*

The disciples gather around Jesus. They marvel and are filled with awe.

The young men roll the circular stone back into place. The camera moves in and the scene ends with a close-up of the circular stone, then a soft dissolve to the next scene.

[SCENE SHIFT]

NARRATOR: *But the Pharisees, who had witnessed the resurrection of Lazarus, went their ways to Jerusalem and told the High Priest what things Jesus had done. And the High Priest gathered his privy council.*

A room in the palace of the high priest Caiaphas. The palace is a rectangular building, consisting of four wings grouped around an open courtyard. All the rooms face the courtyard. A janitress keeps watch at the main gate. We see a large household of men and women slaves bustling about.

The room is the "talinarium," the library, whose furniture and wall decorations show Greek and Roman influence. The council that has been summoned to meet here is the privy council of the high priest.

The high priest, head of the Jewish state, was appointed by the Roman governor, Pilate, and consequently was only interested in being on good terms with the foreign ruler and in carrying out his wishes. Although all good patriots looked upon him as a hireling and corrupt tool of the Roman oppressor, there was no evidence of this being the case. As a politician he was a realist, and he considered it to be for the benefit of the Jewish nation to appease the Romans, giving way in minor political questions, but on the other hand watching over and stubbornly defending the remnants of liberty left to the Jews—their own divine worship, their own justice, their own courts, and their own police force. In case of insurrections the Jewish authorities had the duty of arresting the guilty and delivering them over to the Roman governor. For these reasons the high priest had to consider all rebellious movements as a danger to the nation. The nobility, the priesthood, and the people of substance in the country shared his point of view.

The privy council of the high priest consisted mainly of Sadducees and Pharisees, who were religiously irreconcilable antagonists, but who agreed on the necessity of living in peace with the Romans. Regarding Jesus, Sadducees considered him from a political point of view and the Pharisees from a religious one.

One of the Pharisees who had been present at the resurrection of Lazarus gives his report.

PHARISEE: *People came from far to see Lazarus whom Jesus had raised from the dead, and they were many who believed in Jesus and took him for a Prophet.*

Caiaphas smiles ironically because up to now the whole question has been more a religious than a political one. He says

A Prophet? Where is it written that a Prophet shall come from Galilee?

To this a chief priest adds

And from Nazareth?

Among the counsellors are three men, all known as being just and good and exceedingly sincere in their religious feelings: the old sage and teacher, Gamaliel, and his disciples, Nicodemus and Joseph of Arimathaea. Secretly they approve the teachings of Jesus. Joseph of Arimathaea, therefore, feels compelled to say a word in his defense

Truly he must be a man moved by God.

Nicodemus speaks in a similar vein.

NICODEMUS: *I agree. Where would he obtain the power he has shown if not from God?*
CHIEF PRIEST: *There have been others before him who claimed*

that they were sent by God, and who stirred up the people.
And he is just another one of the same type.
FIRST LAWYER: *And, therefore, a danger to the state.*

At this moment Gamaliel rises with dignity and says

If Jesus is a danger to the state, his preaching will soon come
to nought. But if he be of God, we do well to leave him alone.

His words strongly influence the members of the council.
There is a short pause, then Caiaphas closes the discussion.

Times are dangerous. We will have to keep an eye on him.

Soft dissolve into a close-up of a papyrus sheet. A hand is
seen writing beautiful Hebrew letters, from right to left. The
hand belongs to Lazarus, who is copying one of the books of the
Prophets.

Sitting on the floor, leaning against the wall, is the aged father
of Lazarus. He appears deep in thought.

The camera moves backward and we see Lazarus. Slowly the
image of Lazarus fades from the screen, and Jesus and Mary come
into focus. They are sitting outside the house. Not far from them
is the door to the kitchen.

By means of a trucking-shot Jesus and Mary come into the
foreground. In the background Martha is seen going to and fro
between the kitchen and dining room, carrying plates, baskets
with bread, fruit. Martha tries to catch some of the words of
Jesus, but without success.

Mary is sitting at the feet of the Master listening with a rapt
expression, forgetting everything else. During this, the camera is
moved and focused on Martha, who becomes impatient at seeing
her younger sister sitting idle while she herself is so busy. For this
reason she approaches Jesus and says

Do you not care that my sister has left me to serve alone? Bid
her therefore that she help me.

Mary has jumped to her feet, but Jesus makes a sign indicating that she is to remain. There is silence for a moment. Martha no doubt is already sorry for having given way to her temper.

Jesus gives her a look of mild reproach and says

Martha, Martha . . .

Jesus shakes his head but smiles as he continues

You are careful about many things, but one thing is needful. And Mary has chosen that good part, which shall not be taken away from her.

Martha bows her head in shame. With a lovely smile Mary approaches her sister, embracing and kissing her. Then she sits down again at the feet of Jesus and with her hand invites her elder sister to sit beside her.

Jesus, looking at the two sisters in loving fashion, continues his teaching.

The scene dissolves softly into the Temple in Jerusalem. A priest in a white cloak is standing at the pinnacle of the temple looking toward the south. As soon as dawn breaks he calls down to the priests and Levites on duty for the morning sacrifices.

FIRST PRIEST: *It is dawn.*

The chief priest shouts back

Is it daylight to Hebron?

After a while the priest on watch shouts again

It is daylight to Hebron.

The Captain of the Temple Guard gives an order to open the heavy doors of the Temple. The Levites blow their silver trumpets announcing the morning service.

This shot dissolves softly into the next one.

[SCENE SHIFT]

NARRATOR: *On the following day, which was the Sabbath, Jesus and two of his disciples went up to Jerusalem and came to a pool called Bethesda.*

The pool at Bethesda. This pool was situated just outside the wall, near the sheep market north of Jerusalem and the old "sheep-gate" that opened upon the road leading to Bethany. The pool was a "twin pool," consisting of two pools lying side by side but with different water levels and separated by a colonnade. The pools were enclosed by porches from which staircases led down to the water. The water was supplied from a subterranean, intermittent hot spring, which at certain irregular intervals made the water boil up and seethe like water in a kettle.

The scene starts with a trucking-shot of the pool and the porches, in which a great multitude of blind, halt, lame and withered folk are lying about.

A long shot of Jesus and two of his disciples, John and Peter, entering the porches.

NARRATOR: *It was believed that an angel at certain intervals went down into the pool and troubled the water and whosoever then first stepped in was made whole of whatsoever disease he had.*

The camera passes through the multitude of the sick lying on their pallets or mats or rugs. As it is the Sabbath, relatives have come to visit many of them, but all the sick have their eyes fixed upon the surface of the water, everyone hoping anxiously to be the first to enter when the angel stirs the water again. Therefore nobody takes much notice of Jesus and the two disciples.

Jesus comes to a lame man who is between fifty and fifty-five years old. Jesus and his two disciples are filled with compassion because of the suffering of this man, and they question him about his infirmity.

JOHN: *Have you been in this condition a long time?*

LAME MAN: *Thirty and eight years. Both my legs are lame.*

PETER: *Have you been in the pool?*

LAME MAN: *Not yet.*

PETER: *Why not?*

LAME MAN: *I have no man, when the water is troubled, to put me into the pool. And while I am coming by myself another steps down before me.*

Jesus, who has been listening and watching the face of the lame man, speaks.

Will you be made whole?

The lame man looks in surprise at Jesus, then at the two disciples, and then back to Jesus, wondering whether or not he can be serious. Then Jesus speaks to him with authority

Rise, and take up your bed and walk.

The lame man, still surprised, again looks at Jesus and then at the two disciples. Peter encourages him

Rise.

The lame man shakes his head.

LAME MAN: *But I am lame.*

JOHN: *No, you are whole now.* (Pointing at Jesus) *He has made you whole.*

PETER: *Rise and walk.*

The lame man rises slowly, at first unsteady and tottering, but little by little he gains courage. Involuntarily and from force of habit he uses his crutches, but after having walked a few steps he finds that he is able to stand and also to walk. He lifts up his crutches to show that he can walk without them. The other sick people look at him in astonishment as he shouts

LAME MAN: *I am healed.*
VOICES: *How? How have you been healed?*
LAME MAN: *He just said—rise and walk.*
VOICES: *Who? Who said that?*
LAME MAN: *Him.*

He turns around and points to the place where Jesus was standing a minute before, but Jesus is no longer there. With John and Peter, he has gone away unobserved.

VOICES: *Who?*

The lame man is confused.

LAME MAN: *That man . . .*
VOICES: *What man?*

Perplexed, the lame man does not answer at once. Then he says

He is gone.

And beaming with joy he adds

And I am leaving too. I must find out who he is. I have not even thanked him.

While he has been talking, the lame man has rolled together his cushioned seat, and now he hurries away, greeting his fellow-sufferers by waving his crutches over his head.

[WIPE TO THE NEXT SCENE.]

A road just outside the Bethesda pool, not far from the sheep-gate. The man who has been cured walks along the road. He meets two Pharisees on their way to the Temple. They stop him when they see him carrying not only a pair of crutches, but also a cushioned seat. Then, speaking in a friendly fashion and not in any way commanding, they give him instructions in order to prevent him from profaning the Sabbath.

FIRST PHARISEE: *It is the Sabbath day.*

The lame man looks at them, not understanding at first the purpose of their admonition. Certainly it was the Sabbath, but he had only thought of the man who had healed him and who had bidden him take up his bed and walk.

As the other Pharisee realizes that the man is puzzled by the admonition, he adds

SECOND PHARISEE: *It is not lawful for you to carry your bed on the Sabbath day.*

Now the man understands and answers

He that made me whole, the same said unto me: take up your bed and walk.

The same thought occurs to the Pharisees, and they look at each other and then continue questioning the man.

SECOND PHARISEE: *Who healed you?*
LAME MAN: *I do not know who it was.*
FIRST PHARISEE: *But you know how you were made whole?*
LAME MAN: *He just said—rise and walk.*
FIRST PHARISEE: *Hurry home.*

The man makes off as quickly as possible and the Pharisees walk toward the sheep-gate.

[WIPE TO THE NEXT SCENE.]

Jesus, Peter and John have gone to the Temple and have entered the court of the Gentiles.

This court was enclosed within porches, the most remarkable of which was the porch of Solomon. In these porches the learned scholars and lawyers brought their disciples together and taught them. The teacher sat on a bench or a block of stone while the disciples sat on the floor around him. The disciples would listen and question and the scholars would answer. The purpose of the discussion was always to get to the very heart of the theological problem being debated. Now and then a scholar could be seen closeted with a single, intimate disciple, in a whispering voice teaching him the most secret truths concerning the nature of God.

Jesus, John, and Peter are sitting in one of the porches surrounded by a crowd of listeners.

The man who has been healed and is searching for Jesus passes through the crowd. Jesus calls him and he goes to Jesus, happy to have the opportunity of thanking his benefactor, but Jesus cuts him short, saying in a friendly fashion

> *Behold, you are made whole: sin no more, lest a worse thing come to you.*

The man stammers out a promise and words of thanks and withdraws. He meets the two Pharisees who reproached him for carrying his bed. Pointing to Jesus, he says

> *That is the man who made me whole.*

He accompanies them to Jesus, who realizes the purpose of their visit and is ready for the controversy.

FIRST PHARISEE:　*Why have you done these things on the Sabbath day?*

SECOND PHARISEE:　*Know you not what is written in the Law?*

JESUS:　*Yes, I know that you circumcise a man on the Sabbath, and now you are angry at me, because I have made a man every whit whole on the Sabbath.*

SECOND PHARISEE:　*But it is not lawful.*

JESUS:　*My Father works over, and so must I.*

FIRST PHARISEE:　*You make yourself equal with God?*

The two Pharisees look at each other, shake their heads, and prepare to leave. But Jesus has another word for them

Search the Scriptures—they testify of me.

[WIPE TO THE NEXT SCENE.]

Word has spread through Jerusalem that Jesus has healed a lame man. Therefore, another meeting is held in the palace of the high priest.

Chief priests, lawyers, and Pharisees are present, with them Gamaliel, Nicodemus, and Joseph of Arimathaea. A scribe is reporting what has happened at the Bethesda pool.

SCRIBE: *He just said—rise and walk. And the man rose and walked. Jesus had made him whole.*
FIRST LAWYER: *Profaning the Sabbath.*
FIRST CHIEF PRIEST: *And thus acting against the will of God.*
NICODEMUS (with a knowing smile): *What is the will of God?*
SECOND LAWYER: *To keep the Law.*
JOSEPH: *Is not the will of God to be good—to do good?*
SECOND CHIEF PRIEST: *Not if the Law is broken.*
JOSEPH: *Today Jesus did good. He made a man whole.*
NICODEMUS: *A man who has been lame for thirty-eight years.*
GAMALIEL: *Isn't that a proof that God wished that man to be healed?*
NICODEMUS: *Even on the Sabbath?*
FIRST LAWYER: *No, on the contrary, by breaking the Law Jesus proved that his power to heal is not of God.*

Caiaphas has listened to this dispute with indifference. This theological sophistry is nothing to him and he therefore welcomes the arrival of the two Pharisees who have been talking to Jesus. Knocking on the table, he silences the discussion and turns to the newcomers and asks them

CAIAPHAS: *Any news?*
FIRST PHARISEE: *Yes, Jesus of Nazareth . . .*

CAIAPHAS (interrupting): *We know. He has healed a lame man.*
SECOND PHARISEE: *He has done worse than that.*
CAIAPHAS: *What?*
FIRST PHARISEE: *He said that he is the Son of God.*
GAMALIEL: *We are all God's children.*
SECOND PHARISEE: *He made himself equal with God.*
FIRST LAWYER: *That is: he made himself a God.*
SECOND LAWYER: *A God? He looks like any one of us.*
NICODEMUS: *The stars are not afraid of being mistaken for fire-flies.*

Caiaphas is bored; he also fears another extenuated theological debate.

CAIAPHAS: *He is of course a blasphemer, but what can we do?*
FIRST CHIEF PRIEST: *Let him speak, and his own words will eventually nullify his teaching.*

After thinking over the matter, Caiaphas agrees with him. Gamaliel, Nicodemus and Joseph of Arimathaea shake hands. They are well pleased with the outcome of the meeting.

[WIPE TO THE NEXT SCENE.]

At one of the southern gates, leading from the Temple area to the Ophel and the priests' quarters. Jesus, John, and Peter pass a blind beggar, a young man. Written in Hebrew on a board over his head are the words "I was born blind."

It was a common belief then that sins committed by parents caused their children to suffer, frequently bringing on mental or bodily affliction. Peter asks Jesus

Who did sin, this man, or his parents, that he is born blind?

Jesus answers

Neither has this man sinned, nor his parents: but that the words of God should be made manifest in him.

Then he turns to John

Go and call him.

John approaches the blind man and speaks to him.

JOHN: *Be of good comfort and rise. The Master calls you.*
BEGGAR: *Who?*
JOHN: *Jesus of Nazareth.*
BEGGAR: *The Prophet?*
JOHN: *Yes.*

The blind beggar, filled with hope, puts on his garment, rises quickly, and goes to Jesus. Jesus's actions make the disciples believe that he is going to perform a miracle.

As soon as the beggar reaches Jesus, he cries out.

BEGGAR: *Have mercy on me.*
JESUS: *What will you that I should do unto you?*
BEGGAR (without hesitation): *Something, so that I may receive my sight.*
JESUS: *Believe you, that I am able to do this?*
BEGGAR: *Yes.*

Jesus turns away. Then crouching down he spits on the ground and makes some mud out of the spittle and dust. (This scene of Jesus making the mud is taken from such an angle that we do not see him spitting.) When Jesus has finished his preparations, he rises and anoints the eyes of the blind man with the clay, saying

According to your faith, be it unto you.

And after finishing anointing the man's eyes he adds

Go now and wash in the pool of Siloam.

Some of the people who have been watching take the blind man by the hand and lead him to the pool of Siloam.

[It was generally believed that not only spit but also mud had healing power.]

[WIPE TO THE NEXT SCENE.]

The pool of Siloam [situated southwest of the hill of Ophel]. Here we see the blind man, whose name is Samuel, kneeling, surrounded by friends and curious people. Making a cup with his hands, he dips up the water and washes the mud from his eyes. Then he lifts his head, looking at the sky and at the people around him, who ask him questions.

VOICES: *Do you see anything? What do you see?*
SAMUEL: *I see men as trees, walking.*

Again he dips up water in his hands and washes his eyes.

VOICES: *What do you see now?*
SAMUEL: *Now I see everything clearly.*

Some of the people who are thronging around him say

Is not this he that sat and begged?
Yes.
It is not he, but he is like him.

Samuel puts an end to the discussion.

SAMUEL: *I am he.*
VOICES: *And you are not blind anymore?*
SAMUEL: *No.*

One incredulous passerby holds up his hands before the face of Samuel.

PASSERBY: *How many fingers do you see?*
SAMUEL: *Seven.*
PASSERBY: *And now?*
SAMUEL: *Three.*

PASSERBY: *And now?*

SAMUEL: *One.*

The man looks around triumphantly.

Two Pharisees, their curiosity aroused, approach. They question some of the crowd.

FIRST PHARISEE: *What is the matter?*

SECOND PHARISEE: *Is not he the beggar born blind?*

A VOICE: *Yes, and now he has received his sight again.*

A VOICE: *Jesus of Nazareth made him whole.*

FIRST PHARISEE: *When?*

A VOICE: *Just now, a little while ago.*

FIRST PHARISEE: *On the Sabbath day?*

The two Pharisees approach Samuel.

FIRST PHARISEE: *Follow us to the synagogue and tell the elders the manner in which you have been healed.*

SAMUEL (protesting): *No, first of all I want to see my father and mother. I have never seen them.*

FIRST PHARISEE: *We will send for your father and mother.*

SECOND PHARISEE: *Come, you will meet them in the synagogue.*

A young man in the crowd, a friend of Samuel, offers to help out.

I'll go and tell them.

And Samuel leaves the pool with the two Pharisees.

[WIPE TO THE NEXT SCENE.]

A synagogue in Jerusalem. We see some of the elders, to whom the two Pharisees have already given a report of the healing of the blind man. The group is now on their way to a special room used for examining offenders of the religious laws where Samuel waits. The hearing begins immediately.

ELDER: *How were your eyes opened?*

SAMUEL: *A man that is called Jesus made clay and put it upon my eyes and said to me: Go to the pool of Siloam and wash. And I went and washed, and I do see.*

SECOND ELDER: *Where is that man called Jesus?*

SAMUEL: *I know not.*

The Pharisees dispute among themselves.

THIRD PHARISEE: *This man is not of God because he does not keep the Sabbath day.*

FOURTH PHARISEE: *How can a man that is a sinner do such miracles?*

FIFTH PHARISEE: *Certainly he has a devil.*

FOURTH PHARISEE: *Can a devil open the eyes of the blind?*

One of the elders calls the highly excited Pharisees to order, so that the hearing can continue. The First Elder addresses Samuel.

FIRST ELDER: *What say you of him that opened your eyes?*

SAMUEL: *That he is a Prophet.*

The elders talk together in low tones. Some of them doubt whether the young man had been blind; he might have only been dim-sighted. Two elders decide to examine the parents.

SECOND ELDER: *The parents—have they come?*

OVERSEER: *Yes, they are out here.*

SECOND ELDER: *Let them in.*

Samuel turns toward the door, waiting impatiently for his father and mother, whom he has never seen. As they approach, their faces expressing their great joy, Samuel is too moved to speak. Then he says

Are you my father?

The father is a dyer by profession, as can be seen by his color threaded earrings. To his son's question he only nods and smiles.

SAMUEL: *Speak to me and then I will know.*

The father answers by quoting Isaiah 9:6.

FATHER: *For unto us a child is born, unto us a son is given.*
SAMUEL: *Yes, you are my father.* (Turning to the woman) *And are you my mother?*
MOTHER: *Yes, my son.*

He kisses his father and mother and the elders then start cross-examining them.

FIRST ELDER: *Is this your son?*
PARENTS: *Yes, that is our son.*
FIRST ELDER: *Who was born blind?*
PARENTS: *Yes.*
SECOND ELDER (emphatically): Born *blind?*
PARENTS: *Yes, born* blind.
FIRST ELDER: *How then does he now see?*
PARENTS: *We know not.*
SECOND ELDER: *By what means does he now see?*
PARENTS: *We know not.*
FIRST ELDER: *Who has opened his eyes?*
PARENTS: *We know not.*

The parents evade these questions, for they know that Jesus is considered by the religious leaders as a teacher who is preaching against the Law and the tradition. Fearing to be excommunicated, they try not to say anything that might be misconstrued.

The elders, noticing that the parents choose their words with care, try to trap them by rude treatment.

FIRST ELDER: *You know not . . . you know not . . . you know nothing at all. Are you fooling me?*

FATHER: *No, we know nothing. Ask our son himself; he is of age.*

MOTHER: *Yes, he shall speak for himself.*

The parents are dismissed and the elders examine the son once more.

FIRST ELDER: *What did he to you? How opened he your eyes?*

SAMUEL: *I have told you already, and you did not hear; wherefore would you hear it again? Will you also be his disciples?*

Now the elders are angry and they revile the young man.

SECOND ELDER: *You are his disciple, but we are Moses's disciples. We know that God spoke to Moses. As for this fellow, we know not where he comes from.*

Samuel, now excited and courageous, answers with some arrogance

Why, here is a marvelous thing, that you know not where he comes from and yet he has opened my eyes. Since the world began was it not heard that any man opened the eyes of one that was born blind. If this man were not of God, he could do nothing.

The elders are enraged to be spoken to in this fashion. They shout

SECOND ELDER: *You who are born in sin—do you teach us?*

FIRST ELDER: *Leave the synagogue at once. You are cast out of the congregation.*

Samuel leaves the synagogue but his parents lack the courage to follow him.

[WIPE TO THE NEXT SCENE.]

The court of the Gentiles. On one of the porches Jesus, John, and Peter sit on a heap of stone blocks.

Samuel hurries to Jesus's side.

SAMUEL: *Master . . .*
PETER: *What is the matter?*
SAMUEL: *I have been cast out of the congregation.*

Jesus motions to John and Peter to leave them. Jesus looks earnestly at the young man and asks

Do you believe in the Son of God?

Samuel looks at Jesus in surprise, asking

Who is he that I might believe in him?

Jesus leans forward and says

You have both seen him and it is he that talks to you.

Samuel is quiet a moment and then says

I believe.

With his face reflecting joy and confidence he listens to Jesus. Soft dissolve.

[SCENE SHIFT]

NARRATOR: *One of the counsellors of the high priest, a Pharisee, named Nicodemus, who in secret believed in Jesus, went at night to Bethany to question him concerning the Kingdom of God.*

A trucking-shot, a close close-up of a lantern, carried by a servant in the night. The road leading from Jerusalem to Bethany. We see Nicodemus on his way to Jesus. The servant, carrying the

lantern, leads the way. It is a windy night. The stormy weather
bends the trees, sweeps the road and catches the cloak of Nicodemus
and blows it about him.

Nicodemus was one of the wealthiest citizens of Jerusalem.
Not only a member of the political privy council of the high priest,
he was also a distinguished member of the powerful Sanhedrin. He
was a righteous, God-fearing and cultivated man. He belonged to
the Pharisaic party. His passion for the truth has driven him out in
the night, for he wants first-hand knowledge of the new doctrine.

[WIPE TO THE NEXT SCENE.]

The house of Lazarus in Bethany: the entrance seen from the
inside. A knock at the door. Lazarus appears, an oil lamp in his
hand.

Who is there?

Nicodemus answers

A friend. Nicodemus.

Lazarus opens the door and they greet one another.

NICODEMUS: *I have come to see Jesus.*
LAZARUS: *He is in here.*

Lazarus leads Nicodemus to Jesus.

[WIPE TO THE NEXT SCENE.]

A room in the house of Lazarus. Jesus is seated, talking with
John. He rises as Nicodemus and Lazarus enter. Jesus sits down
again, inviting Nicodemus with a gesture to sit beside him. Lazarus
and John stay with them. Nicodemus puts to Jesus the question in
his mind.

NICODEMUS: *We know that you are a teacher, come from God.*
JESUS: *We?*

NICODEMUS: *Yes, we are many who realize that no man can do
that works that you do except God be with him.* (Pause)
*And we would like to know how we can enter the Kingdom
of God that you speak of.*

Jesus looks searchingly at Nicodemus, then he answers

*Except a man be born again, he cannot see the Kingdom of
God.*

Though Nicodemus is familiar with the figurative language of
that day, the spiritual meaning of the words of Jesus escape him.
Therefore he asks

*How can a man be born again when he is old? Can he enter
the second time into his mother's womb, and be born again?*

Jesus appreciates Nicodemus's eager spirit and tries to give him a
higher, spiritual understanding.

JESUS: *Marvel not that I said unto you, that you must be born
again. But that which is born of the flesh is flesh, and that
which is born of the Spirit is Spirit. Therefore I said unto you:
except a man be born again he cannot enter into the Kingdom
of God.*

All this sounds strange to Nicodemus. It is so entirely different
from the Jewish conception of the Kingdom of God. But with his
ardent thirst for knowledge he sincerely desires to understand.

NICODEMUS: *Born again?*
JESUS: *Yes, born from above.*
NICODEMUS: *Born from above?*
JESUS: *Yes, of the Spirit.*

It is increasingly difficult for Nicodemus to follow the words
and thoughts of Jesus. He repeats pensively

The Spirit?

John and Lazarus have listened with interest to the conversation and now try to help Nicodemus by quoting from the first lines of Genesis

JOHN: *In the beginning God created the heaven and the earth.*
LAZARUS: *And the Spirit of God moved upon the face of the waters. And God said, Let there be light: and there was light.*

Jesus gives a simple analogy to aid Nicodemus. The wind howling outside inspires the analogy.

JESUS: *Hark—the wind blows when it lists and you hear the sound thereof but cannot tell whence it comes, and whither it goes. So it is with every one that is born of the Spirit.*
JOHN: *We cannot perceive the Spirit with our senses but it is there, within us, preparing our second birth—our spiritual birth.*

Nicodemus begins to understand the meaning of the words: born again, born from above. But another question comes to his mind—how to attain to that spiritual birth.

How can these things be? How can I become worthy to enter the Kingdom of God?

John is eager to lend a helping hand.

JOHN: *First we must be transformed from within.*
LAZARUS: *First cleanse the inside of the cup—that the outside is bound to be clean.*
JESUS: *Are you a Master of Israel, and know not these things? If I tell you earthly things, you believe not. How shall you believe if I tell you heavenly things?*
NICODEMUS: *How can I believe in things which are unseen and in Heaven? No man can ascend up to Heaven.*

JESUS: *No. No man can ascend up to Heaven but he that came down from Heaven, even the* Son of Man.

For a moment there is silence. Then Nicodemus says

I know what is required if one is to be found worthy to enter the Kingdom of God, but there is one thing yet that I do not know: where is the gate?

Jesus answers earnestly

God so loved the world that he sent his only begotten Son into the world, that through him it might be saved, and whosoever believes on the Son shall not perish, but have everlasting life.

These last words impress their import on Nicodemus.

NICODEMUS: *To believe in the Son and to love the Father in his Son—is that the gate to the Kingdom of God?*
JESUS: *Yes.*
NICODEMUS (rising): *From now on I will seek with all my strength to find the gate.*
JESUS (also rising): *Seek, and you shall find, and when you find, you shall marvel, and when you marvel, you shall enter the Kingdom and when you have entered the Kingdom, I will give you rest.*

Nicodemus takes leave of Jesus and John, and Lazarus sees him to the door. On his way out he turns to Jesus.

I warn you not to go to Jerusalem.

With an air of resignation, Jesus answers

Nevertheless I must walk today, and tomorrow, and the day following: and the third day I shall be perfected.

Then Nicodemus, deeply moved, leaves.

[Jesus never publicly proclaimed himself the Messiah but undoubtedly he had slowly reached the conclusion that he was the expected Messiah, called by God to establish his Kingdom on earth. But Jesus felt that his mission in the world was an infinitely higher one than just to fulfill the national and political hopes which by tradition were tied to the Messianic dream of the people. Jesus wanted a revolution but one of a spiritual nature. And he gave the Messianic role a new significance by identifying it with "the righteous servant" (Isaiah 53:11) of whom Isaiah had spoken and who through his sufferings would redeem Israel.

When therefore he decided the next day to enter the Holy City, he wished by a symbolic act to emphasize that he came as a Messiah in a spiritual sense. But the multitude thought of the Messiah only in political and military terms.]

The scene dissolves softly into a close-up of an ass's white foal suckling its mother.

NARRATOR: *The next day Jesus went up to Jerusalem, riding upon an ass—thus fulfilling the words of the Prophet: Thy king cometh unto thee, lowly, and riding upon an ass.*

Jesus chose deliberately to make his entry into Jerusalem riding an ass. From olden times the ass had been used by distinguished people: kings, judges and prophets. When a king came riding upon an ass it was a sign that he came with peace. It was therefore to be expected that the Anointed of God would enter the Holy City riding upon an ass.

The close-up dissolves into a long shot in which we see the white she-ass with the suckling foal. The animal is tied near a place where two ways meet. Some people are standing about.

Two disciples, James and Thaddaeus, approach the ass and her foal and loose them. The owner of the asses, seeing what the disciples are doing, hurries over.

OWNER: *Why do you this, loosing them?*
JAMES: *Jesus of Nazareth has need of them.*

OWNER: *For what?*
THADDAEUS: *He is entering Jerusalem today.*
JAMES: *Solemnly.*
OWNER: *Take them.*
JAMES: *They will be returned to you tonight.*

They leave.

The procession, headed by Jesus and surrounded by sheep and their shepherd. The joy of the Galileans has stirred the hearts of the pilgrims in the procession as well as the disciples, and the enthusiasm is spreading quickly. Words of praise are on every tongue, words speaking of Jesus as the Messiah the people are waiting for. To the disciples the procession has become a triumphal march, surpassing their most sanguine expectations. Giving vent to their enthusiasm, long and impatiently held in restraint, they join in the shouting.

VOICES: *Hosanna to the Son of David.*
Blessed the Kingdom of our Father David.
Hosanna in the Highest.
Blessed be he, that comes in the name of the Lord.
Blessed the Kingdom, that comes.
Peace in Heaven, and Glory in the Highest.

"He that comes in the name of the Lord" is the Messiah. All Jews were familiar with that expression.

[WIPE TO THE NEXT SCENE.]

Three old men are standing by the roadside. (They could be the "three wise men from the East.") As Jesus approaches them they get down on their knees, bowing their heads. The shouting from the previous scene is heard in this and the following one.

[WIPE TO THE NEXT SCENE.]

The procession comes to a fork in the road. The Pharisees approach Jesus. The public proclamation of Jesus as the Messiah seems to them to be a very dangerous thing to do, considering the possible political consequences for the nation and also the consequences for Jesus himself. In their opinion, Jesus is acting inexcusably by not forbidding his followers to address him in this way. For this reason they feel justified in appealing to him.

FIRST PHARISEE: *Master, rebuke them!*

Up to now Jesus has been silent. It is as if the whole procession were a dream to him, and he has only allowed himself to be praised. But is not that his own business? Therefore he turns to the Pharisees.

I tell you, if these should hold their peace, the stones would immediately cry out.

Realizing that Jesus does not object to the homage they pay him, the disciples and the pilgrims again shout their praise and continue waving their branches.

The scene dissolves softly into close-up of the hand of a young girl waving some branches. This dissolves into the interior of the subterranean stone quarries of King Solomon.

NARRATOR: *At the same hour revolutionaries from all over Palestine met secretly in the quarries of King Solomon. Tiding had spread that Jesus was about to make his entry into Jerusalem as the Messiah. The revolutionaries, who were constantly seeking a way to get rid of the Romans, were not disposed to let this opportunity slip out of their hands.*

A hundred or more young men, fanatic revolutionaries, have gathered to learn the news that has just come from Bethany. The men are standing and sitting upon the square stone blocks. At one place some stone blocks are piled up forming a pulpit.

A man is just leaving the pulpit, and another man, the leader, mounts it.

You ask for a plan. We have a plan. And if we succeed Jerusalem will be in our hands before sunset.

Two young Galilean pilgrims, who have been sent by the revolutionaries to find out the size of Jesus's procession and how it is being received by the population, hurriedly enter the quarries.

The leader indicates that they are to make their report. Anxious to tell their news and encourage the other members of the "underground movement," they speak at once.

BOTH GALILEANS: *He is entering the city as the Messiah.*
LEADER: *Definitely?*
FIRST GALILEAN: *Definitely.*
SECOND GALILEAN: *And the crowd is enthusiastic.*
FIRST GALILEAN: *Let us all go to meet him.*
SECOND GALILEAN: *And now. We have no time to lose.*
LEADER: *While the iron is hot let us strike.*

Most of the men have risen and gathered around the leader.

LEADER: *Steel your hearts. Let us die, if need be, but do not let us behave as cowards.*
FIRST GALILEAN: *Come. Let us go and stir up the town.*

While the men are leaving in small groups the scene dissolves softly into a shot of a girl's hand waving branches. The shouting of voices rejoicing and praising God is louder.

This scene dissolves softly into one of the procession headed by Jesus. It is just crossing the bridge over the dry brook of Kidron.

The enthusiasm among his followers is greater than ever. All of them believe that Jesus is the promised Son of David. A hope has been kindled that the day of deliverance is at hand. Surely Jesus is the Messiah that should come and institute the Kingdom of God, as foretold by the Prophets.

[WIPE TO THE NEXT SCENE.]

The "water gate" of Jerusalem, south of the Temple area and opening upon a road leading to Bethany, seen from the outside. A crowd of people meet Jesus and bid him welcome. Most of them are pilgrims. The revolutionaries, according to their plan, mingle with the crowd.

[It was common custom for people from Jerusalem to go out and welcome caravans from faraway places and personalities of some importance. The welcome given to Jesus is larger and more enthusiastic than those ordinarily given to pilgrims. This was partly due to the efforts of the revolutionaries.]

[WIPE TO THE NEXT SCENE.]

Close-up of the head of the young donkey trotting patiently after its mother.

[WIPE TO THE NEXT SCENE.]

The top of a palm tree. One of the revolutionaries (whose face we recognize) has climbed up the tree and is busily cutting down branches and handing them to the leader who distributes them to the other revolutionaries. The leader gives them instruction.

And remember: when I make a sign we start chanting the "Hallel."

[The waving of palm branches was used particularly in bidding welcome to kings and persons of distinction.]

[WIPE TO THE NEXT SCENE.]

In front of a house facing the road an old white-bearded patriarch is mounting a kneeling camel. It rises just as the procession from Bethany passes by, with Jesus "meek and sitting upon an ass." The patriarch joins the procession.

[WIPE TO THE NEXT SCENE.]

A down angle shot of the road ahead of the procession. We see the revolutionaries and the pilgrims who have come out from the city, spreading the palm branches on the road like a green mat.

Finally the two bodies of people meet and those from the city greet Jesus with shouts. But now things have taken a new turn. Jesus is no longer praised as the Son of David but openly as the King of the Jews.

VOICES: *Blessed is the King of the Jews.*
Blessed be the King that comes in the name of the Lord.

This is the work of the revolutionaries.

[WIPE TO THE NEXT SCENE.]

A shot from the side across the ass to where we see the leader of the revolutionaries making a sign to his followers to start chanting the "Hallel."

These psalms were chanted on certain solemn religious festivals but they were also chanted as a welcome to the caravans of pilgrims arriving at Jerusalem. The chanting of the "Hallel" together with the shouting of the Hosannas and the waving of palm branches was of utmost significance. The psalms are an antiphony chanted alternately by different voices.

The two bodies of people from Jerusalem and from Bethany, now united, fill the air with their song.

[WIPE TO THE NEXT SCENE.]

A close-up of Jesus. Tears have come to his eyes. Is he weeping at the sight of Jerusalem, the doomed city? Or is he moved to tears by the song and the shouts of joy that greet him? Or does he realize that the danger he is facing in entering Jerusalem is just at hand and that the shouts of the pilgrims, acclaiming him as the King of the Jews, are increasing the danger?

[WIPE TO THE NEXT SCENE.]

The procession headed by Jesus is seen from the water gate, which frames it as it enters.

[WIPE TO THE NEXT SCENE.]

Inside the gate men, women and children stand on the housetops to witness the unusual sight. The news has spread rapidly and the people strain their necks to catch a glimpse of the man who is said to be the King of the Jews.

The water gate seen from inside the city. As the procession passes through the gate, Jesus is greeted cordially and sympathetically by the crowd of people brought into the streets by the shouting. The whole city is moved. Great events are in the making. The disciples are full of joy and expectation. Jesus himself is sitting silently in the midst of the shouting and chanting crowd. The excited multitude think that this is the beginning of a great event. But Jesus knows that it is the beginning of his passion.

[WIPE TO THE NEXT SCENE.]

The procession is moving along the main street which leads to the "triple gate," the chief entrance to the Temple area from the south. The artisans—the glassblowers, matmakers, barbers and sandal-makers, working in their open shops—rise and pay homage to the Prophet, the Messiah, the King.

The chanting and the shouting slowly die down.

At the triple gate is a place where visitors and pilgrims can leave their animals. Jesus gets off the ass he has been riding. With his disciples, and surrounded by the revolutionaries who have mingled with the crowd, he enters the court of the Gentiles.

[WIPE TO THE NEXT SCENE.]

Just inside the triple gate, in the porches at the southern corner of the court of the Gentiles, the merchants selling animals for the sacrifices and the money-changers have their stalls and their shops. Here the sheep and lambs are kept, and here the pigeon-dealers have their doves in cages. Here the money-changers (with a denarius dangling in a thread fixed at the tip of the left ear) have their tables, with their cash boxes and their money scales suspended above. The whole scene is filled with the sounds of bleating and cooing mixed with the voices of chattering and quarreling men.

This market, where the sale of birds and sheep needed for the sacrifices took place, was indispensable to the Temple service. The money-changers were also necessary. The animals sold within the Temple area had been subjected to a sanitary inspection; they were "clean." The money-changers were necessary because the Temple, for religious reasons, refused to accept Greek and Roman coins because they bore the impress of the emperor. Jewish pilgrims from all parts of the world brought with them coins of every kind. Such money could not be used for payments to the Temple and, therefore, had to be exchanged.

At the sight of this sheep market within the Temple the heart of Jesus is filled with indignation.

All eyes are fixed upon him. The multitude and especially the revolutionaries wait eagerly for what he is going to say. His eyes are flaming with righteous wrath and he looks like one of the Prophets. He quotes from their writings.

> *So spoke the Prophets: Your burnt offerings are not sweet to me. I am full of the burnt offering of rams, and the fat of the fed beasts. And I delight not in the blood of bullocks, or of lambs, or of goats. And when you spread forth your hands, I will hide mine eyes from you: for your hands are full of blood. Verily, verily, with the words of the Prophets I say unto you: knowledge of God is more than burnt offering.*

And Jesus points at the people who sell animals for sacrifice, saying firmly

> *Therefore, take these things hence, and make not my Father's house a house of merchandise.*

While Jesus is preaching, the leader of the revolutionaries moves furtively from one to another of his comrades and whispers to them. Now he runs out of the crowd and mounts a bench from which he addresses the multitude

> *Jesus has spoken and his words prove that he is the King and the Messiah we are waiting for. Long enough the people have suffered and tolerated the iniquity of our treacherous rulers.*

It is time that the true patriots of this country take the law into their hands and turn these thieves and robbers out of doors. Come!

Pointing to the sheep market, he now jumps into the midst of the merchants and money-changers, followed by revolutionaries and pilgrims, with whom the Temple market was always unpopular. Some of the revolutionaries make scourges of rope ends, with which they drive out the sheep. Others overthrow the tables of the money-changers.

The multitude apparently is sympathetic to what is taking place and acclaims the actions of the rioters.

The revolutionaries shout

Away from here.
Go, go.
Be gone.
Away with you.
Get you gone.

The merchants protest but it is of no use. The revolutionaries quickly enter the stalls, followed by some of the disciples of Jesus. They snatch the whips out of the hands of the shepherds, who are taken by surprise. Beating the cattle with the scourges and whips and striking at the herds and the merchants, who make futile resistance, they finally put them to flight. The sheep merchants try to hold the animals and pull them out of the stalls. The pigeon-dealers fill the cages with the doves and carry them away on their shoulders; some of the doves escape from their cages. The money-changers also hurry away with their money-boxes and their scales.

During the cleansing of the porches in which the Temple market is installed, Jesus stands by silently. He suddenly becomes aware that he and his disciples have been affiliated with people whose ways are not his ways, whose ideals are contrary to his. He has always kept aloof from them. Some of the disciples, realizing this, gather around him.

The leader of the revolutionaries, with a look of pride and triumph because of the success of the enterprise, approaches Jesus.

We have won the battle. Now we must follow up the victory.

Jesus looks at him reproachfully and shakes his head slightly, without answering.

LEADER: *Come with us up to the Temple. We will proclaim the Kingdom of God and make you the King.*

Jesus does not answer. The disciples answer in his place.

ANDREW: *And the Romans?*
LEADER: *We'll run our daggers through them.*
JOHN: *The Kingdom of God cannot come by killing.*
JAMES: *Only in men's hearts.*

The learned Bartholomew puts an end to the conversation.

Not by force but by the Spirit of God.

Jesus makes a sign to his disciples, and together they leave. The dramatic scene has been played to the end in the course of a few minutes. No resistance has been offered by the people because of the unpopularity of the Temple market.

The Jewish Temple Guard has witnessed the tumults but does not interfere. The Captain of the Temple Guard has been called out but he does not lay hands either on Jesus or on the rioters; he fears that the populace is on the side of Jesus and his followers. It is only when the people catch sight of the Roman troops descending the staircases leading down from the Roman fortress, Antonia, to the northern corner of the Temple area that they take flight with the revolutionaries. In a few moments the court of the Gentiles is cleared of people. The Captain of the Temple Guard, who goes to meet the Captain of the Roman military police, reassures the Roman commander by telling him that some religious fanatics have exchanged some blows in their excitement and it is already over.

By the time the Roman troops arrive, Jesus and his disciples have left the court of the Gentiles through the triple gate. They find many pilgrims gathered with their children. From the enthusiastic faces of their fathers the boys realize that Jesus is the Prophet they have heard so much about. At the side of the street the other boys on their way from school have ranged themselves in a single file, rising on tiptoe in order to catch a glimpse of the Prophet. The boys go to Jesus and gather around him. A little boy chants the "Hallel" and immediately the other boys join in, praising Jesus as the Son of David.

Some priests and lawyers, witnessing this, are alarmed at the possible political consequences. One of them addresses Jesus.

LAWYER: *Do you hear what these say?*

Jesus, with a smile, answers

> *Yes, have you never read: "Out of the mouth of babes and sucklings you have perfected praise"?*

Surrounded by the chanting boys and caressing them, he continues his walk.

The children's voices are also heard during the next scene, fading out slowly.

The porches with the stalls for the sheep and the tables for the money-changers. The sheep merchants and the shepherds, driving the sheep before them, return to the stalls. The money-changers raise their tables, put the money-boxes on them and put up their scales. The scene ends with a close-up of a scale, with the two balances swinging up and down. This close-up dissolves softly.

[SCENE SHIFT]

NARRATOR: *In the mind of the high priest Jesus has changed from a religious sectarian to a political insurgent; he has be-*

*come a peril to the Jewish state. Too much was at stake to
leave unnoticed the conflict between Jesus and the merchants
and the money-changers. The privy council was therefore
summoned for the same day.*

The house of the high priest Caiaphas. The same counsellors
are present as at the two preceding meetings, among them Joseph
of Arimathaea, Nicodemus, and Gamaliel.

CAIAPHAS: *Again one of these useless revolts.*
FIRST CHIEF PRIEST: *If we let him go on in this way the Romans
will make our whole nation suffer because of him.*
JOSEPH: *Why? No harm has been done so far.*
FIRST LAWYER: *Isn't it now clear that he is stirring up the people?*
GAMALIEL: *Prophets are always impulsive.*
CAIAPHAS: *To me he is not a Prophet, but a rebel.*
SECOND CHIEF PRIEST: *A menace to the public order.*
FIRST CHIEF PRIEST: *We must get rid of him.*
SECOND LAWYER: *The sooner the better.*
CAIAPHAS: *But how?*
THIRD LAWYER: *There are grounds enough to arrest him.*
FOURTH LAWYER: *It would be for his own good, if we could take
him into custody. Then he would be hidden from the Romans.*
NICODEMUS: *Does our Law judge any man before it hears him
and knows what he is doing?*
FOURTH LAWYER (sneeringly): *Are you also of Galilee?*

Nicodemus acts as though he has not heard the sneer. Caiaphas
thinks over the matter before speaking.

CAIAPHAS: *No, it is not possible. Not during the feast.*
FIRST CHIEF PRIEST: *Why not?*
JOSEPH: *There might be an uproar among the people.*
NICODEMUS: *That's true. All the people hang upon his words.*
FIRST CHIEF PRIEST: *On the other hand it is too dangerous to
leave him at liberty.*
GAMALIEL: *Truly, he suffers because of his popularity.*

SECOND LAWYER: *Yes, his popularity in itself is dangerous.*

THIRD LAWYER: *How?*

SECOND LAWYER: *Because it* might *be used by others. Indeed, that may already have happened.*

SECOND CHIEF PRIEST: *At any rate some measures must be taken. But how?*

CAIAPHAS: *Perhaps we might be able to change the mind of the people.*

FIRST CHIEF PRIEST: *You mean, deprive him of his popularity.*

FIRST LAWYER: *Or even make him unpopular?*

CAIAPHAS: *In any case, turn the people away from him.*

THIRD LAWYER: *How can that be done?*

CAIAPHAS: *I think we can leave it to our lawyers and Pharisees to find out how to proceed in that matter.*

He rises. The meeting is closed.

The scene dissolves softly into a shot of a small loom. In close-up we see the hands of a young woman pushing the shuttle backward and forward.

The camera glides backward and sideways and we then see the whole room. We are in Bethany. Mary is weaving. Her sister Martha is sitting beside her, preparing the yarn. Jesus is with them, deep in thought. His eyes are closed. The two sisters look at him now and then but do not speak.

A faint noise like men's voices in the distance is heard. Suddenly Jesus opens his eyes and rises. He is seen leaving the room, going out to the terrace and mounting the outer staircase leading up to the roof where the disciples are gathering together. They do not hear him and are taken by surprise. Jesus asks them

What was it that you disputed among yourselves?

The disciples do not answer. Ashamed of themselves, they look at each other. Jesus answers for them

You disputed among yourselves as to who should be the greatest in the Kingdom of God.

The disciples hang their heads as Jesus continues

*So shall it be among you, that whosoever will be great among
you shall be your minister: and whosoever will be the chiefest
shall be the servant of all. For even the Son of Man came not
to be ministered unto, but to minister.*

Peter takes courage and asks

*Behold we have forsaken all, and followed you—what shall we
have therefore?*

To this Jesus answers

*There is no man, that has left house, or parents, or brethren,
or wife, or children, for the Kingdom of God's sake, who
shall not receive manifold more in this present time, and in
the world to come everlasting life.*

The disciples are satisfied with this answer. It does not occur to
them that the words "manifold more" are meant in a spiritual
sense.

Jesus returns to the room below.

[To the Jews of that age it was an accepted fact that those
who would be admitted as the chosen ones of the Kingdom of God
would be raised immediately to honor and power and greatness.
It was therefore not surprising that the disciples should openly discuss the matter of who should be accounted the greatest in the
new Kingdom.]

Jesus sits by the two sisters. Again he loses himself in thought.
Shutting his eyes, he leans against the wall. For a while we stay
with him, then the camera moves slowly sideways and forward
and at the end of the scene we only see a close-up of the loom and
the hands of Mary pushing the shuttle backward and forward.

NARRATOR: *While time was weaving Jesus's fate, he felt more
lonely than ever. He almost despaired because of the very men*

who had been living with him day after day, who had heard
him preaching and teaching and who had witnessed his mighty
works. Though they loved him and were faithful to him, they
simply could not comprehend his mission on earth.

The close-up of the loom and the hands of Mary dissolves
softly.

[SCENE SHIFT]

NARRATOR: *The lawyers who were trying to destroy the popu-*
larity of Jesus were already at work.

[WIPE TO THE NEXT SCENE.]

The Sanctuary of the Temple, near the entrance and close to
the northern wall. To one of the ground flagstones an iron ring is
fixed to make it possible to lift the stone. Under this stone is a
hollow filled with dust from the Sanctuary.

We see some women accused of adultery, their heads shaved.
Accompanied by Levites, a priest is bending over the hollow, taking
up some dust and putting it into a cup of water. The water mingled
with dust from the Temple was given to these women as a symbolic act of purification.

A young woman, weeping piteously, her head shaved, is led
through the hall. She is followed by a priest and Levites and executioners, who are taking her to the place of execution to be stoned.

NARRATOR: *This woman, who had been taken in the very act of*
adultery, according to the Law of Moses should be stoned.

On their way to the court, at the gate of Nicanor, this procession meets some lawyers and Pharisees whom we have seen at the
meeting of the privy council. They have already passed by when
they stop, acting upon a sudden impulse. After consulting together
in whispers, they command the priest, the Levites, and the executioners to follow them and to bring the young woman along.

[WIPE TO THE NEXT SCENE.]

The court of the Gentiles. Jesus stands on a stone block. A great multitude has gathered round him. All his disciples are with him. Judas stands a little to one side. During the scene Judas suddenly turns and discovers by his side a young Pharisee. They greet each other, with friendly smiles. They stand together during the whole scene. The young Pharisee is impressed by the personality and words of Jesus.

[The preaching of Jesus is quoted in extenso, but it depends on the scene-shifting as to how much of it shall be used.]

JESUS: *I am the true vine; I am the vine, you are the branches. As the branch cannot bear fruit of itself, except it abide in the vine, no more can you, except you abide in me.*

The lawyers and Pharisees whom we have seen at the gate of Nicanor arrive, and behind them the executioners with the woman. The crowd gives way to the counsellors of the high priest, who push the woman toward Jesus. Weeping loudly she hides her face in her arms.

Jesus has stopped his teaching and invites the counsellors to state their business. He himself sits down to listen.

FIRST LAWYER: *We know that you are good and that you teach the way for one to find goodness of heart. Therefore we have come to ask you a single question.* (Points at the woman) *This woman is taken in adultery, in the very act. Now Moses in the Law commanded us, that such should be stoned: but what say you?*

If Jesus objects to the execution, he defies the Law of Moses and publicly he has stated that he has not come to destroy the Law, but to fulfil it. On the other hand, if he consents to the execution he will lose some of his popularity, especially among the women, who are grateful for the way he has always defended them and placed them on equal terms with men.

When the lawyer begins accusing the woman, Jesus, a reed in his hand, bends forward and begins making designs in the sand

—crosses, one next to the other. He continues doing so even after the lawyer has ceased speaking, as though he had not heard him.

When it appears that Jesus does not intend to give an answer, the lawyers ask him a number of questions, whose purpose is to entangle him in a discussion.

SECOND LAWYER: *What is your opinion?*
FIRST LAWYER: *Shall she be stoned or not?*

No answer from Jesus.

FIRST PHARISEE: *She has led the man into sin.*
SECOND PHARISEE: *And the sins of the flesh are abominable to God.*
FIRST LAWYER: *You shall judge her.*
SECOND LAWYER: *And whatsoever you judge, it shall be valid in Law.*

There is still no answer from Jesus. The lawyers and the Pharisees look at each other and shake their heads.

The young woman has raised her head. Her eyes wander from the lawyers to the Pharisees, to the executioners, and then to Jesus, her new judge, who, apparently ignoring her, continues making designs in the sand.

Impatiently the lawyers try to press Jesus for an answer.

FIRST LAWYER: *Say, shall this woman be stoned or not?*
SECOND LAWYER: *Her fate is in your hands.*

At last Jesus replies

He that is without sin among you, let him first cast a stone at her.

And Jesus again stoops down and continues making designs in the sand.

The lawyers and the Pharisees do not know what to say.

They know that Jesus has a certain power which enables him to look into the past and the future of other people. They are not innocent of "the sins of the flesh." One by one they leave, the eldest first. Jesus is left alone. He has not offended the Law of Moses and he has not endangered his popularity. Jesus looks up and, seeing no one but the woman, pretends to be surprised.

Where are your accusers?

The woman speaks through her tears.

WOMAN: *I know not.*
JESUS: *Has no man condemned you?*
WOMAN: *No.*

The woman falls to her knees, awaiting her doom. Jesus speaks

Neither do I condemn you.

At first the young woman cannot believe that she has escaped a cruel death and is free. But from the expression on the face of Jesus she at last realizes that it is true and she bursts out weeping, not convulsively, but loudly and with a feeling of relief. Her face is bathed with tears of joy.

Then, a close-up of Judas and the young Pharisee. They speak in whispers.

YOUNG PHARISEE (in sincere admiration):   *He is great in debate, your Jesus.*
JUDAS: *It is he who has been offended. Is it not so?*
YOUNG PHARISEE (nodding pensively):   *You are right.*

He invites Judas to come with him for a private talk and they leave the place arm in arm.

The weeping of the woman is heard during this interlude. Now we see her again, still kneeling before Jesus. She is calmer and rises quietly and walks over to Jesus. She bends down and kisses the hem of his garment, saying

Thank you.

Jesus, looking at her with compassion, answers

Go, and sin no more.

The woman nods and, adjusting her kerchief so that her face is almost covered, she runs away. Jesus turns and completes the design he has been making in the sand.

The scene ends with a close-up of the sand with the crosses and the reed in the form of a cross.

[During the early days of their relationship, Judas had sincere devotion and faith in Jesus. But by nature he was a skeptic and after a time he looked upon Jesus with a critical eye. Not of spiritual bent, he interpreted the words of Jesus literally and noticed with disapproval how often Jesus appeared to contradict himself. In the discussions between Jesus and the Pharisees he was often inclined to agree with them rather than with Jesus. Doubt crept into his mind, but he allowed himself to suffer humiliations, privations, and persecutions, partly because he was strongly attracted by the personality of Jesus and partly because, being a Jew, he never ceased to hope for the Kingdom of God.

The royal entry into Jerusalem had inspired him with new hope but now it was dwindling away. Judas was a skeptic and a doubter, but in fact he was no traitor. As the action of the film progresses, the wavering of Judas between faith and doubt is shown particularly by gestures and mime, but also by exclamations of approval and disapproval, improvised on the spot.]

The close-up of the sand with the crosses and designs made by Jesus dissolves softly into the next scene.

A room in the house of Lazarus at Bethany. It is dusk of the same evening. Jesus is sitting with Lazarus and Mary. There is an atmosphere of melancholy and sadness caused by the words of Jesus.

Mary and her brother are silent but their hearts are full of love as they listen to Jesus.

JESUS: *Verily, verily, I say unto you: the hour is come.*

After a short while he continues

I have yet many things to say unto you, but you cannot hear them now.

Martha enters with a lighted candle which she puts in a candleholder. She is as solemn as her brother and sister.

At the sight of the candle the thoughts of Jesus turn in a different direction.

Yet a little while is the light with you. (Pause) *While you have light, believe in the light, that you may be the children of light.* [John 12:35–36.]

While Jesus is speaking, the camera approaches the candle. The scene ends with a close-up of its light. Soft dissolve.

[SCENE SHIFT]

NARRATOR: *But the lawyers and certain of the Pharisees and the Sadducees took counsel how they might entangle Jesus in his talk and turn the people against him. And on the following day when Jesus went to the Temple, they were ready to put their plan into action.*

Jesus teaching in the court of the Gentiles. A great multitude has gathered around him in which there are groups of Pharisees, Sadducees, and lawyers. They have come in order to destroy Jesus's influence with the people. Judas is seen with the young Pharisee he met.

Jesus, who senses the ill-feeling of his enemies, begins his preaching by denouncing the lawyers and the Pharisees.

JESUS: *The lawyers and the Pharisees sit in Moses's seat: but do not you after their works: for they say and do not. They do all their works to be seen of men: they pay tithe of mint and anise and cumin but omit the weightier matters of Law, judgment, mercy and faith.*

Voices in the crowd shout

That is unjust.
The Pharisees are good men.

During these words we observe the faces of the hearers. The Pharisees and the lawyers are offended. Judas disapproves of the open provocation and he does not make any secret of his feelings to his friend the young Pharisee. People in the crowd watch the faces of the Pharisees and the lawyers closely in order to learn the effect of the words of Jesus.

As soon as Jesus has finished speaking, the Pharisees step forward.

FIRST PHARISEE: *Tell us, by what authority do you say these things?*
SECOND PHARISEE: *Who is he that gave you this authority?*

Jesus answers with a question

I will also ask you one thing: and answer me. The baptism of John, was it from Heaven or of men?

The two Pharisees are at a loss for an answer and they turn to the group of Pharisees and lawyers standing nearby. Then they turn again to Jesus.

FIRST PHARISEE: *We cannot tell whether it was from heaven . . .*
SECOND PHARISEE: *Or of men.*

JESUS (quietly): *Neither can I tell you by what authority I do these things.*

The Pharisees, after yet another conference, approach Jesus once more and this time they ask him an important political question. But the question is disguised with flattering words.

FIFTH PHARISEE: *Master, we know that you are true and teach the way of God in truth. Tell us therefore: what think you, is it lawful to give tribute unto Caesar, or not?*
JESUS: *Why tempt you me?*
SIXTH PHARISEE: *We do not tempt you. We are in doubt ourselves.*

Jesus, appreciating the spirit of the Pharisees, asks

Show me a denarius.

[A denarius was a silver coin stamped with the portrait of the Roman emperor and a superscription giving his name. Sometimes there was also another superscription saying that this coin was the emperor's property.]
One of the Pharisees hands him a denarius. Jesus shows them the coin.

JESUS: *Whose image is this?*
FOURTH PHARISEE: *Caesar's.*

Jesus looks at the coin for a moment and then hands it back to the owner. He says

Render unto Caesar the things which are Caesar's; and unto God the things that are God's.

[If Jesus had answered in the negative, it would be an offense to the Roman authorities. If he answered (as he actually did) in the affirmative, he would lose popularity among all patriots, who were opposed to paying taxes to the Roman forces. Now they felt deceived, for their hope that Jesus was a national Messiah was now crushed. On the other hand, Jesus was as good a patriot as anyone and there could be no doubt of his nationalistic feelings and sympathy, but he was opposed to any insurrection.]

In close-up we see the Pharisees feeling triumphant over what they have accomplished, and in another there appear Judas and the young Pharisee. Judas has upon his face a look of despair, reflecting the general feeling of the people. Jesus notices Judas and the Pharisee departing together.

The crowd around Jesus has grown thin. Regardless of this, Jesus continues to denounce the lawyers and the Pharisees

> *Woe unto you, you blind guides, which say, Whosoever shall swear by the Temple, is nothing; but whosoever shall swear by the gold of the Temple, he is a debtor! You fools and blind: for whether is greater, the gold, or the Temple that sanctifies the gold?* [Matthew 23:16–17.]

We follow Judas and the young Pharisee, who walk to a bench in one of the porches and sit. The voice of Jesus has faded away. Judas is quite disheartened.

JUDAS: *What a disaster.*
YOUNG PHARISEE: *If he continues like that it will soon be all over with him.*
JUDAS: *With all of us who are his disciples.* (Pause) *I wish it were over.*
YOUNG PHARISEE: *Are you deceived?*

Judas does not answer.

YOUNG PHARISEE: *I pity you.*

Two elder Pharisees come to them and the young Pharisee rises in order to make room for them, at the same time making a sign to Judas to remain seated.

YOUNG PHARISEE: *This is Judas, one of Jesus's disciples.*

They examine Judas closely for some minutes. In truth, he does not make a very imposing impression. Then one of them asks him, in a sympathetic voice

FIRST PHARISEE: *Are you still his disciple?*

Judas looks at him in surprise.

FIRST PHARISEE: *Have you still faith in him?*
JUDAS (hesitating): *Yes.*
FIRST PHARISEE: *And no? You doubt?*
JUDAS (faintheartedly): *I hoped that he was the one who would redeem Israel.*
FIRST PHARISEE: *No, he is not the one we are waiting for.*
SECOND PHARISEE: *Why don't you break with him?*

Unsure, Judas does not answer.
The Pharisee, who is sympathetic, continues in a persuasive tone

Why do you listen to a man who has led you astray?

Judas is wavering, irresolute. Suddenly, he rises

I must go.

He leaves hurriedly. The two elder Pharisees look after him and then at each other. The First Pharisee says

The end is approaching.

Soft dissolve into the next scene.

NARRATOR: *That same evening Jesus's friends in Bethany made a supper for him.*

A close-up of a narrow alabaster flagon, used for precious perfumes, containing ointment of spikenard in a niche in one of the rooms of Lazarus's house at Bethany. Mary lifts it out of the niche.

By means of a trucking-shot we follow Mary to the door of another room where the supper is being held. She stands at the door while Jesus speaks. We approach him.

I say unto you: wheresoever two are together, God is with them. And wheresoever someone is all alone I shall be with him.

Martha is serving. Lazarus, his father and the disciples are at the table with Jesus. All are reclining at the table, according to oriental custom. Jesus, these last days, has constantly spoken of his approaching death. With her greater sensitivity and with a woman's intuition Mary is more capable perhaps than the men of knowing how near he is to his end. Perhaps she will not be at his side when death comes, and for this reason she has decided to use the spikenard symbolically as an ointment.

As soon as Jesus has finished speaking, Mary approaches with the flagon in her hand. She halts at his side, breaks the neck of the flagon, and pours the precious contents of the bottle over his head, not drop by drop, but all at once. While she is doing this, those who are present hold their breath in apprehension. With great simplicity Mary accomplishes the ceremony and with equal simplicity Jesus allows himself to be anointed. All who are present feel they have witnessed a solemn act—that is, all but one, and that is Judas. He is too profane to be impressed by this solemn ceremony. To Judas's way of thinking, Jesus contradicts himself and once more gives proof of his inconsistency. One day the teaching is: give all that you have to the poor. The next day Jesus himself allows an extravagance like this. The spikenard is worth three hundred denarii and is equivalent to a laborer's yearly wages. Judas cannot restrain his indignation and says loudly

Why was not this ointment sold for three hundred denarii and given to the poor?

Judas has taken the flagon from Mary's hand and now he points to it. Then he flings it into a corner of the room. Judas has not reproached Jesus but Mary, and she blushes deeply. She acted impulsively out of love, and now she is being humiliated.

Jesus defends her

Let her alone. Why trouble you her?

Mary turns to Jesus. A faint smile of gratitude lights her face as he continues

You have the poor always with you; but me you have not always. For in that she has poured this ointment on my body, she did it for my burial.

Mary begins to cry.

In spite of his anger Judas is moved by Mary's proof of love and by the gravity of Jesus's words. Now he is sorry that his temper got the better of him. Ashamed of himself, he approaches Jesus, who with a lovely gesture of forgiveness invites him to sit at his side.

The scene ends with a close-up of the broken flagon.

A soft dissolve into Judas walking in one of the porches of the court of the Gentiles. First we see him in close-up but this changes slowly into a medium shot and then into a long shot. He approaches a group of Pharisees, among them his young friend and the two elder Pharisees to whom his friend introduced him the day before. As soon as they catch sight of him they stop him and he joins the group. The usual greetings are exchanged.

FIRST PHARISEE: *You are still clinging to him?*
JUDAS: *Yes.*
THIRD PHARISEE (ironically):   *To the bitter end?*

Judas does not answer. He has been humiliated so often for the sake of Jesus that once more makes little difference. The Second Pharisee, who sincerely sympathizes with Judas, takes up the conversation.

SECOND PHARISEE: *You still believe him to be the Messiah?*

JUDAS: *Yes.*

FIRST PHARISEE: *But if he is the Messiah, he must prove it.*

JUDAS: *That is what I am waiting for.*

FOURTH PHARISEE: *For the proof?*

JUDAS: *Yes. A clear proof.*

YOUNG PHARISEE: *That he is the Son of God?*

JUDAS: *Yes.*

THIRD PHARISEE (ironically): *You have not been waiting long enough?*

JUDAS (after a pause): *Why is he hesitating? That is what I do not understand.*

FIRST PHARISEE: *We ask the same question.*

SECOND PHARISEE: *We too desire him to show us a sign from Heaven.*

FOURTH PHARISEE: *But he always refuses.*

THIRD PHARISEE (ironically): *I wonder if it is because he lacks the power?*

JUDAS: *Oh no. Think of all his mighty works.*

FIRST PHARISEE (fatherly): *You believe, and you believe not.*

SECOND PHARISEE: *Nor will we believe, except we see signs.*

THIRD PHARISEE (sarcastically): *But we will see no signs.*

FOURTH PHARISEE: *For he is no Prophet and no Messiah.*

Judas, who has been watching for Jesus all the time, suddenly sees him.

JUDAS: *There he is. Look how the crowd is rushing toward him.*

FIRST PHARISEE: *Let us also go.*

They all start to leave. Judas hurries away in advance of the others.

[WIPE TO THE NEXT SCENE.]

In the court of the Gentiles Jesus speaks to the crowd. Judas stands between the other disciples and the group of Pharisees, but there are many other lawyers and Pharisees mingling with the crowd. Many revolutionaries are also present. They are openly hostile to Jesus because he has refused to be their leader. But many of the pilgrims, especially those from Galilee, believe in him and give him their support. Perhaps they remember previous rebellions which the Romans crushed pitilessly.

The Pharisees begin their conspiracy by asking Jesus a question which they feel he will evade.

FIRST PHARISEE: *How long do you make us doubt? If you be the Messiah, tell us plainly.*

Jesus is even more energetic than usual. His voice has a tone of authority which demands attention.

JESUS: *I told you, and you believed not: the works that I do in my Father's name, they bear witness of me. Though you believe not me, believe my works: that you may know and believe, that the Father is in me, and I in him. I and my Father are one.*

LAWYER: *Where is your Father?*

JESUS: *You neither know me, nor my Father; if you had known me, you should have known my Father also. I am come in my Father's name and you receive me not, though the works, which the Father has given me to finish, bear witness of me, that the Father has sent me.*

In the crowd we notice the man whose lameness had been cured and the man who had been born blind. Both of them are eager to testify to the power of Jesus.

LAME MAN: *He made me whole.*

MAN BORN BLIND: *I received my sight.*

Jesus speaks to the lawyer who asked the last question.

JESUS: *You believe me not, because you are from beneath; I am from above: you are of this world; I am not of this world.*

PHARISEE: *Who are you?*

JESUS: *Even the same that I said unto you from the beginning. I am the light of the world; he that follows me shall not walk in darkness but shall have the light of life. I say unto you: If a man keep my saying, he shall never see death.*

PHARISEE: *Now we know you are mad. Abraham is dead, and the Prophets, and you say: "If a man keep my saying, he shall never taste of death."*

LAWYER: *Are you greater than our father Abraham, who is dead?*

PHARISEE: *Whom make you yourself?*

JESUS: *I do nothing of myself. I only do what I see my Father doing. But he that is of God hears God's words: you therefore hear them not, because you are not of God.*

PHARISEE: *Are we not of God?*

JESUS: *Nay, if God were your Father you would love me: but I know that you have not the love of God in you.*

PHARISEE: *Are we not right that you are mad?*

JESUS: *I am not mad; I honor my Father, and you dishonor me. But who of you can accuse me of any sin?*

FIRST REVOLUTIONARY: *Tell me whom you mingle with and I'll tell you what you do.*

SECOND REVOLUTIONARY: *You eat with publicans.*

THIRD REVOLUTIONARY: *And you go with harlots.*

Some of the Pharisees make signs to the revolutionaries to keep silent. And one of the Pharisees makes himself the spokesman of them all.

PHARISEE: *What sign showest you unto us?*

JESUS: *Destroy this Temple, and in three days I will raise it up.*

The Pharisees burst out laughing, and one of them answers

This Temple took six years to build, and will you build it up again in three days?

They shake their heads in disbelief. But many people believe in him, and they make manifest their belief.

FIRST PILGRIM: *When the Messiah comes, will he do more miracles than these which this man has done?*
SECOND PILGRIM: *He raised Lazarus from the dead.*

The people disagree, and they all speak at once.

VOICES: *Of truth this is a Prophet.*
No, he is the Messiah.
Nay, shall the Messiah come out of Galilee?
We know this man and where he comes from: but when the Messiah comes, no man knows where he comes from.

When the Pharisees and the lawyers notice the crowd's excitement, some of them fear trouble and appeal to the Captain of the Temple Guard to interfere. The camera follows them.

PHARISEE: *Why do you not seize this man?*
LAWYER: *Do you not see how he is stirring up the people?*
CAPTAIN: *That would mean fighting and killing.*

He points to himself and the Temple police who crowd around him.

CAPTAIN: *And we are the people who would be killed.*
PHARISEE: *We'll hold you responsible for that.*
CAPTAIN: *And I'll answer to it.*

The camera follows these Pharisees and lawyers back to the crowd surrounding Jesus. The discussion goes on with greater vehemence. Jesus tells a parable:

JESUS: *I am the good shepherd: the good shepherd gives his life for the sheep. Therefore does my Father love me, because I lay down my life for the sheep.*
VOICE (scornful):   *How long shall we yet suffer you?*

Jesus does not listen to the shouting but continues

*Yet a little while I am with you, and then I go unto him that
sent me. You shall seek me and shall not find me: and where
I am, thither you cannot come.*

The Pharisees put their heads together and talk among themselves.

PHARISEE: *Whither will he go, that we shall not find him?*
PHARISEE: *Will he kill himself?*

Jesus does not listen; he is absorbed in what he is saying.

*Yes, therefore does my Father love me, because I lay down
my life. No man takes it from me, but I lay it down of myself.*

Jesus has spoken with great solemnity. Now he changes his tone
and addresses the Pharisees.

JESUS: *I speak that which my Father said unto me, and you
should do the same.*
LAWYER: *Our Father is Abraham.*
JESUS: *If you were Abraham's children, you would do the works
of Abraham. But I say unto you that Abraham, whom you
call your Father, rejoiced to see my day; and he saw it, and
was glad.*
PHARISEE: *You are not fifty years old, and you have seen
Abraham?*
JESUS: *I say unto you, before Abraham was born, I am.*

Again the people disagree about what he says.

FIRST REVOLUTIONARY: *Why do you listen to him?*
SECOND REVOLUTIONARY: *He is mad.*

But some of the pilgrims defend him. One says

These are not the words of a madman.

Some revolutionaries approach a heap of stones intended for repairs of the Temple building, whilst others of them shout

FIRST REVOLUTIONARY: *Yes, stone him.*
SECOND REVOLUTIONARY: *He is profaning the Temple.*
THIRD REVOLUTIONARY: *He is blaspheming God.*

Jesus is calm, without fear. He turns to those who would stone him.

You seek to kill me, because my word has no place in you. And because I have told you the truth.

The revolutionaries come back with stones. But there is no fear in Jesus as he speaks to them

Many good works have I shown you from my Father; for which of those works do you stone me?

A fight breaks out between the revolutionaries and the pilgrims, who try to prevent them from throwing the stones. During the fight some of the revolutionaries shout

For a good work we stone you not, but for blasphemy. And because that you, being a man, make yourself God.

With power and authority Jesus says

Verily I say unto you: All these things shall come upon this generation. O Jerusalem, Jerusalem, you that kill the Prophets, and stone them which are sent unto you.

Once more some Pharisees and lawyers approach the officers of the Temple Guard.

PHARISEE: *Why do you not put an end to this?*
FIRST OFFICER: *Never spoke man like this man.*

PHARISEE (with a stern look): *Are you also misled?*
LAWYER: *You will be called to account for that.*

Throughout this, interspersed scenes have shown Roman soldiers and officers, quartered in the nearby Roman fortress Antonia, observing what is going on in the court of the Gentiles. The Roman Captain is filled with indignation. And as it does not appear that the Temple Guard will do anything to end the disorder, he sends some soldiers to disperse the mob.

In a down angle shot, we see the place where Jesus speaks to the multitude. Jesus concludes

> *You believe not, because you are not of my sheep. My sheep hear my voice, and I know them, and they follow me: And I give unto them eternal life.*

After this Jesus and his disciples leave, but the crowd remains, continuing to discuss, debate, and dispute.

Suddenly news spreads that the Roman soldiers are descending the staircases leading from Antonia to the court of the Gentiles. The crowd disperses. When the Romans arrive they find the place deserted, and they return to their quarters.

The down angle shot of the deserted place with its pavement of square stones dissolves softly into the next scene.

NARRATOR: *The riotous incidents in the court of the Gentiles were soon known about in the palace of the high priest, who, fearing reprisals on the part of the Roman Governor Pilate, summoned his privy council to meet at once.*

The palace of Caiaphas: the "tablinarium." The privy council in session.

FIRST CHIEF PRIEST: *If we let him alone Pilate will take away the few privileges we have left.*
SECOND CHIEF PRIEST: *I wonder whether he is aware of what has been happening.*

CAIAPHAS: *You can be certain he is.*

SECOND CHIEF PRIEST: *Let us go and tell Pilate what we know and we shall at least be clear ourselves and not have his wrath upon us.*

NICODEMUS: *Shall we make ourselves his spies?*

PHARISEE: *Even though we do not always agree with Jesus, he is after all one of our own people.*

JOSEPH OF ARIMATHAEA: *And a good Jew.*

GAMALIEL: *Of course we will stand up for him.*

CAIAPHAS: *As far as possible.*

A servant enters and hands a wax tablet to Caiaphas

A message from the Governor.

Caiaphas unties the tablet and reads it

I am wanted at once, as might have been expected.

He points at the First Chief Priest, Nicodemus, and Joseph of Arimathaea, saying

You, you, and you go with me. (Turning to the others) *You had better stay until we come back in case we have to take any important action.*

Then he leaves the room followed by the First Chief Priest, Nicodemus, and Joseph of Arimathaea.

[WIPE TO THE NEXT SCENE.]

Pilate's residence, the Palace of Herod. Caiaphas enters the reception room. Pilate talks with his chancellor and some secretaries who have just laid some rolls of papyrus on a table. Oil lamps of silver and bronze are alight and charcoal burns in the warming-pans.

[The conversation which takes place between Pilate, Caiaphas and his three counsellors would be held in Greek.]

To Pilate the case of Jesus is only a routine matter, one among hundreds of other similar cases, and it will soon be a forgotten episode. He holds a slip of papyrus he has just received from one of the secretaries, invites the high priest and the three counsellors to sit down. He remains standing himself, facing them while speaking.

It is because of this . . .

He studies the slip of papyrus in his hand and continues

Because of Jesus of Nazareth I have summoned you. You think probably that I know nothing of what is going on in this city, but believe me I do. The men in my service are neither blind nor deaf. This . . .

He again consults the slip of paper.

Jesus of Nazareth has for months been carefully watched. Nothing is hidden from me and I am fully informed. (Emphatically) *This man must be put away before the feast; it is high time. I can run no risks. Understood?*

After a short silence Nicodemus speaks

May I say a few words?

Pilate nods assent.

NICODEMUS: *You are mistaken if you think he is acting seditiously against the Roman authorities. He has never had anything to do with politics.*
JOSEPH: *If anything he is only a religious fanatic.*
PILATE: *Fanatics are always dangerous.*
CAIAPHAS: *I agree, but in my opinion the best thing to do is to leave him alone for a while. We have been provoked by him ourselves but we feel that in time the people will turn away*

from him and he will be forgotten. He has already lost some of his popularity.

PILATE: *His followers have hailed him as a king.*

FIRST CHIEF PRIEST: *He has never proclaimed himself as king.*

PILATE: *Maybe not. Today the people follow him. Tomorrow they force him to follow them. That is the danger. I know who the people are that follow him.*

CAIAPHAS: *You overestimate him. He is a visionary, a dreamer.*

PILATE: *Dreaming of a kingdom.*

NICODEMUS: *A kingdom of God, not a political kingdom, but a spiritual kingdom.*

PILATE (frowning): *To me a kingdom is a kingdom, and a king is a king. To me this man is a rebel.*

NICODEMUS: *You have no* proofs *of that.*

PILATE: *He is a suspect and that is enough. It is my will that he be arrested and handed over to me before the feast; that means not later than tomorrow night.*

CAIAPHAS (startled): *But that is impossible.*

FIRST CHIEF PRIEST: *To arrest him in broad daylight—that would mean fighting and killing and bloodshed.*

PILATE: *Then at night? Where does he spend his nights?*

NICODEMUS: *In Bethany.*

PILATE: *Then take him there.*

NICODEMUS: *It will not be easy to lay hands on him there either.*

PILATE: *Why?*

NICODEMUS: *He has many friends in Bethany.*

CAIAPHAS: *Why must he be handed over to you tomorrow instead of at a more convenient time?*

PILATE: *Because I have received reliable information that the pilgrims have planned a public demonstration in his favor.*

CAIAPHAS (sincerely astonished): *When?*

PILATE: *On the first day of the feast, the day after tomorrow.*

CAIAPHAS: *That is a surprise to me.*

PILATE: *Not to me. I am even aware that they have planned to set the city on fire. But I'll wait on you until tomorrow night. If you have not delivered him over to me by then, I'll take the matter in my own hands.*

CAIAPHAS: *That is against the edict of Caesar.*
PILATE: *Not in the case of a rebellion.*
NICODEMUS: *But he is* not *a rebel.*

Pilate pretends that he does not hear Nicodemus's last remark and turns to Caiaphas.

PILATE: *Tomorrow night.*
JOSEPH: *What do you intend doing to him?*
PILATE: *I'll make short work of it. To the cross with him. What else?*

A deep silence. Caiaphas thinks what is best to do and say. The others await his decision. At last he speaks.

CAIAPHAS: *We have always tried to come to an agreement with you.*
PILATE: *Where there is a will, there is a way.*
CAIAPHAS: *In this case also we will act in good faith. We will issue an order that all who know where Jesus is must inform us, and then the Temple Guard will be able to take him alone.*

Nicodemus and Joseph of Arimathaea look at each other in surprise. They are troubled.

Pilate shrugs his shoulders as if to say "It is not my business, but yours," and then he says

As you desire it.

He indicates that the audience is at an end. Caiaphas and the three counsellors leave.

[WIPE TO THE NEXT SCENE.]

[A fair appraisal of the character of Pilate is only possible if the difference between the Roman and Jewish conceptions of the state and the individual is taken into consideration. To the Romans the state was of supreme importance; to the Jews, the individual.

It will also help to understand Pilate's condemnation of Jesus if we take an analogy from events of our own time. As a Roman governor, Pilate was guilty of the same kind of corrupt conduct as were the governors Hitler sent to the European occupied countries; in brutal and reckless fashion each was quick to suppress any signs of rebellion by the people. Pilate was acting under the same kind of pressure. The philosophy of law he was ordered to follow was that it was better to let ten innocent people die than to let one guilty person escape. All historical evidence agrees in characterizing Pilate as a hard and uncompromising man whose suspicious nature always obeyed his reason rather than his feelings. He possessed the Roman conqueror's contempt for the conquered people, and he also abhorred the Jewish mentality and spirit which was as different from the Roman as the Orient from the Occident. The Jews' eternal meditation on religious problems, their fanaticism, their ritualism, their hatred of everything which was un-Jewish—all this no doubt had aroused his antipathy, as had their religious fervor. He was too much the intellectual and too unimaginative to appreciate the Jews.]

Caiaphas's house. He and his three companions return from the meeting with Pilate. Those who have been waiting for them can scarcely restrain their excited curiosity. After they have entered the room, the high priest calls a secretary and gives him an order

> *Write a commandment that all who know where Jesus is shall reveal it so that the police may take him.*

The secretary starts writing immediately.

PHARISEE (terrified): *But this means the cross.*

CAIAPHAS (sneering): *You understand nothing. Can't you see that the commandment is a warning to Jesus? The wisest thing he can do is to take the hint and flee, across the border. Then he will be safe and we and the Romans will be rid of him.*

LAWYER: *The less trouble we have with him the better.*

GAMALIEL: *And if Jesus doesn't take to flight?*

CAIAPHAS: *It will be his own fault. We have a clear conscience.*

The secretary has finished writing the commandment and places it before Caiaphas. With his signet ring Caiaphas puts the seal underneath—at the same time setting the seal upon the fate of Jesus.

The scene ends with a close-up of the seal, which dissolves softly into the next scene.

NARRATOR: *That very day the high priest's commandment was issued, and in order not to expose his friends in Bethany to any danger Jesus spent the night in an olive grove on the Mount of Olives. His disciples were with him and the name of the place was Gethsemane.*

The garden of Gethsemane, on the slope of the Mount of Olives. It is surrounded by a wall with a gate, just inside which is a square white house occupied by the overseer. During the day people work in the grove. Jesus and his disciples enter the garden. The workers have left their tools: the oil-mill, the oil-press, the wheel for drawing water for the water-pipes, mortars, large and small vessels, and baskets. The disciples seem depressed because of the turn of events. Jesus is lost in his own thoughts and has about him an air of sadness. He realizes that his hour is approaching.

They all walk in silence, looking for a place where they can lie down. Next to Jesus walk Peter, James, Andrew, and John. The path they are following is right over against the Temple which crowns the great walls of the Holy City. The mountain fortress on the other side of the valley, in its power and strength, is a strange contrast to the pastoral scene on this side of the valley. They have arrived at a glade among the trees. The leaves of the olive trees frame a lovely view of the Holy City. At the sight of all these walls and buildings of massive stone, and bearing in mind those stern words of Jesus concerning the priesthood and the Temple: "Behold, your house is left unto you desolate," John stops suddenly and turns to Jesus.

Master, see what manner of stones and what buildings are here.

Jesus looks at the Holy City and answers solemnly

JESUS: *Behold, the days will come, in the which there shall not be left one stone upon another that shall not be thrown down.*

PETER: *Master, when shall these things be?*

JESUS: *When you shall see Jerusalem compassed with armies, then know that the desolation thereof is nigh.*

PETER: *And what sign will there be when these things shall come to pass?*

JESUS: *The sun shall be darkened, and the moon shall not give her light, and the stars shall fall from Heaven. When you see these things come to pass, know you that the Kingdom of God is nigh at hand. Then you shall see the Son of Man coming in the clouds of Heaven.*

JAMES: *But before . . .*

Jesus interrupts him

But before all these things happen they shall lay hands on you and persecute you, and you shall be hated of all men for my name's sake.

With an expression of sadness he looks about the faces surrounding him

But if the world hates you, you know that it hated me before it hated you, and if they have persecuted me, they will also persecute you. They shall deliver you up to be afflicted, and shall kill you: and they who kill you will think that they do God service. But he that endures to the end, the same shall be saved. In your patience possess you your souls.

Some of the disciples sit, with heavy hearts. Jesus remains standing.

The scene dissolves softly into the next one.

NARRATOR: *And the next morning the high priest's commandment was read aloud in all synagogues. By order of Pilate, Jesus was made an outcast among his own people.*

We see the commandment, written in Hebrew and with the seal of the high priest. Two hands hold it and by means of a superimposition we see, at the same time, the document and the Ruler of the Synagogue who is reading it aloud.

The scene dissolves softly.

NARRATOR: *On this day which was the day of the unleavened bread Jesus sent two of his disciples to Jerusalem to prepare the Passover, for the Law bid that the Paschal lamb should be eaten within the walls of the Holy City, and Jesus would not flee from his destiny.*

The garden of Gethsemane. By means of a trucking-shot we see ten of the disciples lying fast asleep. The gliding movement continues until we come to Jesus, who has evidently just called Peter and John. He is giving them instruction in a low voice.

JESUS: *Go and prepare the Passover that we may eat.*
PETER: *Would you have us prepare it?*
JESUS: *When you have entered the city, a man will meet you, bearing a pitcher of water; follow him into the house he goes into.*
JOHN: *Whose is that house?*

Jesus pretends not to hear the question.

And you shall say unto the good man of the house: "The Master said: my time is at hand. I will keep the Passover at your house. Where is the guest chamber where I shall eat the Passover with my disciples?"

John cannot conceal his astonishment.

JOHN: *And he will let us keep the Passover at his house?*
JESUS: *He will show you a large, furnished upper room; there make ready.*

The two disciples silently leave the grove. Jesus returns to the other disciples, who are still sleeping.

The scene dissolves softly into the foot of a papyrus document, the order of the day. In a close-up we see the signet of Pilate, his hand carrying the signet and the wax seal.

NARRATOR: *On the same day Pilate put his seal to an order of the day forbidding the Jews from holding any meetings and assemblages except divine services in the Temple and the synagogues. No crowding in the streets or the marketplaces would be tolerated. The Roman rounds were doubled and no more than three persons were allowed to walk or talk together.*

Soft dissolve to John and Peter entering the Holy City by the water gate which opens to a path leading down to the well of Gihon. The water-carriers from the southern part of the city ordinarily used this gate.

The two disciples soon catch sight of a man carrying a jar on his shoulder and follow him.

[WIPE TO THE NEXT SCENE.]

A street, one side of which is occupied by a timberyard. The disciples follow the water-carrier at a distance.

[WIPE TO THE NEXT SCENE.]

One side of the street is a walled courtyard. Inside the gate to the right and to the left are small buildings used for storing wine. There are casks of wine in the courtyard. In the middle of the courtyard is a large building shaded by old trees.

The servant, noticing that he is being followed by two men, turns to them questioningly.

JOHN: *Where is the goodman of the house?*
SERVANT: *Come with me.*

He enters the house, followed by the disciples. Inside, the members of the family and the servants are busily preparing the Passover which is to take place that same evening. One of the servants is preparing the *charoseth*, a mixture of bitter almonds, nuts, figs, dates, and cinnamon. Another servant washes the bitter herbs. Others are working at the oven, making the unleavened bread, called *matzoth*. A servant takes the flat loaves out of the oven. All this is seen only in passing. The servant leads the two disciples to the goodman of the house, who is tapping wine for the evening. He is surprised to see them. Peter speaks.

The Master said: my time is at hand—I will keep the Passover at your house. Where is the guest chamber where I shall eat the Passover with my disciples?

The face of the goodman brightens and he answers

Tell the Master that he is welcome.

Apparently the goodman is one of the many secret disciples of Jesus. He has probably been warned by someone that Jesus and his disciples would spend the night in Jerusalem and though it is dangerous to do so he is ready to receive him. [The situation reminds us of the underground movement in the occupied countries of Europe during the last war. Those who belonged to the underground never asked in vain for shelter.]

The goodman beckons them to come with him.

I'll show you; I have a large upper room.

The two disciples follow the goodman outside and climb an outer staircase to the upper room. By using this outside staircase Jesus will be able to come and go unseen by those of the household.

They enter the room. The table is partly set with vessels, cups and dishes. The lamps are filled with oil. In a corner of the room is a handwashing basin.

While the goodman is explaining things to them, the scene dissolves softly into the document of the order of the day, full size; we have already seen Pilate's hands affixing his seal to it. The order is written in Latin, Greek, and Hebrew.

NARRATOR: *In the early hours of the morning the order of the day was issued by Pilate and, according to common practice, read aloud at all the gates of Jerusalem.*

By means of superimposition we see the document with the seal, and the herald accompanied by a drummer who marks every single section with a roll.

The scene dissolves softly into a street-crossing with a market-place in the background. We see Judas carrying a basket.

NARRATOR: *Judas also went to Jerusalem that day to buy food and provisions.*

Judas turns a corner. To the right is a group of several Jews discussing the high priest's commandment. A Roman patrol arrives. It scatters the group, directing the Jews to go home separately.

[WIPE TO THE NEXT SCENE.]

Another street. Judas stops at a store and buys different sorts of food. The camera is now placed inside the store facing the street, so that we see the interior of the store in the foreground and the street in the background.

In the street we see the two Pharisees, to whom Judas has been introduced, walking together. They stop walking, surprised to see one of Jesus's disciples. They cross the street and greet him.

FIRST PHARISEE: *What are you doing here?*
JUDAS: *Buying food for tonight.*
SECOND PHARISEE (surprised): *Are you going to keep the Passover in Jerusalem?*
JUDAS: *Yes.*
SECOND PHARISEE: *All of you?*
JUDAS: *Yes.*
FIRST PHARISEE: *Jesus too?*
JUDAS: *Yes. Why?*
FIRST PHARISEE: *I thought he had fled.*
JUDAS: *Why should he flee? He has not done anything wrong.*

SECOND PHARISEE: *Where did you spend last night?*

JUDAS (smiling): *It is a secret.*

FIRST PHARISEE: *Where are you going to eat the Passover tonight?*

JUDAS: *It is a secret too.* (Apologizing) *I do not even know my-self.*

SECOND PHARISEE: *Why all these secrets?*

FIRST PHARISEE: *If Jesus is the Messiah, whom has he to fear?*

JUDAS: *He is the Messiah.*

FIRST PHARISEE: *Today he is the Messiah. Yesterday you were in doubt.*

The two Pharisees look at each other. They sympathize with the young man and wish to help him. At the same time they consider it their duty to inform the high priest. Therefore they urge Judas to follow them. He does.

[WIPE TO THE NEXT SCENE.]

Outside the palace of the high priest. The Pharisees again urge Judas to follow them inside.

FIRST PHARISEE: *I have a few words to say to the high priest. Come and keep him company for that long* (pointing to the Second Pharisee).

Again hesitating, Judas finally gives in to their coaxing.

[WIPE TO THE NEXT SCENE.]

A private room in the high priest's palace. The two Pharisees, who seem to be at home there, enter, followed by Judas. The first Pharisee indicates to the others that they are to remain where they are.

Stay here, it will not be long.

He leaves the room. The second Pharisee and Judas sit down and continue the conversation they have been having while walking.
    [In the following conversation the Pharisee does not try to lure or outwit the young man. He is seriously troubled about Judas,

whom he considers as one who has been led astray and to whom it would be a service to lead back to the right way. And the Pharisee is as interested as Judas is in finding some proof that Jesus really is the Messiah.]

SECOND PHARISEE: *Look, you have been mistaken in him. All of you have been mistaken in him. Believe me: his downfall will come soon. The clouds are gathering. Stay out of danger for your own sake. Take courage and protect your own destiny.*
JUDAS (disheartened): *How will it come to pass?*
SECOND PHARISEE: *He will be given over to the Romans.*
JUDAS: *That means death.*
SECOND PHARISEE: *Yes.*
JUDAS: *On the cross.*
SECOND PHARISEE: *Yes, and God's will be done.*
JUDAS (with conviction): *But God will not let him die.*
SECOND PHARISEE: *Not if he is the Son of God.*

The Pharisee, struck by a new thought, continues

Perhaps that is the sign from Heaven we are waiting for.

He looks like a man to whom a heavenly secret has just been revealed. Judas stares at him.

JUDAS: *What?*
SECOND PHARISEE: *If he dies on the cross it will be proven that he was a false Prophet. But if God miraculously saves his life, it will prove that he is the Messiah, that he and God are one.*

Judas repeats with conviction

God will not let him die.

The Pharisee is carried away by his thoughts

Then he will have stood the test. If he descends from the cross, even we will believe in him. Then, in truth, the Messiah will have come to Israel.

Apparently Judas is swayed by these new ideas and he is like one hypnotized when the Pharisee turns to him and says

> *It is in your power to make possible that sign from Heaven. What a deed you will have done. Perhaps God has chosen you just for that deed.*

The first Pharisee enters.

FIRST PHARISEE: *The high priest wants to see you.*
JUDAS: *No!*

He is a little flustered and, wondering what it is all about, he follows the two Pharisees to the high priest.

[WIPE TO THE NEXT SCENE.]

The private office of the high priest. The three men enter. Caiaphas receives Judas with a cordiality which cannot fail to impress him. He then goes directly to the business at hand.

CAIAPHAS: *I have just been told that Jesus is going to eat the Passover here in Jerusalem.*
JUDAS (a little uneasy because of his talkativeness): *Yes.*
CAIAPHAS: *He must do so at his own risk.*

Judas does not answer. He is standing with downcast eyes. The high priest changes his tone and speaks to Judas more confidentially.

> *If we do not him give over to the Romans tonight they will fall upon us and the whole nation will have to suffer.*

Judas raises his head suddenly, as in self-defense.

JUDAS: *I'll not betray him.*
CAIAPHAS: *But you betray the people.*

Judas does not answer. The high priest takes Judas by the hand.

CAIAPHAS: If *Jesus is the Messiah—and you believe he is, don't you?*
JUDAS: *Yes.*
CAIAPHAS: *Then God will take care of him. But if he is a deceiver you know what the Law says: "You shall exterminate the evil from your midst."*

Judas's resistance is weakening. The high priest is able to press home his point.

CAIAPHAS: *After supper tonight you will know where Jesus is going to spend the night?*
JUDAS (fainthearted): *Yes.*
CAIAPHAS: *Then you must come here and inform me—yes?*
JUDAS (reluctantly): *Yes.*

Judas is a victim of conflicting feelings. His mind, that of a simple villager, has suddenly been forced to face problems which are too much for it. He turns to the high priest and speaks fervently and persuasively. But his words are directed to his own conscience as much as to the other man, as he seeks to reassure himself

> *Whatever I do I know it will be for his glory, for I believe in him: I believe he is the Son of God; that God is in him and that God has given his power to give eternal life to all those who believe in him . . .*

He is almost carried away by the idea that he has been chosen by God to be an instrument of his divine purpose.

The high priest listens indulgently to the youth. Then he smiles, and interrupts him.

CAIAPHAS: *You almost persuade me to become one of his disciples.*
JUDAS: *I wish that you were.*
CAIAPHAS (still smiling): *I don't think that I am fit for that.*

The high priest makes a sign to the two Pharisees and to Judas and says

Come.

They follow him.

[WIPE TO THE NEXT SCENE.]

The "tablinarium," where the counsellors are gathered waiting for the high priest's return. He enters, followed by the two Pharisees and Judas, who is humble and impressed by the presence of all the distinguished people. The high priest goes immediately to his seat and speaks to the counsellors

> *Jesus has not fled. He has not taken our hint. He will have himself to blame for what befalls him. In sheer defiance he is going to eat the Passover in Jerusalem. This has just been told me by this young man who is one of his disciples* (pointing at Judas). *He does not know where Jesus will eat the Passover as it has been kept a secret even from his disciples. But after supper tonight he* (again pointing to Judas) *will know where Jesus will spend the night, so that we can send the police to take him. I suppose you agree with me that this is how we should act.*

Gamaliel rises.

> *Before we come to any decision I would say a few words, but I beg you to command this young man to leave us while I speak.*

The high priest makes a sign to the second Pharisee to accompany Judas out of the room. As soon as they have left, Gamaliel speaks.

GAMALIEL: *My advice is: refrain from this man and let him alone, for if he be of God you will find yourselves in a fight against God. Therefore let us straightway refuse to give him over to Pilate. But our "no" must be a determined "no."*

CAIAPHAS: *No matter what the consequences will be?*

GAMALIEL: *Yes, we are in the right according to the promises of Caesar. We must insist that a signature is a signature.*

CAIAPHAS: *We must not allow ourselves to be guided by our personal feelings. The state is at stake.*

GAMALIEL: *But this is not just a matter concerning Jesus. It is a matter concerning public security as a whole.*

CAIAPHAS (impatiently): *The matter is urgent. We have pledged ourselves to deliver him up tonight, and a man's word is a man's honor.* (Pauses, apparently deeply moved) *As for Jesus, you may believe me or not, but it is with a heavy heart that I give the Jew Jesus over to the Romans. On the other hand, all things considered, is it not preferable to sacrifice one man to save the lives of many?*

LAWYER: *Including our own lives.*

The high priest pretends not to hear the interruption and continues

Isn't it expedient for us that one man should die for the people, and that our nation perish not? (Pause) *I would like to know who agrees with me and who does not.*

A hush covers the assembly. Gamaliel, Nicodemus, and Joseph of Arimathaea shake hands and then rise without saying a word and leave the "tablinarium." The high priest turns to the others and asks

And you?

The majority lift up their hands. Two or three sit silently with their eyes cast down. They do not vote.

The high priest indicates that they are to let Judas in. Judas enters. The high priest addresses him.

CAIAPHAS: *Now, the matter is settled, and I expect you tonight.*

JUDAS: *Yes.*

CAIAPHAS: *After supper.*

JUDAS: *I'll come.*

CAIAPHAS (as an admonition): *And see that you tell no man these things.*

JUDAS: *No.*

The high priest strikes a gong near his seat. The camera rapidly approaches the gong and the scene ends with a close-up of it.

For Jesus the hour has come.

[Caiaphas was doubtless in his way a patriotic Jew with good intentions, a man with experience and a knowledge of human nature, a man who would not hesitate to compromise and who was well versed in the art of diplomacy. He was also a cold, calculating politician. And with good reason. The Near East at that time was subject to perpetual shifting and changes. In the controversies between the great powers of that day lay the possibility of a free Judaea. The Jews themselves were not strong enough to shake off the yoke of their oppressors. History only too soon proved that Caiaphas was right in his efforts not to irritate the Romans, but to live on good terms with them and to hope that in due time God would give the Jews back their freedom.

When Caiaphas decided to sacrifice Jesus, was it not possible that he, in spite of his hard character, did so with a heavy heart simply because Jesus was a Jew? There is no reason not to believe that Caiaphas did what he did in order to save the people from the cruel reprisals of Pilate. How many political and religious idealists both before and after Jesus have been killed because of political or religious necessity, and always in the name of the people?]

The close-up of the gong dissolves softly into the room where Jesus and his disciples are about to celebrate the feast of the Passover. The disciples arrive in small groups. Among those already present is Judas. We see him talking to John, Andrew and James.

JUDAS: *Where do we sleep tonight? In Gethsemane?*

JOHN: *Yes. Why?*

JUDAS: *I must go and see someone after supper. I'll come a little later.*

He leaves John and joins some others.

The last group arrives, with Jesus. The master of the house welcomes him cordially. The room is lighted by two lamps which have just been brought in by servants. All that is needed for the supper has been prepared: the wine, the unleavened bread, the bitter herbs, and the roasted lamb that will be served later. The table is already laid. After inviting the guests to take their seats, the master of the house withdraws to celebrate the Passover with his own family.

The table is long and low. Two-thirds of it is covered by a cloth and around this part the guests recline on cushions, five at each side and three at the end. The table is shaped like a horseshoe, leaving one end free which is uncovered and the servants serve from here. The cushions are pushed close to the table and lend support for the left arm and elbow, thereby leaving the right hand free to eat with.

Jesus occupies the seat of the head of the house at the table. His place was not, as generally supposed, at the end of the table but at one of the sides, the second place from the unlaid end. At his right is John, and on his left, in the place of honor, is Judas.

Jesus and the disciples take their places at the table. The disciples know that a search is being made for Jesus. They also know he is thinking of his death, so it is not surprising that a mournful air hangs over the gathering. Jesus's eyes look with affection upon his friends and disciples.

They begin the supper. The servants have mixed wine and water in a large cup and one of them hands this to Jesus who, before giving thanks, says

> *I have desired to eat this Passover with you before I suffer. For I say unto you, I will not any more eat thereof, until it be fulfilled in the Kingdom of God.*

He then gives thanks for the wine

> *Blessed are you, Jehovah, our God, who has created the fruit of the vine.*

He tastes the wine and presents the cup to the disciples who each take a sip.

A servant brings Jesus a basin and a pitcher of water and pours water on the hands of Jesus. The other servant places the dish of bitter herbs and another with salt water before Jesus, who pronounces a benediction and dips the bitter herbs in the salt water, eating of them himself and offering them to each of the disciples.

The scene softly dissolves into one of the outer wall of the houses. The camera starts to move vertically downward. When it approaches the ground floor, the shot of the outer wall dissolves into one of the inside room in which the owner of the house and his family are celebrating their Passover. Here, too, all the festive lamps are lighted, and we witness the next stage of the Passover ceremony: the breaking of the unleavened bread.

The unleavened loaves of bread are placed before the master of the house. He takes one and breaks it into two parts. One half, the *afikoman*, is laid aside and covered with a cloth; it is to be eaten after supper. Then he breaks the other half, takes a piece himself, and offers it to each one of the others. No one eats, however, until they see him begin himself.

The scene inside the room dissolves softly into one of the outer wall. We are again in the street and the camera shifts to move toward a neighboring house. During the trucking, we listen to the faint sounds of joyful voices, singing psalms, chanting prayers. As soon as the camera is focused upon the outer wall of the neighboring house, it dissolves into a scene of the inside of a room where the family is gathered around a gaily decorated table which is just being removed. We witness the next stage of the Passover ceremony.

While the second cup of wine is being filled and handed to the father, the youngest in the party, a boy of seven or eight, rises and addresses the father, and asks the meaning of the feast.

Why on all other nights we do not dip even once, but on this night we dip twice? Why on all other nights do we eat meat roasted, boiled or stewed, but on this night only roasted?

The inside of the room dissolves into the outer wall of the house and the camera moves to another neighboring house. The outer wall of this dissolves into the inside of the house and we see another family, consisting mostly of elderly people. Here the father of the house is an old man and the youngest is a young man of twenty. Here too the table has been temporarily removed. The young man is asking the last of the three questions prescribed by the Law

Why on all other nights do we eat leavened or unleavened bread, while on this night we eat only unleavened bread?

The old man rises and tells of the captivity in Egypt and the deliverance

This is done because of that which the Lord did unto us when he brought us out of the land of Egypt. At that time Moses called for all the elders of Israel and said unto them: draw out and take you a lamb and kill the Passover and color the lintel and the two side-posts with the blood.

The inside of the room dissolves into the outer wall and the camera moves to the outer wall of the house next to the one in which Jesus is celebrating the Passover. The outer wall dissolves into the inside of a room which is a little smaller than the other rooms we have seen. For this reason the occupants do not recline on their cushions but sit cross-legged on them. Here, the father is just concluding the account of the captivity

When the Lord saw the blood upon the lintel and on the two side-posts he passed over the home and would not suffer the Angel of Death to come in and smite those in the home.

After this the father raises the second cup in his right hand, drinks, and then hands the cup over to the company, and each one drinks from it. All begin to sing the first part of the "Hallel"

Praise you the Lord, Praise, O, you servants of the Lord, praise the name of the Lord. Blessed be the name of the Lord, from this time forth and for evermore. From the rising of the sun unto the going down of the same the Lord's name is to be praised.

The inside of the room dissolves into the outer wall and the camera moves vertically upward to the upper room of the same house. Here again the outer wall dissolves into the inside of a room where a family of pilgrims is gathered. We hear them singing the last verses of the first part of the "Hallel"

Tremble, you earth, at the presence of the Lord, at the presence of the God of Jacob, which turned the rock into a standing water, the flint into a fountain of waters.

Now the Paschal meal begins. The table is replaced in the midst of the family. The Paschal lamb, distended by means of two branches of a pomegranate tree, is put on the table. An old maid servant takes care of the handwashing. She has a basin, a water pot, and a towel in her hand, and goes about from one guest to another.

According to custom, the head of the family now should hand each one of those present a "sop" consisting of a piece of the roasted lamb and some of the bitter herbs wrapped in a piece of unleavened bread that has been dipped into the *charoseth*. We see the house-father start preparing the first sop. Then the inside of the room dissolves into the outer wall and the camera moves slantingly along the outside staircase to the outer wall of the upper room where Jesus is with his disciples. The outer wall dissolves into the inside of the upper room. Jesus has formed a spoon out of a piece of bread and filled the "spoon" with a piece of the roasted lamb and some bitter herbs which he dips into the *charoseth*.

It is the custom to hand a sop to someone at the table as a sign of friendship. Jesus has already handed sops to all the disciples except Judas. At the moment the camera brings the scene into focus, Jesus is handing the sop he has just made to Judas, looking at him sadly and affectionately. He speaks to him in a low voice so that his words can only be heard by Judas.

What you do, do quickly.

Struck with astonishment, Judas looks at Jesus. He realizes that Jesus has seen into his heart and knows what he plans. There is no hint of disapproval in Jesus's eyes and no tone of reproach in his voice. Judas puts the sop on the table, rises, and leaves the room. The other disciples pay little attention to his departure for their thoughts are occupied by the feast.

The outer staircase. Hesitatingly, Judas descends the steps. He stops, thinks, turns around, as if he would return, but finally decides to keep his promise to the high priest.

The upper chamber. The third cup is now filled and handed to Jesus who, after having pronounced the benediction, passes it to the disciples.

Knowing of his approaching death, Jesus speaks the simple yet profound and majestic words of his farewell discourse.

JESUS: *A new commandment I give unto you. That you love one another. By this shall all men know that you are my disciples, that you love one another even as I have loved you. (Pause) And greater love has no man than this, that a man lay down his life for his friends. But if I go and prepare a place for you, I will come again and receive you unto myself; that where I am, there you may be also.*

PETER: *Whither go you?*

JESUS: *Whither I go, you cannot follow me now, but you shall follow me afterwards. But whither I go you know, and the way you know.*

THOMAS: *We know not whither you go, and how can we know the way?*

JESUS: *I am the way, the truth, and the life: no man comes unto the Father but by me.*

PHILIP: *Show us the Father, and it suffices us.*

JESUS: *Have I been such a long time with you, and yet have you not known me, Philip? He that has seen me has seen the Father; and how say you then: show us the Father?* (Pause) *I came forth from the Father, and I came into the world: again, I leave the world, and go to my Father.*

PETER: *Lo, now you speak plainly. Now we believe.*

JESUS: *Do you now believe? Behold the hour comes, yes, is now come, that you shall be scattered, every man to his own, and shall leave me alone: and yet I am not alone, because I go to the Father.*

While Jesus speaks, the disciples listen with deep interest and loving hearts.

Judas on his way to the high priest's palace. He selects the most deserted streets and lanes. But every so often we see the tents of the pilgrims, outside of which are small fires, over which the lambs have been roasted. The air is filled with the sounds of singing, prayers and joyful talk. From the housetops people watch the solitary wanderer.

The upper chamber. The fourth (and last) cup is filled and handed to Jesus. He puts the cup on the table and takes the half of the bread called the *afikoman* which had been put aside to be eaten after supper. After giving thanks, he breaks the bread and distributes the pieces among the disciples, saying

Take, eat; this is my body, which is broken for you.

The disciples, deeply impressed by the strange words and the solemnity of his tone, take the bread and eat.

Then Jesus takes the cup of wine, gives thanks and hands it to the disciples.

JESUS: *This cup is the new covenant in my blood, which is shed for you. This do, as often as you drink it, in remembrance of me.*

PETER: *Will you not drink of it yourself?*
JESUS: *I will not drink of the fruit of the vine until that day when I drink it new with you in my Father's Kingdom.*

The disciples all drink of it.

Again, Judas on his way to the high priest. A Roman patrol passes by. Except for these few Roman soldiers, no people are seen in the street. The Jews are not allowed outdoors on this evening, except to go to the place where they are staying overnight.

The upper chamber. The eleven disciples have gathered around Jesus. The last to sip of the wine puts the cup down on the table. All of them are looking at Jesus, who now lifts up his eyes to Heaven and prays aloud for his disciples

Father, the hour is now come. I have manifested your name unto the men which you gave me. I have given unto them the words which you gave me; and they received them and have known surely that I came out from you, and they have believed that you did send me. I pray for them: Holy Father, keep through your own name those whom you have given me, that they may be one, as we are. As you have sent them into the world, even so have I also sent them into the world. And for their sakes I sanctify myself, that they also might be sanctified through the truth. But I pray not for these alone, but for them also which shall believe in me through their word that they all may be one; as you, Father, are in me, and I in you, that they also may be one in us; that the world may believe that you have sent me.

Judas enters the high priest's palace.

The upper chamber. The disciples have been listening to the prayer earnestly and tears have come to the eyes of many of them. After finishing the prayer, Jesus turns to the disciples and says

Hereafter I will not talk much with you. Arise, let us go hence.

Some of the disciples put out the lamps. The door to the outer staircase opens and the owner of the house enters. Jesus embraces him cordially, kissing him on both cheeks.

Through the open door we can hear the second part of the "Hallel" being sung in a neighboring house. Jesus and his disciples spontaneously join in

The Lord is on my side; I will not fear; what can man do unto me? The Lord takes my part with them that help me: Therefore shall I see my desire upon them that hate me. It is better to trust in the Lord than to put confidence in man.

Singing the hymn, they leave the room which remains dimly lighted. The sound of the hymn slowly dies away and the room remains empty.

On festival occasions the guests cleaned their hands with large pieces of bread which after they threw on the floor. We see a dog entering the room and greedily eating the pieces of bread.

Judas sits in the anteroom adjoining the private office of Caiaphas. The sound of the gong is heard and a moment later a servant appears. He makes a sign for Judas to follow him.

Judas enters Caiaphas's office. He receives him kindly but seriously. A human life meant more to the Jews than to the Romans.

CAIAPHAS: *Where will he spend the night?*
JUDAS: *In Gethsemane.*

Out of curiosity, but also with some compassion, he inquires after Jesus.

CAIAPHAS: *How is he? In low spirits?*
JUDAS: *No. Tonight he said that he would not eat the Passover any more until it be fulfilled in the Kingdom of God. That means . . .*
CAIAPHAS: *What?*

JUDAS: *That the Kingdom of God is near at hand, and* . . .
CAIAPHAS: *And?*
JUDAS (almost triumphantly): *That Jesus is the Messiah.*

Judas speaks the last words hesitantly because a Kingdom of God with Jesus as king means the end of the priesthood and the whole priestly system.

Caiaphas shakes his head discouragingly. As a realist, he feels that all this is absurd.

A secretary enters the office holding a wax tablet and Caiaphas ends the conversation.

> *This man will take you to the Captain of the police. You will give him the information he needs. He has been informed about the matter.*

Nodding kindly, Caiaphas indicates that the audience is concluded. The secretary and Judas leave the office together.

Jesus and his disciples, having left Jerusalem through the water gate, follow the road under the East wall and are about to cross the brook Kidron, using the same bridge which Jesus had used a few days ago. The moon is full and the fields are sprinkled with hundreds of the small black goatskin tents set up by the pilgrims. From the tents voices are heard singing the "Hallel."

The disciples are tired and dispirited. They gather about Jesus. Sometimes they walk and at other times they just stand still. They halt on the bridge. They have been deeply moved by the words Jesus spoke to them after supper. They cannot forget his prophecy that in his fatal hour they would leave him. What has given him such a thought? They ask him questions, at times they speak at once.

ANDREW: *How say you, my hour is come?*
JOHN: *Your Father in Heaven will not suffer you being done any harm.*
PETER (simple-heartedly): *Nor will we* . . .

JAMES: *We will support you.*

PHILIP: *Of course. We will not leave you alone.*

With a sad smile Jesus hears their protests. Then he answers them

> *It is written, I will smite the shepherd, and the sheep shall be scattered.*

Peter is filled with ardor.

PETER: *I am ready to go with you, both into prison, and to death.*

THADDAEUS: *So am I.*

MATTHEW: *And I.*

JOHN: *I will not abandon you.*

BARTHOLOMEW: *Neither will I.*

And they all say the same. Peter is especially disturbed by Jesus's words and feels compelled to reinforce his assurances:

> *I will lay down my life for your sake.*

Jesus looks at him with love and affection and asks

> Will *you lay down your life for my sake?*

Peter feels injured because of the doubt expressed by Jesus, and, speaking vehemently, he once more affirms his intention of standing with Jesus.

> *Even if I should die with you, I will not leave you alone and I will not deny you in any wise.*

Jesus looks at him with love, but also with sadness.

> *I tell you, Peter, the cock shall not crow this day, before that you shall thrice deny that you know me.*

Jesus has said these words in a calm voice and the disciples know that when he predicts in this tone his predictions come true. Therefore, they dare not protest. Confused and perplexed, they look at each other silently and at Peter, who for once is at a loss for words. He is glad when Jesus indicates that they are to continue their walk.

Judas and the secretary arrive at the building where the Jewish police force is quartered. They enter the guard-room and the secretary addresses a police sergeant

Bring this young man to the chief captain for he has something to tell him from the high priest.

The secretary hands the wax tablet to Judas.

Take this and give it to the chief captain and he will understand.

The secretary leaves the guard-room while the police sergeant leads Judas into an adjoining room. The police sergeant speaks to the chief captain

A secretary from the high priest requested that I bring this young man here; he has something to say to you.

The police sergeant withdraws. The chief captain takes Judas by the hand and draws him aside.

CHIEF CAPTAIN: *What is it that you have to tell me?*
JUDAS: *I was told to give you this.*

He hands the wax tablet to the chief captain, who unties it and reads what it says. Then he turns again to Judas.

CHIEF CAPTAIN: *How many disciples has Jesus with him?*
JUDAS: *Eleven.*
CHIEF CAPTAIN: *Come, let us go at once.*

Judas and the chief captain go back into the guard-room together. Judas waits while the chief captain chooses a score of
policemen armed with staves. He also selects two sergeants who
are armed with swords as he is.

Jesus and his eleven disciples reach Gethsemane. The night is
quiet. Only the distant sound of the "Hallel" can be heard. Jesus
and Peter, John, and James walk ahead; a short distance behind
the other disciples. Inside the gate near the oil mill, Jesus turns
to the eight disciples and signals them to stay where they are.

Sit you here and watch, while I go and pray.

The night is cool and the eight disciples are weary. They lie
down and, muffled in their cloaks and sheltered by the oil mill, they
soon fall asleep.

Jesus and the three other disciples walk to a part of the garden
where the trees and plants grow wild. Jesus, who appears distraught,
stops at a group of trees and indicates a place to the three disciples
where they may stay.

Tarry you here, and watch.

They sit down and look with compassion at Jesus, who for a
moment stands before them with an expression of sadness. Heaving
a deep sigh he says

My soul is exceeding sorrowful unto death.

Then he withdraws. They look after him with wonder and sympathy. John and James bow their heads and wrap the upper parts
of their cloaks around them. They do this in order to pray, but
they are soon overcome with weariness. Suffering makes one weary.
Peter too has wrapped his cloak around his head but he has not
fallen asleep. He listens to the soft steps of Jesus.

Jesus has withdrawn about a stone's throw from the three
disciples. We see him kneeling down. He is deathly pale.

The three disciples. Peter is still listening, and we hear Jesus's
prayer.

Abba, Father, all things are possible unto you, take away this cup from me: Nevertheless not what I will, but what you will.

Though distant, the words can be heard distinctly. Then we hear heavy sighs. Peter now bows his head forward until it touches his knees and he too falls asleep.

[Scholars have always been puzzled how the writers of the Gospels could know the wording of the prayers of Jesus in the garden of Gethsemane, since the three disciples with him all fell asleep. The few words which Jesus, according to Mark and Matthew, used for his prayers can only be a very brief outline of them. The only explanation appears to be that the three disciples (or perhaps one or two of them) woke up at intervals, in which they may have heard the brief fragments quoted in Mark and Matthew. We must remember that Jesus had only withdrawn a stone's throw and he did not say his prayers silently or in a low voice. Rather he poured out his heart loudly lamenting and with a flood of tears. Here this problem has been worked out in such a way that we never *see* Jesus himself praying. We *see* the three disciples and with them we hear the prayers of Jesus. And when all three of them are asleep we just hear in the distance sounds of his lamenting, sighing, and groaning, mingled with a few inarticulate words, which also might have penetrated through their drowsiness to their consciousness.]

The disciples. Although they are asleep, we hear the indistinct murmurings of Jesus. Suddenly there is a loud cry of despair. The disciples awake. They realize that the cry must have come from Jesus and they are startled. John wants to hurry to his aid, but Peter holds back. For a moment they listen and tears come to their eyes. Murmuring prayers, they again wrap their cloaks around their heads and go to sleep. And again we hear Jesus praying. After a while all noise ceases.

A deserted street in Jerusalem. Judas and the chief captain of the police with the score of policemen are on their way to Gethsemane.

Gethsemane. The group of three disciples, still asleep. Jesus appears, sad and sorrowful, like a man who is in need of sympathy. And he finds his three closest friends sleeping—sleeping while he is desperately fighting the struggle of the soul. Jesus reproaches them mildly.

Sleep you?

The disciples awake and look at Jesus, whose face bears witness of his suffering.

Jesus addresses Peter in particular.

Watch you and pray, lest you enter into temptation. The spirit truly is willing, but the flesh is weak.

When Jesus warns them that it is time to watch and pray, they understand that it is: "not for my sake, but for your sake." They too are in danger. They nod assent but their eyes are heavy with weariness. James and Peter at once cover their heads, bow forward, and fall asleep. John has the willpower to keep awake, and he remains sitting upright. When Jesus leaves he is more lonesome than ever.

Now his thoughts are concerned with his disciples. The cup waiting for him is also waiting for them, unless he saves them by drinking it himself.

With John, we can hear Jesus praying in the distance, though the sounds are distinct.

O, my Father, if this cup may not pass away, except I drink it, your will be done.

Jesus, in his humanity, hopes there may be a way out, an escape from the cross. Above all, his desire is that his Father's will be done. While praying, he waits for his Father's answer.

John has fought bravely against sleep, but at last he succumbs. He bows his head without covering it. Again Jesus's prayers are heard, more passionate than before and accompanied by heavy sighs and groans. We hear sobbing and convulsive crying, and then silence.

Jesus approaches the three disciples. This time he comes like a father who, though in danger himself, must look after his children who also are in danger. He finds them asleep again. He calls them by their names but they sleep soundly. He calls them again, and they awake but "they know not what to answer him." They are startled at the look of him, weak and exhausted. He is bathed in cold sweat, like someone sick with a fever. After a short while he turns around and leaves the three disciples. And as their eyes are exceedingly heavy they are soon wrapped in sleep again.

The bridge crossing the Kidron. Judas, the chief captain and his men cross the bridge on their way to Gethsemane.

Gethsemane. We see the three sleeping disciples and we hear, not far off, the indistinct voice of Jesus lamenting and pouring out his stricken soul. A loud plaintive cry wakes Peter.

We hear these words of Jesus

O, my Father, if you be willing, then let this hour pass from me—this evil hour that is coming and drawing nearer. Nevertheless not my will but yours be done.

Jesus has suffered the crucial moment of his struggle and the battle has been won. Peter wraps his cloak around his head.

Slowly, the sighing and groaning of Jesus decreases and comes to an end. We hear nothing more. For a moment or two only the three sleeping disciples. Then Jesus returns. Now he is calm. He sits on the stump of a tree, his face serene.

Suddenly he listens intently. He rises and calls the three disciples, who are drowsy with sleep. Jesus feels that danger is approaching. The three disciples rise to their feet and they all listen.

Then Jesus catches sight of Judas, standing in a glade in the moonlight. The appearance of Judas is something Jesus has been waiting for, an answer from God. And he gives up all thought of fleeing.

Judas, having seen Jesus, approaches him quietly, kisses him cordially, with great sincerity. He has now steeled himself with the thought that he is an instrument in God's hand. Jesus has somewhat the same thought. Nothing will come to pass unless it is God's will.

[Through the whole film we will have been seeing men kiss each other when they meet, so that the kiss of Judas will appear a common practice.]

Jesus becomes aware of the danger and he and the three disciples move toward the oil mill to join the other disciples. They wake them. The moonlight illumines their troubled faces.

The sounds Jesus has heard increase. Shortly, the chief captain and men arrive at the open gate. They enter the garden and walk toward the group around Jesus.

Having accepted his fate, Jesus steps forward.

JESUS: *Whom seek you?*
CHIEF CAPTAIN: *Jesus of Nazareth.*
JESUS: *I am he.*

The policemen draw back and some of them stumble, perhaps surprised at Jesus's calm. They were prepared to meet resistance, fear, and flight, but not this. And, being Jews, some of them most likely disapprove of the work they are ordered to do, while others perhaps fear the supernatural power Jesus has often manifested.

JESUS: *Whom seek you?*
CHIEF CAPTAIN: *Jesus of Nazareth.*
JESUS: *I have told you, that I am he.*

Some of the disciples, among them Peter, John, James and Andrew, hasten to Jesus's rescue and begin quarreling with the policemen.

JAMES: *What manner of conduct is this?*
JOHN: *Why all these weapons?*
PETER: *Have you set out to capture a robber?*
ANDREW: *Are you Jews?*

The chief captain responds to their reproaches

I do my duty.

With a gesture of authority Jesus silences the four disciples and then he addresses the chief captain

I was daily in the Temple teaching, and you took me not. If you therefore seek me, take me, but let them go.

The chief captain answers

I will take no one but you.

Jesus walks to him, but the disciples rush forward to prevent the policemen from laying hands on him. Jesus, however, turns and says

My hour is come. God's will be done.

He advances and surrenders to the policemen, stretching out his hands so that they can bind them. Some of the disciples attempt a futile attack on the policemen in order to free Jesus. A brief hand-to-hand fight takes place. The chief captain loses patience and shouts

Take them, all of them.

The policemen draw their staves and the sergeants their swords. Facing this superior force the disciples flee. Some of them climb the wall, while others hide in the thicket of the garden. "And they all forsook him, and fled."

From their hiding-places they see Jesus being led away.

[SCENE SHIFT]

NARRATOR: *And they led Jesus and brought him to the high priest who had called a meeting of his privy council before handing Jesus over to the Romans.*

The high priest's palace has a gate in which there is a wicket with a portlid. This can be worked from within and is closed with a grate. A close-up of the portlid. Then, a close-up of the face of a woman, the janitress, appears. She is spying. The noise of tramping feet is heard.

By means of a trucking shot there is a slow transformation into a long shot of the deserted street and the front of the palace. We see the Jewish policemen approaching with Jesus in their midst. The janitress opens the gate for them and they enter. Only a few people have noticed the procession. The last of the policemen make them move on.

NARRATOR: *While all the other disciples fled, Peter followed Jesus afar off, to see the end.*

Peter approaches the palace, taking care not to be seen. He remains outside the gate waiting for an opportunity to get into the courtyard. He hides in the shadows so that he cannot be seen by the janitress. The whole palace seems to be in a state of alarm. Members of the privy council arrive. Messengers are let in and out, among them one with a wax-tablet in his hand, which he insists on delivering to the high priest himself. The janitress leaves the gate open for a few minutes in order to follow the messenger into the courtyard. Peter takes advantage of the opportunity to slip inside. Here a fire has been kindled in a large warming-pan around which servants and some of the policemen have gathered to warm themselves. Peter sits among them.

Peter sees Jesus in the opposite corner of the courtyard surrounded by policemen. The chief captain is at his side. Caiaphas's secretary approaches the chief captain, and speaks to him in a low voice, seeming to give him instructions. The chief captain nods and makes a sign to Jesus and two of the policemen to follow him. They enter the colonnade surrounding the courtyard and disappear into the building.

NARRATOR: *While the high priest was waiting for his privy counsellors, Jesus was led away to Annas who was father-in-law to the high priest.*

A room in the palace. Annas is sitting on a low couch reading the Scriptures. The chief captain introduces Jesus and leaves the room.

Annas is an old man, accustomed to wielding authority. He was high priest before his son-in-law, Caiaphas. He is a man of wealth and of great influence, and he is curious to meet Jesus. His conversation with Jesus, therefore, is not a trial or even an investigation.

He is silent for a long time, studying Jesus who stands before him.

ANNAS: *So you are Jesus of Nazareth?*

Jesus does not answer.

ANNAS: *We warned you strictly not to come to Jerusalem, and behold, you have filled the city with your teaching.*

There is still no answer from Jesus.

ANNAS: *What is the meaning of your doctrine?*
JESUS: *I spoke openly to the world; I ever taught in the synagogue and in the Temple, and in secret I have said nothing.*
ANNAS: *I know, but answer my question.*
JESUS: *Why ask me? Ask those who heard what I have said unto them: behold, they know what I said.*

Annas studies Jesus and then bids the chief captain to come and lead him away. He then resumes his reading.

Jesus is led into the adjoining room which is the anteroom of the tablinarium where the privy council is held.

The chief captain gestures to Jesus to sit down and also seats himself.

In the courtyard. Apparently nobody is aware of Peter's presence. All are quietly talking and warming their hands over the fire, the flames lighting up their faces. Only a maidservant who passes the fire on her way to the water cistern becomes suspicious. Perhaps she has seen Peter with Jesus in the court of the Gentiles. Looking at him carefully she says

Are you not one of his disciples?

Peter is taken by surprise and is completely at a loss for words. In his confusion he says

I know not, neither understand, what you say.

She looks at him disbelievingly and we follow her as she continues her trip toward the cistern. She keeps her eyes on him while filling her jar. Peter's anxiety is reflected in his face.

We follow the maid back to the fire. She stops and looks at him sharply. This time she does not speak to Peter but to the crowd gathered around the fire. She points at him and says

This man was with him; he is one of them.

Peter is better prepared now. Rudely and sneeringly he repudiates the accusation

I am not. I know not what you say.

But a spark of suspicion has been ignited. Peter is surrounded by people who whisper and look at him belligerently. The crowd has become hostile. A manservant shouts

Surely, you are one of them, for you are a Galilean.

Peter begins to curse and swear indignantly, and says

I know not this man of whom you speak.

And immediately, while he is still speaking, the cock crows. Peter calls to mind the words of Jesus: "and when he thought thereon he wept." He turns away in order to hide his tears. But all the people standing by look at him in surprise and wonder. Have they done him some wrong? At any rate they leave him alone. A little later he gets up and leaves the courtyard and the palace.

The tablinarium. Jesus is led to the high priest, who sits with his counsellors. Gamaliel, Nicodemus and Joseph of Arimathea are not present.

This meeting is a matter of form, necessary only in order to hand Jesus over to the Romans. Jesus faces the council. They test him in order to find out how deep-rooted is his belief that he is the Messiah.

PHARISEE: *Did you not say: "I am able to destroy the Temple of God and to rebuild it in three days"?*
CAIAPHAS: *What is it that you are accused of?* (Pause) *Answer you nothing?*

The high priest bends forward and, giving Jesus no chance to evade the crucial question, asks

Are you the Messiah? Tell us.

His voice vibrates with excitement; he is both hoping and expecting that Jesus will deny it. But Jesus does not deny it; rather he affirms it as he addresses the high priest

If I tell you, you will not believe. And if I ask you, you will not answer me.

Raising his voice and addressing the whole council he adds

But hereafter shall the Son of Man sit on the right hand of God.

Then the high priest repeats his question

Then you are the Messiah?

The question is asked to draw a denial, but Jesus refuses to avoid the danger. With guileless sincerity, he answers

You say that I am.

For a while there is deep silence. The counsellors look at each other and many shake their heads with regret. The man will not be saved.

The high priest again addresses Jesus, not in excitement but with sympathy

You should not have allowed yourself to be addressed as a king. The Romans thought you were planning a revolt.

In a low, sad voice Caiaphas speaks his final words to Jesus

It is with heavy hearts that we hand you over to the Romans.

Caiaphas makes a sign to the chief captain who is standing near the door. Handling Jesus gently, the chief captain leads him from the room. Soft dissolve.

NARRATOR: *And in the night Jesus is led away and delivered to Pilate, who takes the seat of judgment in a place called Gabbatha.*

A close-up of the judgment seat of Pilate, a carved ivory chair, placed in the Roman praetorium. This chair was called "Bima" or "Curul."

Soft dissolve into the "Gabbatha."

During his visits to Jerusalem Pilate would occupy the palace-citadel built by King Herod only thirty or forty years before. Inside its walls is the large paved or flagged square called in Aramaic "Gabbatha." On a raised platform stands the ivory chair. Beside the judgment seat there is a space for the court clerks.

One of the clerks is preparing a new sheet of papyrus; another one is nibbing his reed pen. In front of the platform the prosecutor, the counsel of defense, and the accused will take their places. A regiment of soldiers, commanded by a centurion, encircle the platform.

The trial takes place on Friday morning at six.

Jesus is brought in, accompanied by two Jewish lawyers, members of the privy council of the high priest, who are to act as his counsel of defense. Jesus is delivered over to the centurion.

[Jesus has been taken prisoner in the night and has been led in great secrecy to the high priest's palace. In equal secrecy he was taken that same night to the Romans, and the trial was set for an early hour in order to avoid arousing suspicion among the pilgrims.]

Jesus is the first case that day, so the ivory chair is still empty. Pilate arrives. As a military person of high rank and belonging to the *"Herrenvolk"* of that epoch he has a military walk and his steps on the pavement are heard all over the "Gabbatha." He gives Jesus only a cursory glance, ascends the tribune and takes his seat. Pilate turns to the prosecutor and asks him

What accusation bring you against this man?

[According to the proceeding in the Roman courts of law the prosecutor first made his accusation, the *accusatio*. Then the judge examined the prisoner, the *interrogatio*. And at last the counsel of defense spoke, the *excusatio*. After this the Judge pronounced the sentence.]

The prosecutor rises, holding the written bill of indictment, and reads

This man, Jesus of Nazareth, who has been handed over to us by the privy council of the high priest, is said to be a successor in direct descent from King David, of the first Jewish dynasty. I cannot prove the truth hereof. But I can prove that we have had the good fortune to lay hands on one more rebel from Galilee, the great breeding ground of revolts against the Roman government. He has long been disturbing the Jewish people, provoking them to rise against their Jewish rulers and thus causing disturbances of peace and order. In doing so he threatened Roman interests and undermined Roman authority. But we soon discovered that he was more than a dangerous political agitator, stirring up the people throughout all Judea. We learned that he openly proclaimed himself to be the Messiah, the leader sent by the God of the Jews to deliver them from Caesar and from Rome. At his entry into Jerusalem last Sunday he was hailed as a king. And whosoever makes himself a king is an enemy of Caesar. It is our duty not only to trace, but also, with the utmost rigor, to suppress any attempt at insurrection. Indulgence would be interpreted as weakness. In the name of Caesar and the Roman people I charge the prisoner of high treason, according to lex Juliana, *and I claim punishment of death.*

Pilate, who has been fully informed in advance about all the charges against Jesus, has listened with indifference. Now he turns to Jesus, asking him questions in Greek which are translated by one of his defense counsel.

PILATE: *What do you answer to this?*

Jesus is silent.

PILATE: *Answer you nothing?*

Jesus remains silent. But the accusation must be proven. Pilate desires an admission of guilt from Jesus himself.

PILATE: *Are you the King of the Jews?*
JESUS: *So you say.*

Pilate is not satisfied with this.

PILATE: *Are you a king then?*
JESUS: *My kingdom is not of this world; if my kingdom were*

of this world, then my followers would have fought for me,
but now is my kingdom not from hence.

PILATE: *So then you are a king?*

JESUS: *You say that I am a king. To this end was I born, and*
for this cause came I unto the world, that I should bear wit-
ness unto the truth. Everyone that is of the truth hears my
voice.

Pilate shrugs his shoulders.

PILATE: *What is truth?* (Short pause) *Whence are you? Do you*
not speak to me? Know you not that I have power to crucify
you and have power to release you?

Now Jesus answers with great dignity

You could have no power at all over me, except it were given
you from above.

After this Pilate cannot do anything but ratify the sentence of
death. However, according to custom, he says to the two Jewish
lawyers

What can you state in his defense?

One of the lawyers steps forward

We can only repeat that Jesus is a religious fanatic but not
deliberately a political revolutionary. We therefore ask the
prosecutor not to press the charge and we ask humbly for the
Governor to show the greatest possible leniency.

Even before the lawyer has come to the close of his plea, Pilate
makes a sign to the prosecutor to bring the indictment for his
signature. Before signing the document he rises in the seat and
addresses Jesus in Latin

Ibis ad crucem (Go to your cross).

And to the centurion

> *I, miles, expedi crucem* (Go, soldier, prepare the cross).

He puts his seal on the death warrant. The centurion salutes Pilate.
Dissolve into the document and the hands and signet of Pilate,
which also dissolves softly.

[SCENE SHIFT]

NARRATOR: *Jesus's doom was sealed. He was sentenced to death
by Pilate as a rioter and a rebel. He came to Jerusalem to die
for his faith and he died for his people.*

A hall in the citadel. Jesus has been placed on a raised marble
bench. His hands are still bound.

Roman soldiers surround him, laughing at him. A soldier is
just putting a purple woolen military cloak around him and
fastening it with a clasp at the shoulder.

FIRST SOLDIER: *Now, you are just like a king.*

Jesus submits silently and patiently to the jesting. Another
soldier has plaited a crown of bramble-bush thorns in mockery.
The purpose of putting a crown on Jesus's head was not to wound
him but to mock him by likening him to Roman emperors who
on ceremonious occasions wore plaited crowns of leaves.

The soldier who has just finished plaiting the crown puts it on
the head of Jesus.

SECOND SOLDIER: *You will soon be in your kingdom; in the
meantime, here is your crown.*

A third soldier puts a reed into his hands.

THIRD SOLDIER: *And here is your scepter.*

In turn the soldiers sneeringly bow before him, salute him,
and mock him, shouting

Hail, the King of the Jews.

Jesus is able to endure all the insults because he rests in God. He is heard whispering the old prayer, "Shema"

Hear, O, Israel: The Lord is our God. The Lord is one: and you shall love the Lord with all your heart and with all your soul and with all your might.

The two Jewish lawyers who have acted as his defense counsel pass by. When they see how Jesus is being treated by the soldiers they stop and rebuke them sharply.

FIRST LAWYER: *For shame!*
SECOND LAWYER: *Stop that.*
FIRST LAWYER: *Otherwise we will lodge a complaint against you.*

A soldier enters carrying on a long pole the *titulus* for Jesus's cross: a square tablet with a coating of gypsum and with the inscription in Greek, Latin, and Hebrew: *The King of the Jews.*
   The lawyers' attention is diverted from Jesus. They ask the soldier

FIRST LAWYER: *Who ordered that inscription to be written?*
FOURTH SOLDIER: *The Governor.*
SECOND LAWYER: *Himself?*
FOURTH SOLDIER: *Yes.*
FIRST LAWYER: *That must be a mistake.*
SECOND LAWYER: *Let us go and speak to him at once.*

The First Lawyer addresses the soldier

Come with us.

The two lawyers and the soldier with the titulus leave the hall. The soldiers continue mocking Jesus. When a soldier attempts to adjust the reed, the crown slips to one side. The soldier tries to straighten it but it falls off Jesus's head and rolls along the floor, bringing a roar of laughter from the soldiers. One of them shouts to Jesus

You almost lost your crown.

One of the soldiers picks up the crown and puts it back on Jesus's head.

We follow the two lawyers hastening back to the "Gabbatha." Pilate is already busily engaged with the next case. During a pause the lawyers approach the Governor and make their complaint.
The First Lawyer points to the tablet and says

We have come to ask you not to allow that *to be used.*

Pilate is annoyed at the interruption and answers curtly.

PILATE: *Why?*
FIRST LAWYER (pointing at the tablet): *It says that he is crucified as the King of the Jews.*
PILATE: *And?*
FIRST LAWYER: *That is not correct.*
SECOND LAWYER: *He is crucified because he said that he was the King of the Jews.*
PILATE (cutting them short): *What I have written, I have written.*

He turns his back on the lawyers and continues his conversation with the Roman officials.
Shrugging their shoulders, the lawyers leave.
Soft dissolve.

NARRATOR: *On this day, as on all other days, the divine service within the Temple began with the offering of the incense.*

A close-up of a golden vessel into which incense is poured.
The camera glides backward and we see a priest in white, the

vessel in his hands, start walking toward the Sanctuary. He is joined by another priest, clad in white, who carries a golden fire-pan filled with live coals that have been taken from the altar of burnt offerings.

We follow the two priests into the Sanctuary, passing by the golden candlestick. In the center of the Sanctuary is the incense altar. The priest with the fire-pan places the live coals on the altar, after which the other priest sprinkles them with incense.

The priest with the fire-pan leaves the Sanctuary while the other priest falls to the floor, worshipping God.

The camera approaches the altar and the scene ends with a close-up of the altar with the burning incense—symbol of the prayers of believers.

The scene dissolves softly.

NARRATOR: *And the Romans took Jesus and led him away to be crucified.*

The main street, which parallels the northern wall. There are few people about; everyone is asleep after the feast. The shops are closed. The only sounds are those of the roar of the wild beasts in the circus nearby and the quick footsteps of soldiers. Quietly some doors open and frightened people look out and ask those in the street if anything is wrong. When they are told that the Romans are out, they hurriedly retreat into their houses, shutting fast doors and windows with bolts and crossbars. The footfalls of the Roman soldiers become louder.

The camera moves so that we are also able to see the procession surrounding Jesus enter the street. Jesus is being led from Herod's palace to the gate opening on the road leading northward.

The procession is headed by a herald who announces in a loud voice the prisoner's crime. He is accompanied by a drummer who makes a rolling noise on his drum at certain intervals in the announcement. A soldier walks behind the herald and the drummer carries the titulus which later will be placed on the cross. He is followed by the centurion and a few soldiers.

Then follow four executioners with Jesus in their midst. The executioners carry carpenter's tools and implements, for instance, a ladder, boards, ropes.

According to Roman custom the man who has been sentenced to death must himself carry the cross-beam to the place of execution. We see the cross-beam laid on Jesus's shoulders. He bends his neck under the heavy burden.

Soldiers follow along at the end of the procession. One of the soldiers carries on the head of a lance the crown of thorns.

Jesus is pale and weak. As the procession approaches the camera we see how his feet fail him. Slowly his strength gives way and, stumbling over a stone in the pavement, he sinks to his knees. The procession halts. One of the executioners helps him up and replaces the cross-beam on his shoulders.

Meanwhile a few people have become bold enough to draw near, particularly some women and children. One of the women feels compassion for Jesus and says to one of the soldiers

Look how he sweats. May I help him to wipe his face?

The soldier nods his assent.

[Women in Palestine at that time frequently wore a napkin which hung loosely over the shoulders or around the neck. Among the Jews it was considered a sign of compassion to wipe the face of another human being who was in distress.]

The woman, moved with pity, hands Jesus her napkin. He takes it and presses it against his face and then gives it back to her. The centurion now shouts an order that they are to continue. And the procession moves on, Jesus bearing his cross.

The scene dissolves softly into a close-up of the altar with the burning incense at the Sanctuary of the Temple.

The camera moves backward and the priest who has been worshipping God rises and leaves the Sanctuary. We follow him through the entrance hall to the steps leading up to the holy place. At the foot of the steps the believers have gathered. Standing at the top of the steps and lifting his hands over the people of Israel, the priest pronounces the Aaronic benediction, the same benediction which is used today in Christian churches

The Lord bless you and keep you, the Lord make his face to shine upon you and be gracious unto you: the Lord lift up his countenance upon you and give you peace.

During the last words the scene dissolves softly into the procession with Jesus, which has passed the Genath gate and now is outside the first northern wall. Golgotha is not far away. It is an open rocky landscape covered with gardens.

Somewhere along the road, Jesus stumbles once more and the procession stops. The executioners again help him to rise and they also attempt to place the cross-beam on his shoulders but the centurion interferes.

No, it's no use; we must find someone to carry the cross for him.

He looks about.

A Greek Jew, Simon of Cyrene, who is actually on his way home at this moment, meets the procession. The centurion calls him and commands him to carry the cross.

CENTURION: *Carry that cross for him. He is exhausted.*
SIMON: *Why do you ask me? You have men enough.*
CENTURION: *I didn't ask you. It was an order.*

Simon, grumbling, lifts the cross to his right shoulder with the help of one of the executioners.

The procession moves on, with Simon behind Jesus, who is leaning on one of the executioners.

Soft dissolve.

The Temple. At the end of the morning service the Levites on duty gather on the steps leading to the Sanctuary. Two priests with trumpets are with them. The Levites commence their psalm, and at each blast of the trumpets the people fall to the ground in worship of God.

By means of a trucking-shot the scene ends with a close-up of the trumpets and dissolves softly into the next scene. Meanwhile the music is still heard, the song subdued and the trumpets prominent.

Golgotha, a long shot. This was about a hundred meters from the Genath gate and a little off the road which followed the northern wall to King Herod's palace.

Roman soldiers have been posted all around the place to prevent people from approaching the place of execution. The crowd is small.

If it were not for the crosses the place would resemble a timber yard with piles of rough-hewn beams and boards. Two men are sawing a beam which is placed on two vertical beams. There is a bundle of faggots on the ground. [Sometimes the executioners would hasten the victim's death by kindling a fire at the foot of the cross.] A heap of sand lies to one side.

The carpenters whom we see are the executioners. They do not look bloodthirsty, but more like artisans engaged in their profession. One of them carries water from a nearby cistern and pours it into a barrel. Another is bent over a tub washing his bloody hands with the help of another man who pours water from a jar.

The sound of hammer strokes and axe blows fills the air. Also we hear sighs, groans and wailing and doleful cries.

Jesus is to be crucified along with two revolutionaries who have committed murder. One of them is already hanging on a cross and two executioners are just nailing his feet to the vertical beam of the cross. The other one is about to be hoisted up upon his cross.

The cross-beam is laid on the ground. The man sentenced to death is stretched out upon the cross-beam, his arms extended and his hands nailed to the beam. Then the cross-beam is hoisted up and placed upon the raised vertical beam.

By means of ropes, ladders, and long hooked poles the cross-beam is hoisted up to the top of the vertical post and fastened by nails and ropes. Spur-shores are placed between the cross-beams and the vertical beam. Midway up the vertical beam a wooden saddle which supports the body is fixed, called the *sedile*. Then his feet are nailed to the vertical beam.

The executioners prepare the cross for Jesus midway between the two crosses for revolutionaries. A hole is hewn in a rock. The vertical beam, ready to be planted in the ground, is lying near the hole.

Three or four executioners raise the beam, pushing the foot of it into the hole until it sinks into position. They put wedges into the hole around the foot of the beam to hold it firm. The vertical beam was not too high, for the feet of the sufferer had to be less than a man's height above the ground.

One of the executioners hums a gay tune while working and another one joins in singing the refrain.

When Jesus arrives, the cross-beam is lifted from the shoulders of Simon of Cyrene and placed on the ground.

According to Roman law those sentenced to death on the cross must be placed naked on "the tree," but in Palestine they were allowed to wear a loin-cloth.

Jesus is ordered to remove his clothes. Simon of Cyrene offers to help him, but the executioners send him away.

Glimpses of others at the scene are interspersed while Jesus is undressing.

When we return to Jesus, he is stripped and stretched out on the ground, his arms extended on the cross-beam. They have not yet been nailed to the cross. A rope is tied around his wrists and they are straightened out toward the ends of the cross and fixed tightly. This is seen in a trucking close-up shot along the cross-beam from one end to the other, and then the executioners mark on the beam the place where the nails will be driven. The string is loosened and holes are made with an auger to receive the long nails. Again the arms are straightened out and the string fastened to the ends of the beam in order to prevent the sufferer from drawing back his hands and making it difficult to drive in the nails.

While this is happening we hear Jesus saying

Father, forgive them, for they know not what they do.

From a new angle we see one of the executioners drive the nails through the hands, first the right hand and then the left. The actual cruelties of this scene are not shown directly. We see the executioner's back and the hammer being lifted up after each stroke. We hear, as it descends, the dull thud and the moaning of Jesus.

Now we see the top of the vertical beam of Jesus's cross and a Roman soldier handing the titulus to an executioner who stands on a ladder. The executioner fastens the titulus on the beam so that it will appear just above the head of Jesus when he is placed on the cross. The camera slowly approaches the titulus until it covers the whole screen, while different sounds are heard: the bleating of sheep, the horns from the Roman Governor's palace, the answering blasts from the Roman fortress. We also hear dogs barking and the cries and moans of the crucified.

After a while the titulus dissolves softly, and the camera moves backward to a long shot. Jesus hangs upon the cross. Two executioners are about to nail his feet to the upright beam. We hear the strokes of the hammer and see the points of the long nails pierce through the beam.

The front of the cross. The ladder still rests against the cross and an executioner stands on it. A Roman soldier hands the crown of thorns to the executioner who places it on Jesus's head. The executioner descends the ladder and removes it from the cross. The paleness of death is already on the face of Jesus. With great difficulty he raises his eyes and in a loud voice cries

Eloi, Eloi, lama sabach thani?

His eyelids close and he turns his head heavily and slowly from one side to the other. Tears come to his eyes and roll down his cheeks.

Again the camera approaches the titulus until it fills the screen. After a few moments it dissolves into a short scene showing one of the revolutionaries on his cross. He shouts disdainfully at Jesus

If you be the Messiah, save yourself and me.

The scene dissolves back to the titulus and different sounds are heard.

The scene changes to show three executioners looking at Jesus. One of them says

He would destroy the Temple and build it in three days.

The scene dissolves back to the titulus and the camera moves backward so that we see Jesus. In a faint voice he is heard gasping

I thirst.

A Roman soldier draws near with a sponge that has been moistened with vinegar. The sponge is fastened to the head of a lance. The soldier lifts the sponge to the mouth of Jesus who turns his head away. While he is lifting the sponge, he shouts

You saved others, but yourself you cannot save.

Again the camera approaches the titulus. Soft dissolve into the next scene.

We recognize several of the revolutionaries in the crowd.

FIRST REVOLUTIONARY: *He said he was the Son of God.*
SECOND REVOLUTIONARY: *Let God deliver him now, if he will have him.*

The scene dissolves softly back to the titulus which shortly again dissolves into a shot of four executioners. According to the Law the executioners took possession of the garments of a political offender. They are sitting on the ground casting lots to determine what each of them should take. The garments of Jesus consisted of his cloak (*simiah*), his headgear, his girdle, his sandals, and his *kiton,* which is woven in one piece. They cast lots by drawing a square on the ground which is divided into nine smaller squares. The object is to get the most points. The one who gets the *simiah* says

I never dreamt I would wear a royal mantle.

Soft dissolve to the titulus. The camera glides backward until we see Jesus again, his strength almost spent. He cries in a loud voice

Father, into your hands I commend my spirit.

"And having said thus he gave up the ghost." [Here dissolves are not complete but superimpositions, so that the titulus remains subdued behind the different interspersed scenes.]

Jesus's cross shown from a different angle.

The centurion and a soldier approach the cross. It was the duty of the centurion to make sure that those crucified were really dead and he motions to the soldier to pierce the side of Jesus with his spear. The soldier does so and "forthwith came there out blood and water."

A long shot. The centurion seated with a few soldiers who have been ordered to remain until all the crucified are dead. The executioners have left. The soldiers have opened their knapsacks and start eating.

By means of a dissolve the soldiers and the crosses of the two revolutionaries slowly disappear. The cross with Jesus remains. We see the shadow of the cross lengthening until it extends beyond the frame of the image.

NARRATOR: *Jesus dies, but in death he accomplished what he had begun in life. His body was killed, but his spirit lived. His immortal sayings brought to humanity all over the world the good tidings of love and charity foretold by the Jewish prophets of old.*

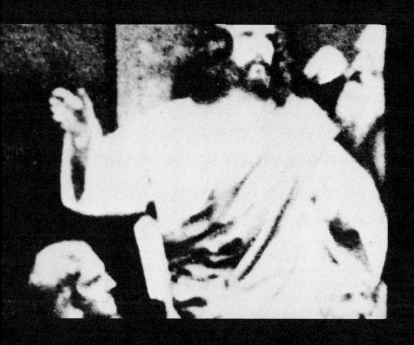

WORKING
WITH DREYER

by Preben Thomsen

With ironical remarks, Dreyer slashed our speed as we drove through North Zealand to catch the ferry at Hundested, reminding me in little didactic hints about his film of Johannes V. Jensen's "myth," *Did They Make the Ferry?* The grim vision of death on the road in a rumbling little delivery van, created by Dreyer in the forties, seemed if possible clearer just then than when I had seen it on the screen with my schoolmates. The scenes had evidently been so sharp and simple as to have etched themselves on my mind's eye. I was caught up again in that film's mood. And the all-seeing and all-observing passenger beside me sensed it, being highly amused and almost triumphant when his remarks made me take my foot off the accelerator.

We caught the ferry and crossed to Odsherred. Some time later we sat on the terrace in front of the vicarage, looking across Sejro Bay. The scene had changed. The mood had changed. He got up and surveyed the landscape, then proceeded to interpret it by suggesting certain rearrangements. You could, for example, have felled

a few more of those trees, which blocked the view of the hills where
they flatten out to the sea over in the west. It would have given
that golden touch to the scene—to say nothing of the Dreyer touch.

I undertook to have most of the hedge felled, but in the same
moment had to promise him not to send for a gardener during the
month or so he envisaged spending at Norre Asminderup. For we
were bent on working . . .

I hurried out to empty the library he had brought from the
car. And at once we started to arrange all the books, and the large
buff office envelopes on which, in a neat copperplate hand, he had
written names like "Jason," "Corinth," etc. We intended to make
a film script of Euripides' *Medea,* based on the vast material that
Dreyer had collected over the years, and that, with a systematist's
sense of order, he had arranged as if in preparation for a thesis.

I was certainly made to work. With sympathetic cruelty,
Dreyer woke me every morning before the cock crew, and was not
at all pleased unless I had given him his breakfast and was ready
to sit down at the desk by cockcrow. He had no need of either
clapper-board or any other exterior means to get me to function.
Rarely have I found myself so efficient as during that summer,
although only occasionally allowed to go out and air my brain.
Dreyer's radiation kept me fixed to the chair.

If with his immense intuition he sensed that I was grinding
to a halt and needed to be left alone, he would go and sit in the
half-shade of the weeping birch with a book of Greek poetry or
other source material, waiting for me to come out as soon as possible with a fresh scene to read to him. And as often as not he
would regret that he had not stayed at the desk to be present at the
birth. Now it had to be done all over again.

I had chiefly been allotted the dialogue. Assisted by Euripides,
and, in his paternal way, by Dreyer, it was my job to get Jason,
Medea's nurse, the Princess of Corinth and more especially Medea
herself to speak. Dreyer had already thought out the scenes himself,
and with such visualized and detailed clarity that all I had to do
was to take down what he dictated from the notes picked with his
neat hands from the buff envelopes. With his inward eye he had
envisaged a scenario which lay ready fixed. Now it was his task and

mine to move the figures about in this film scenography and also bring them to life in their dialogue. This meant, first and foremost, that he and I should come together in a dialogue that would enable us to meet the figures jointly. That was where the difficulties naturally began to arise, but at this point also I learnt a fantastic lot from the great film poet: from his stubborn, almost fanatical determination to experience his own work from within.

Our talk turned mostly on Medea. She was to be the subject of the film. It was her mythological womanliness that Dreyer wanted to explore in depth. He would sit far into the night in the wide black chair that had belonged to the clergyman-poet Grundtvig, discussing Medea with me. And the more we talked about her, the nearer we got to her. As Grundtvig had employed Norse myths, Dreyer would use the Greek myth about the woman forced to avenge herself. He thought of one means after another of understanding her demoniac behavior. He related her to the female characters he had created in earlier films: Joan of Arc, a martyr to patriotic and religious fanaticism; Anne Pedersdotter of *Day of Wrath,* going down before the world which wanted to create her in the image that had very little to do with her real self; and Gertrud, who became a victim of the worldly limitation of existence by ambitions. Medea is related to these women. But she will not be sacrificed. She kills and sacrifices others. Her vengeance is not even satisfied by getting rid of her rival when Jason has jilted her; but, driven by an inner, tragic compulsion, she sacrifices her own children. It was this compulsion that Dreyer wanted to depict. He would thus go a step further than in his earlier films, where his archetypal women characters ended as sacrifices.

For Medea herself sacrifices what is of the greatest value to her, her children. Therefore the sacrifice is the judgment over her. But at the same time we had throughout to establish Medea as the one who is herself a sacrifice. Dreyer was insistent that all who saw the film should be able both to understand Medea and sympathize with her. There must be something moving and gripping in his Medea, he would say. The words were extremely typical of him when he spoke of this conception of the figure. He could use such words without tempting one to accuse him of sentimentality. He wanted

above all that Medea should be "relevant." At one point he produced a newspaper cutting from one of the buff envelopes, to show
me that a Medea incident could occur today. It was a report in a
French paper about a woman who had murdered her children from
jealousy. He also liked to talk of a certain Miss Jensen in a dairy
shop in a working-class district of Copenhagen who would be able
to appreciate the mythological Medea as an expression of something
within herself. It was an aspect of Dreyer's rather aristocratic approach as an artist, yet at the same time an expression of his idealis-
tic dream of translating an old Greek tragedy into his own clear
and concise imagery for quite ordinary people of today, thereby
opening their eyes to the mythological drama in their own inner
world. With his Medea film he would, as it were, pave the way for
a young new cinema audience for the great film he had dreamt of
and toiled for since his own early youth. The Euripides drama
would be a visual prophesy of his real mythological work on the
struggle of the good against the demons in man's world. In this film
the good would be embodied in the person who was for Dreyer the
archetype of all archetypes, namely Jesus of Nazareth. So it was not
only because Dreyer sat in Grundtvig's chair in a country vicarage
that our talks ended, evening after evening, in a discussion that
was theological.

It was quite simply because the subject of Jesus embraced the
whole sum of his subjects. I well remember how he put me down
one evening when we sat discussing the untameable mind of Medea.
He accused me of being negative. Surely I could see that Medea was
another of those cases whom Jesus would have pitied. The cinema
projector spotlighting the figure of Medea in Dreyer's imagination
borrowed its rays from that source of good light in the history of
man. So Medea must also reflect real humanity, even charity. And
as Euripides pulls no punches when he makes Medea murder her
children with her sword, almost in an ecstasy of blood lust, so
Dreyer in his film would have her rock them to death while singing
a lullaby, after giving them poison under pretence that it is medi-
cine. Medea's possessed mind must always contain the possibility of
cure.

And when one night he allowed me to read the English script

of the Jesus film that he had done in the United States in the forties
I could suddenly see a connection between his earlier works and
Medea, and finally his interpretation of Jesus. What binds them
together and makes them human is the deep impression of thirst for
compassion and justice.

His great female figures perish in this thirst. And Jesus, who
is able to quench the thirst in others, is Himself crushed by the
social structures that would prevent Him from exercising compassion. They are sociological phenomena that in Dreyer's art express
the demonic reality. Ultimately, Medea, too, foundered on a political alliance, namely the opportunistic connection between her husband and the royal house of Corinth. Jason's marriage policy en-
forces the tragic necessity under which Medea slays.

In the Jesus film Dreyer also wishes to illustrate how the pale
cast of thought becomes reality in the political security measures
adopted by the Roman state to protect itself against any form of
rebellion. The impersonal intrigue which in Dreyer is personified in
the governor Pilate is the real evil of the world which surrounds
Jesus. And in such a delineation of the political possibility of power
Dreyer seeks to tell his visual "myth" of Jesus. In doing so he
wanted to make the historical events both relevant and immediate.
The question that remains is whether at the same time he over-
simplifies the problem of Jesus, making one person too absolutely
the villain of the piece, namely Pilate, representing the totalitarian
state.

For our common edification we read the New Testament together. I pointed to the passages which for me indicated the intention of the New Testament authors to represent the whole gallery
of people surrounding Jesus as guilty of His death. Dreyer then
said that with his film he wanted to take the opportunity, once and
for all, of standing up for the Jewish judges. With his work he
wanted to strike at European anti-Semitism. He had got this idea
from reading a book by the American Jewish historian Dr. Solomon
Zeitlin, who describes Caiaphas as a sort of Quisling. Dreyer also
wanted to defend Caiaphas. Nor did he think that by depicting so
much human innocence about Jesus he was taking some of the sting
out of the drama. And when I asked him if in doing so he was not

also acquitting the Christian Church, he replied ironically that he certainly hoped not. Nevertheless there can be no doubt that the New Testament, the source book of the Christian Church, hits the Church harder than Dreyer's film script, because the evangelists have the courage to depict the disciples as cowards and accessories, while Dreyer lets them off very gently, indeed almost sentimentally.

Although one may suspect Dreyer of having thought along humanist and political lines more than along religious ones in his interpretation of the Jesus story, yet I still think that we should have seen a film with the immediacy and relevancy only his genius could have given to one on this subject.

We met again when I agreed to adapt and translate the script with a view to its Danish publication. I sensed in the great film poet's willingness to allow his work to come out in print a connection with a feeling that in his heart of hearts he had ceased to believe that it would ever be visually realized. He was getting tired. He, too, had so often run his plan and his dreams against the pale cast of a brick wall. It may not have been actually a Pilate that had stood in his way. Rather it was a case of many little "Pilates," who instead of seating themselves on a Gabbatha of stone in powerful Roman fashion had settled rather too comfortably on their heaps of bank books and so had blocked his work of art: not only, indeed, this work of art, his film about Jesus, but several of his other great film ideas. The Medea film never came to anything either.

TRIBUTES TO
CARL DREYER

Jean Renoir: Dreyer's Sin

Did God give us the world so that we could take it apart and analyze it? This is what man is doing today. The investigations of the scientist are confined to the body and its surrounding elements. The investigations of the artist are aimed at knowledge of the soul.

So long as the artist keeps the results of his discoveries to himself the damage he can do is limited. The trouble is he wants everyone to know.

We know the results of the spreading of knowledge of the quality of matter by the scientist: the atom bomb.

The spreading of the knowledge of man by artists is even more formidable than nuclear fission; it is a sin which can only be pardoned if the sinner is a genius. This is the sin of Dreyer. God will forgive him for it was He who bestowed upon him his extraordinary perception.

There is spirit and there is matter. There is God and there is the Devil. Does a pebble merely consist of matter? To what extent are the elements which surround us aware of themselves and of us and of their universe, be it small or great? Is there a hierarchy? Do we find pure spirits—or at least, a pure spirit—at the top of the ladder? Must we be content with the reactions of the pebble at the lowest rung of this ladder? Is there a way of giving a soul to this pebble? A very few privileged people have succeeded. In the Middle Ages they were called saints. Today we call them artists. Their function in this world of ours is to increase the spiritual quality while, at the same time, preserving the purity of the pebble.

Strangely enough and through a sort of irony which seems to delight in the forces which take us from chaos to the music of Mozart, these distributors of the spirit rely on matter itself in their struggle against materialism. They are not very numerous; just one or two in each century. Dreyer is of their company and, like all great artists, he poses the problem of submission to nature and, at the same time, the evasion of this same nature. He sets this problem and he solves it. What is more, he gives us the arguments and the arms to solve it for ourselves.

I speak of Dreyer as if he were still with us because for me and for many others he *is* still here—and he always will be.

Dreyer knows nature better than a naturalist. He knows man better than an anthropologist. It is possible that he does not know the proportions of oxygen, hydrogen or nitrogen contained in the branches of the old oak tree under which he meditated as a child, but he knows the long watches of the tree during the winter nights. He knows the pain caused by the snapping of a snow-laden branch. He knows the thrill of the spring rains. He knows the caress of the evening breeze refreshing the leaves in the dry evenings. Anyone armed with the necessary test-tubes, scalpels and chemical reactors can analyze the nature of a tree. But to know a tree as one knows a friend, to have insight into its grandeur and its weakness, to observe not without irony its desire to dominate—its pitiless destruction of rival plant life; in other words, to identify oneself, even if only for an instant, with plant life, is more difficult. And if the object of your interest is not just a tree but a man, this undertaking calls for more than simply the right tools. It calls for an exacerbated sensibility, a needle-sharp perception and a rigorous humility; all this plus an insane pride. It presupposes the belief that we have the right to stick our noses into the affairs of others. After all, there is no proof that ants are in any way flattered at the idea of our analyzing their formic acid. The examples of man interfering in the lives of other creatures could be written in blood on the countless pages of innumerable books.

Two or three times during the course of my life I have come close to Dreyer, but I cannot claim to have known him in the flesh. Humanly speaking, I can boast that I have known him very well—just as he can claim intimate knowledge of the old oak tree in question. The fact of the matter is that I am not at all sure he ever saw this old oak. It is quite possible that he is perfectly indifferent to old oak trees. Perhaps the idea of an old oak tree has never even crossed his mind.

The truth is that I have created this oak, and I have done so purely for my own convenience. If one wants to get close to a being like Dreyer it is necessary to have a solid basis on which to work. Dreyer never needed this oak tree with its branches so high they are hidden from sight—this friendly oak within whose shadow I stand. He had no need of it because he *is* the oak tree in question.

The problem of realism as opposed to transposition, of concrete as opposed to abstract, does not arise here. The reason why I bring it up at all is because I feel it; and some of my doubts can perhaps help me penetrate the labyrinthine ways of the mind of the man I admire.

As far as most of us are concerned there are two ways of looking at the truth: from the outside and from the inside. The cult of truth seen from the outside is purely academic. The reproduction of nature without the personal touch of the artist is of no interest. This was summed up by Pascal when he said: "Man is the only thing of interest to man." If I see a landscape without any figures in it, this landscape is just a reproduction. Take the case of an actor who has been given the part of a cook to play, and supposing he is a bad actor but a conscientious one, he will go and watch cooks at their work, initiate himself in the jargon they use in their trade and finally acquire the appearance, the aspect and the deportment of a real cook. The clothes he wears to play his part will have been worn by a cook and will not have been cleaned since then for fear of removing authentic kitchen stains. The result of all this will probably be that our man, either on the stage or on the screen, will remain what he really is, a bad actor. In spite of the authentic outside trappings he will not convince anyone.

Let us now go to the other extreme and take the case of a good actor who has been given the same role. I do not think this man would have the slightest desire to read up his subject. It is possible that he might have a word or two with some cooks but he is not likely to wear himself out seeking the authentic tools of the trade, an authentic costume or the authentic language of cooks. It is even possible that he may be a new Charlie Chaplin, not dressed at all like a cook but with a spiritual awareness of the problems of cooks which would be immediately recognized by the public, which would see in him a real cook.

If this theory is taken to the point of absurdity the only answer is the abandonment of realism as seen from the outside and the creation of a world which is simply the issue of the imagination of the artist. This is abstract art, and in my humble opinion, apart from certain cartoons, this is not a cinematographic method to be recommended. To my mind the artist is all the more visible in a landscape in that he does not show himself. He is hidden behind a bush or something, but he soon reveals himself. He is recognized by his approach, his intonations, the light in which he bathes his picture or the positioning of the elements in his landscape. In other words, a good way for the artist to get to his public and to be recognized is to hide himself and let the public find him.

I have said that this does not apply in Dreyer's case and I will repeat this a hundred times if necessary. A man of these dimensions is neither concrete nor abstract. He is concrete inasmuch as his personages are of a disturbing reality, both externally and internally. When Dreyer asked Falconetti to have her head shaved to play the part of Joan of Arc in prison, he was not asking for a sacrifice to mere external truth. I think that primarily this was an inspiration for Dreyer. The sight of this admirable face deprived of its natural adornment plunged Dreyer into the very heart of his subject. This shaven head was the purity of Joan of Arc. It was her faith. It was her invincible courage. It was her innocence, even stronger than the knavery of her judges. It was the resistance to oppression and tyranny; it was also a bitter observation of the eternal brutality of those who believe themselves to be strong. It was the ineffectual protest of the people. It was the affirmation that in human tragedies it is always the poor who pay; and also that the humility of these poor people makes them closer to God than the right and the powerful could ever be. That shaven head said all this and much more to Dreyer. It was and remains the abstraction of the whole epic of Joan of Arc. What is miraculous is that this is also the case with the spectators who continue to come and purify themselves in the pure waters of Dreyer's *Joan of Arc*.

Dreyer is over and above all theories. He takes his arms where he finds them. The ways chosen by his inspiration to reach out to us, his spectators, are of little account. What is important is that he remains with us, not only because of *Joan of Arc* but also through his other films; and we are involved in a way which goes far beyond day-to-day banality.

Federico Fellini

To add something new, original or striking about the work of Carl Dreyer, to describe afresh his precise, pristine vision would be difficult and require some length because so much of the critical discussion regarding him is so inflated and extended. I know only a few of his films, but I remember being enthralled and bewitched by the extraordinary imaginative force of this great master who contributed so decisively to making film an authentic act of art and expression.

The films of Dreyer, so rigorous, so chaste, so austere seem to me to come from a distant, mythical land, and their creator a kind of artist-saint, but it is also true that I find in these films a familiar dwelling place where an artistic vocation has been completely lived, experienced, and expressed.

François Truffaut

When I think of Dreyer, there come to mind those *white* images and above all the great silent close-ups of *The Passion of Joan of Arc*, the succession of which is equivalent to the uninterrupted staccato dialogue of the actual trial of Joan at Rouen.

Then, I recall the *whiteness* of *Vampyr*, but this time it is accompanied by sounds, by cries, foremost among them the fruitless wails of the Doctor whose perturbed shade disappears into a cask of flour at the bottom of a mill from which no one can deliver him. After the commercial failures of the two masterpieces, *Joan of Arc* and *Vampyr*, Carl Dreyer waited eleven years before being able to work again, and that was on what is probably his best film, *Day of Wrath* (1943), which deals with a case of sorcery at the beginning of the sixteenth century. It is in *Day of Wrath* that one sees the most beautiful female nude in cinema, at once the least erotic and the most carnal, the nude white body of Marte Herlof, the old woman who is judged a witch and burned at the stake.

Ten more years went by before Dreyer was rediscovered with

Ordet, a film which tells of lost and recovered faith. In my mind, *Ordet* lives in the milky *whiteness* of its unerring images but also for its sonorous, hallucinatory vision that evokes an emotion stronger than does the superb screenplay itself. In the last part of the film, the center of the screen is filled by a coffin in which rests the heroine whom the protagonist, a madman who believes himself to be Christ, has promised to resurrect. The quiet of the bereaved house is broken only by sound of men's footsteps on the plank floor, a sound characteristic of new shoes, of "Sunday" shoes . . .

The other Dreyer images that come to mind rise from *Pages from Satan's Book* (a tribute of the young director to the work of D. W. Griffith) or from *Love One Another* (1922), which is a precursor of the Godard of *Les Carabiniers.*

Commercially, Dreyer had a difficult career and if he was able to live for his art, it was thanks to the receipts of the film theater which he programmed and directed in Copenhagen. A deeply religious artist and a devoted film enthusiast, his life was driven by two dreams that were never realized: to make a film on the life of Christ and to work in Hollywood.

Dreyer was a short man, seemingly mild and yet formidably obstinate, stern and yet sensitive and warm. His last public act was characteristic: three weeks before his death he brought together the eight principal Danish film men and together they drew up a letter of protest against the dismissal of Henri Langlois of the Cinémathèque Française.

When Dreyer joined the ranks of those great artists who have left us—after Griffith, Stroheim, Eisenstein, Lubitsch—it was then that one understood that it was just these men who had been the distinguished first generation of film.

Editor's Note

THE TEXT:

The text for this edition of Dreyer's film manuscript, *Jesus*, is based on Dreyer's original English language version, which was written in Independence, Missouri in 1949–1950. When Dreyer wrote the script there was every reasonable expectation that his film would be produced, but subsequently the financial backing went elsewhere. Three major films on the life of Jesus were produced subsequently: George Stevens's *The Greatest Story Ever Told*, Nicholas Ray's *King of Kings,* and Pier Paolo Pasolini's *The Gospel According to St. Matthew*. With Preben Thomsen and Merete Riis, Dreyer prepared a Danish translation of the script which was published after his death in 1968. I would like to extend my gratitude to the Danish Ministry of Foreign Affairs for permission to use Ib Monty's biography of Dreyer, Jean Renoir's appreciation and Preben Thomsen's memoir. These articles were written for a booklet on Dreyer published by the Press and Information Department of the Danish Ministry of Foreign Affairs in 1969.

311

Federico Fellini and François Truffaut generously contributed their appreciations and the translations of these are my own. Especial thanks are due to Miss Dedria Bryfonski and Mrs. Penny Butler for their aid in preparation of the manuscript.

THE CONTRIBUTORS:

Ib Monty is Director of the Danish Film Museum and a member of the editorial board of the Danish film journal *Kosmorama*. Preben Thomsen is a clergyman and dramatist. His plays, *Atalja* and *Gyngehesten* (*The Rocking Horse*) were presented by the Danish National Theater. Federico Fellini's films include *La Strada*, *La Dolce Vita*, *8½*, *Satyricon*, *The Clowns*. François Truffaut's, *The Four Hundred Blows*, *Jules and Jim*, *Stolen Kisses*, *The Wild Child*, *Bed and Board*. Jean Renoir's, *Rules of the Game*, *Grand Illusion*, *The River*, *Picnic on the Grass*.

ROBERT CORNFIELD